WITHDRAWN

THEY FOUGHT AT
ANZIO

THEY FOUGHT

AN

UNIVERSITY OF MISSOURI PRESS

JOHN S. D. EISENHOWER

AT
ZIO

COLUMBIA AND LONDON

Library of Congress Cataloging-in-Publication Data

Eisenhower, John S. D., 1922-
   They fought at Anzio / John S.D. Eisenhower.
      p.   cm.
   Summary: "Eisenhower examines the Allies' Italian campaign—which included
some of World War II's longest and bloodiest battles—with an emphasis on the
Anzio offensive from the perspectives of the individuals who fought, both
commanders and foot soldiers, highlighting his analysis with quotations from
personal accounts and memoirs"—Provided by publisher.
   Includes bibliographical references and index.
   ISBN 978-0-8262-1738-7 (alk. paper)
   1. World War, 1939–1945—Campaigns—Italy.   2. Anzio Beachhead, 1944.
I. Title.
   D763.I8E34 2007
   940.54'2157—dc22   2007000113

Designer: FoleyDesign
Typesetter: BookComp, Inc.
Printer and binder: Thomson-Shore, Inc.
Typefaces: ITC American Typewriter and Palatino

TO
Andrew J. Goodpaster

CONTENTS

Contents

BOOK FOUR: THE CRISIS

BOOK FIVE: BREAKOUT AND THE CAPTURE OF ROME

MAPS

ACKNOWLEDGMENTS

Since 1989, when my book on the Mexican War was published, I have benefited from the assistance and encouragement of three people: my wife, Joanne, Professor Louis D. Rubin, Jr., and Mrs. Dorothy (Dodie) Yentz. Four books have followed, and my debt to these three has grown. There is not much I can add except another Thank You.

Mitchell Yockelson, of the National Archives and Records Administration (NARA) has always been of invaluable help. He is an expert on both world wars and is unfailing in providing pertinent official documents.

Kate Flaherty, of the National Archives, though promoted to another office, took time out from her regular duties to assist Joanne and me in our search for photographs. Her efforts saved us days of digging. She was ably assisted by Teresa Roy.

Louise Arnold-Friend, of the Military History Institute, Carlisle, Pennsylvania, is always there with her expertise, willing to help.

The Eisenhower Library in Abilene, Kansas, under the directorship of Daniel D. Holt, is always ready to assist. Stacy Meuli, his assistant, is one I always call on. Kathy Struss, of the photographic files, did yeoman's work in finding photos apparently not available elsewhere.

Carlo D'Este, a comrade-in-arms for many years and a distinguished military historian, was of great help, including providing me with his personal copy of General John P. Lucas's diary, without which this book would never have been the same.

Colonel John D. (Sailor) Byrne, my old boss in the English Department at West Point, provided invaluable background, based on his service as commanding officer, 39th Field Artillery Battalion, 3d Infantry Division.

James F. C. Hyde, Jr., Esq., of the 69th Armored Field Artillery Battalion, which landed at Anzio with the 3d Division, provided valuable anecdotes based on personal experience. His wife of many years, Enid Griswold Hyde, made Jim's contribution possible since he lost his sight at Anzio.

Mrs. Avis Dagit Schorer, of the 56th Evacuation Hospital, supplemented the material in her fine book, *A Half Acre of Hell,* with personal correspondence.

Mrs. John P. (Rosemary) Lucas, Jr., kindly provided photos of her late father-in-law.

No military book is better than the maps that indicate tactical situations and troop movements. For three years now, I have worked happily with Christopher Robinson, of Laurel, Maryland. Besides his obvious professional competence, I would like to thank him for his patience and good humor.

I have corresponded with a good many people, but I would like to mention the following in particular:

William H. Martin, Jr., of Victoria, Texas, for information on the Rapido River crossing.

Doug Cook, of Escondido, California, for material pertaining to the 1st Armored Division.

James E. Duncan, East Berlin, Pennsylvania, for background on the 509th Parachute Infantry Battalion.

John Shirley, whose excellent book, *I Remember,* provided much material for the accounts of the breakout from Anzio. He has supplemented that material with personal correspondence.

I would also like to mention the generosity of Mrs. Kenneth F. Kauffman, for sending a manuscript on artillery positions at Anzio; Durham Caldwell, for supplying an article by Jimmy Dolan on the Ranger action at Anzio; John A. Tysor, President, the USS *Ancon* Association, Baltimore, Maryland; Colonel Philip A. Wyman, a friend of many years, who provided background on his artillery battery from the 88th Division going into Rome.

And finally, my thanks to the staff of the University of Missouri Press, especially Beverly Jarrett, editor-in-chief, and Sara Davis, senior editor. I owe Professor Robert H. Ferrell a debt of thanks for introducing me to the University of Missouri Press some years ago.

BOOK ONE

THE ROAD TO THE
RAPIDO

Map by Chris Robinson

PROLOGUE

I t was Monday, June 5, 1944, and the time had come for Lieutenant General Mark W. Clark to make a triumphal entry into Rome. Only the day before, the lead elements of his Fifth U.S. Army had entered the southern neighborhoods of the Eternal City and the occupying German forces had left in haste. Nobody was quite sure which unit, British or American,[1] had first entered the city proper, but that detail mattered little to Clark so long as the credit for the capture of this great prize was accorded to the Fifth Army.

To accompany him in his big moment, Clark had selected two key officers. One was his chief of staff, Major General Alfred M. Gruenther, and the other was Major General Edgar E. Hume, whom Clark had designated as the temporary governor of the city. As a vehicle, the jeep was ideal for the publicity-conscious Clark; it was so configured that the senior passenger, sitting up front in the place of honor beside the driver, was readily visible, in plain view of the gaze of the onlooker and the lens of the cameraman as well. The other two passengers, huddled in the cramped rear seats, seemed almost superfluous.

As Clark and his party drove into Rome they were greeted by the scenes of deliriously rejoicing Italian civilians. "There were gay crowds in the streets," he later wrote, "many of them waving flags, as our infantry marched through the capital." Flowers were being stuck in the muzzles of the soldiers' rifles, and many Romans "seemed to be on the verge of hysteria in their enthusiasm for the American troops."[2]

All of a sudden, however, Clark felt a twinge of consternation. Neither he nor his driver knew where they were. The conquering hero of Rome was lost! Still, they hated to admit this indignity, and they continued to

1. Though designated as the U.S. Fifth Army, the command included British, French, and at times New Zealand and other troops.
2. Mark W. Clark, *Calculated Risk,* 365.

bounce through the streets, their eyes straining to pick up any landmark that would lead them to Capitoline Hill, where Clark had instructed his four corps commanders to meet him to plan further operations. But for a while no sign presented itself.

Their embarrassment eventually subsided, however. Clark and his party found themselves at St. Peter's Square, where General Hume, who had some knowledge of Rome, could get his bearings. As they paused, gazing up at the great dome of St. Peter's, a priest walking by stopped to say hello.

"Welcome to Rome," the priest said, unconscious of the three stars on the bumper of the jeep or even the three stars on Clark's cap. "Is there any way in which I can help you?"

"Well, we'd like to get to Capitoline Hill."

The priest gave directions and then added how proud he was of the American Fifth Army. He gave his name and proudly announced that he was from Detroit.

"My name's Clark," the general said, probably expecting a reaction that did not come. After a few more pleasantries between priest and general, the priest started to take his leave.

Suddenly, however, dawn broke and Clark's new friend stopped. "What did you say your name is?" Clark was now identified. To the crowd gathered around, the priest grandly announced that they were in the presence of the commander of the Fifth Army. The crowd roared its approval and appreciation, and a youth climbed on his bicycle to lead the party to Capitoline Hill.[3] Clark's tour of the city was of course duly recorded by photographers. The picture of Clark, sitting confidently in the front seat of his jeep, looking like the master of all he surveyed, became part of history.

Though he tried to portray his entry into Rome in a humorous light, Clark's arrival in the Italian capital was the high point of his long and sometimes controversial career. It represented the culmination of months of heavy, dogged fighting over perfect defensive terrain, usually in abominable weather and against a skillful and determined enemy. The campaign, originally visualized as an easy matter, had turned out to be anything but.

The timing of the fall of Rome could not have been better for the morale of men who had performed the thankless task of making this day possible. The very next day, June 6, 1944, the Anglo-American forces under General Dwight D. Eisenhower would cross the English Channel from

3. Ibid., 366.

Britain to France in the long-awaited Operation Overlord. From then on, Overlord would occupy center stage.

Yet the Italian campaign was no small affair. Taken by itself, it would eventually entail over 313,000 Allied casualties and about 336,000 German, including prisoners.[4] To understand the story, one must begin nine months earlier, at the inception, at a small port thirty miles south of Naples, named Salerno.

4. Eric Morris, *Circles of Hell: The War in Italy, 1943–1945*, 437.

Allied Landing at Salerno, 9 September 1943

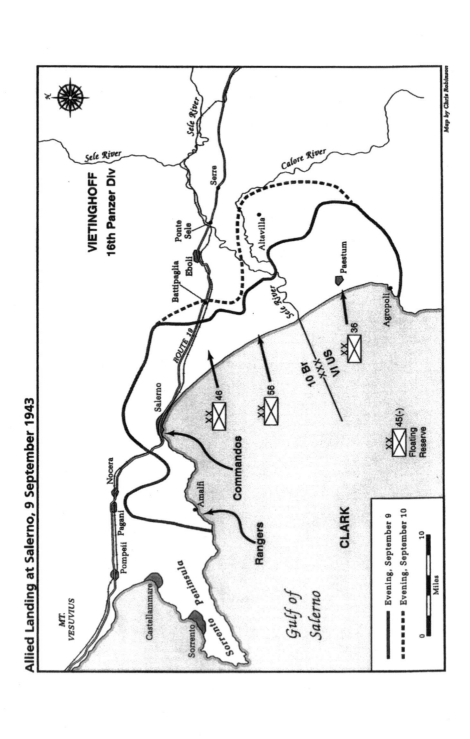

Map by Chris Robinson

CHAPTER 1

THE BEGINNING

The Landing at Salerno

On the evening of Wednesday, September 8, 1943, Lieutenant General Mark Wayne Clark, U.S. Army, stood on the bridge of the USS *Ancon,* sailing into the Gulf of Salerno, Italy.[1] The Allies were about to launch the Italian campaign which, though they had no way of imagining it, would include the dramatic Anzio battle.

The *Ancon,* a comfortable vessel, was the flagship of Vice Admiral Henry K. Hewitt, USN, Commander of U.S. Naval Forces in the Mediterranean. Hewitt, a man from the Class of 1906 at the Naval Academy, had amassed a wealth of experience in active naval operations, including the delivery of General George S. Patton's Seventh U.S. Army to the beaches of Sicily the previous July. Hewitt's counterpart, Clark, age forty-six, was coming into combat at a high level for the very first time.

Hewitt's task required all the expertise he had attained. He was charged with transporting the various army units to the landing area from widely scattered locations: the 36th Infantry Division from Oran, in Algeria; the 45th from Sicily; the 46th British from Bizerte, Tunisia; and the 56th British from Tripoli, Libya. Much of that task had been accomplished. As of September 8 Hewitt had already concentrated his convoy just off Salerno. What still remained was the debarkation itself and the problem of follow-up. The Allies had to build up land forces at Salerno faster than could the enemy.

---

1. " . . . flagship *Ancon* was the only complete AGC [Amphibious Command Ship] in the Western Task Force; so well equipped, in fact, that Admiral Hewitt was tempted to requisition her for his own use. He did not long resist the temptation, and 'Hotel Ancon,' as she was nicknamed, became his flagship for Salerno" (Samuel Eliot Morrison, *Sicily, Salerno, Anzio,* 64).

Lieutenant General Mark W. Clark and Vice Admiral Henry K. Hewitt, aboard the USS *Ancon*, c. September 8, 1943. National Archives.

Despite their differences in background and experience, Clark and Hewitt worked smoothly together, because each knew exactly the role he was to play. Hewitt would be in command of the entire task force, army and navy, until Clark's troops were established ashore, at which point Clark, as army commander, would take over. Clark did not envy Hewitt's job of assembling and landing the four hundred and fifty ships of varying sizes and shapes of the convoy. As he watched the assembling of vessels from the bridge of the *Ancon*, Clark felt nearly awed by the magnitude of Hewitt's responsibilities. "Thank God," he later quoted himself, that "I don't have the job of getting them assembled and into shore."[2] Hewitt, on the other hand, did not seem overwhelmed by the difficulties. He was, however, anxious to get this chore finished so he could get on to other missions. "When can you take over?" he asked that evening. Clark, in no very great hurry, managed to stall for the moment.[3]

2. Clark, *Calculated Risk*, 183.
3. Ibid., 186.

The Strategy of the Italian Campaign

The landing at Salerno was a high-risk proposition, and nobody was more aware of that fact than General Dwight D. Eisenhower, at that time the Allied Commander in the Western Mediterranean. The German forces in Italy, he knew, included sixteen divisions, against which, if concentrated, he could land only four Allied divisions until later reinforcement. He was, in fact, invading Europe on a shoestring.

That situation, so lamentable from the Allied viewpoint, had been brought about by a basic difference in British and American concepts of how to defeat Hitler. The Americans focused their attention on one long-range objective: to cross the English Channel and drive across France toward Berlin. The British, especially Prime Minister Winston Churchill, deemed the Allies too weak for such an invasion until the year 1944 at least. So the American strategists, headed by Army Chief of Staff George C. Marshall, found themselves dragged from one operation to another in the Mediterranean throughout the year 1943.

The slippery slope of Allied commitment to the Mediterranean had begun back in the summer of 1942, when Roosevelt and Churchill substituted an occupation of French North Africa in place of a cross-Channel invasion that year. It continued at Casablanca in January 1943, when the Combined Chiefs of Staff, under their political leaders, had agreed to invade Sicily after the fall of Tunisia. In June of 1943, the decision had been made to invade Italy following the fall of Sicily. Since Overlord could not be launched until nearly a year from then, General Marshall had reluctantly acceded to these various decisions, but only on the condition that the lion's share of resources be sent to the United Kingdom, in preparation for the cross-Channel invasion, rather than to the Mediterranean.[4]

Avalanche, as the Salerno landing was code-named, therefore represented a compromise. It would be executed, but on a shoestring.

From the viewpoint of the man who would be ultimately responsible for a limited campaign in Italy, Eisenhower, the arithmetic was disheartening. The first-line German divisions scattered throughout Italy were capable of concentrating anywhere in the peninsula within days. So Eisenhower, as he had before and would do after, had placed all his hopes on achieving overwhelming air superiority. As he wrote later:

---

4. President Franklin Roosevelt looked to Marshall for the detailed strategic direction of the European war. In the very broadest decisions, such as that to invade North Africa in late 1942, he of course reserved the last word for himself.

> . . . in some respects the operation looked foolhardy; but it was undertaken in the faith in the ability of the air forces, by concentrating their striking power, to give air cover and emergency assistance to the beachhead during the build-up period, and in the power of the Navy to render close and continuous gunfire support to the landing troops until they were capable of taking care of themselves.[5]

Eisenhower's troubles continued, however. His hopes for receiving the airpower he deemed sufficient to overcome his weakness in ground forces were quickly dashed. Instead of doubling his current bomber strength of six groups of heavy bombers as he requested,[6] he was told to make do with what he had. General Marshall was being consistent in his determination to send everything possible to Britain, even to the point of taking risks in the Mediterranean.

So Eisenhower now harbored double misgivings about Avalanche. When he received formal orders to execute it anyway, he felt he had no choice but to obey.[7]

The Tactics

Planning for the invasion of Italy was simple in one respect. Due to the location of the British and American forces at the close of the Sicily campaign, it was foreordained that Montgomery's Eighth Army would drive up the Italian boot on the right and Clark's Fifth Army would go on the left. The Eighth Army's task in securing a footing was easy; in fact it had slipped two divisions across the Strait of Messina six days before Avalanche, on September 3. But Clark's Fifth Army could land in any of several places, and it was necessary to pick where. His ultimate objective was the port of Naples, but there were several routes by which to reach it. Allied Force Headquarters, in Algiers, had considered several possibilities, of which Salerno was only one. Another was the Calabria region, the toe of the Italian boot, already partly occupied by Montgomery. Another area was the Gulf of Gaeta, north of Naples.

All three alternatives had disadvantages. Calabria, for one, had been rejected because the Strait of Messina is located about 150 miles from

---

5. Dwight D. Eisenhower, *Crusade in Europe,* 187.

6. Four groups of B-17 Flying Fortresses and two understrength groups of B-24 Liberators.

7. John S. D. Eisenhower, *Allies,* 360–61.

Naples over rugged terrain. An advance from that area would be too tedious and expensive in resources.

Gaeta, on the other hand, afforded good landing conditions. Maneuver room between the beaches and the surrounding hills, for example, was more than adequate. However, that area lay outside the range of Allied fighter planes based in Sicily, and General Eisenhower ruled it out.

That left Salerno, which also had its shortcomings. The principal disadvantage was the limited maneuver space between the beaches and the surrounding hills. Salerno did, however, lie within Allied fighter range, and that consideration took top priority. So Salerno it was.

The overall ground command for the Italian invasion was vested in Britain's most experienced commander, General Sir Harold Alexander. Alexander bore two titles. First, he was Eisenhower's deputy commander, but, far more important, he commanded the 15th Army Group,[8] the headquarters of which were located in Sicily. Once Clark's Fifth Army was ashore, Alexander would have two armies fighting on the Italian mainland. In general terms Clark would be based on the Tyrrhenian Sea and Montgomery on the Adriatic. But the Salerno operation was a one-army affair, so the detailed planning for the landing had been done at Clark's headquarters.

Clark's Fifth Army, while American in name, consisted of more British troops than American. The army consisted of two corps, the British 10 Corps,[9] under Lieutenant General Sir Richard L. McCreery, and the U.S. VI Corps, under Major General Ernest J. Dawley, together about 55,000 men.[10] The planned landing sites were spread out over a distance of about thirty-six miles, from Maiori on the Sorrento Peninsula on the left to Paestum on the right.[11] Because of the concave shape of the Salerno shoreline, the beaches on the left ran nearly east-west and those on the right nearly north-south. The town of Salerno lay almost at the left, or north end,

8. The number fifteen had been coined in Sicily, where the two armies under Alexander's command were the American Seventh Army and the British Eighth. The number of the army group had been unchanged, even though the American Fifth had replaced the Seventh.

9. British custom calls for corps designations to be by Arabic numerals whereas American custom calls for Roman. Hence this text will designate the 10 British Corps and the VI U.S. Corps.

10. Clark, *Calculated Risk*, 185.

11. The actual right flank was at Agripoli. However, the nearby Paestum is the town known to history.

of the landing area. The beaches were generally satisfactory, but the rugged mountains surrounding the beachhead were broken by only two exits, that of the Sele River Valley a little bit south of the midpoint, and the Vietri Pass, near the extreme left of the line. The Vietri Pass led to Nocera, Vesuvius, and eventually to Naples. Of the two passes, the Vietri Gap possessed the greater strategic importance, but the Sele River Gap to the south was tactically the most dangerous.

A major danger point for a landing force in the Salerno area was the Sele River, which cut the landing area in two. A river splitting a landing area is bad enough in any circumstance, but the Sele presented an additional hazard: its delta had built up large sandbars on the sea, preventing landings over an eight-mile stretch of coastline. The two embarking corps, therefore, would for some distance be incapable of mutual support. The British 10 Corps and the American VI Corps could not join up, in fact, until they both had driven inland about thirteen miles. The planned point of juncture was a bridge over the Sele River named, appropriately, Ponte Sele. On the south, or American, side of the beachhead, the path of the invading troops would also be forced to cross the Calore River, a stream that flows into the Sele from the south. Because the Sele River gap was located somewhat toward the southern part of the beachhead, the American VI Corps on the right would have space to land with only one division, whereas the British 10 Corps could land two.

In the wider landing area on the left, the British 10 Corps consisted of the 46th Infantry (Oak Tree) Division and the 56th Infantry (Black Cat) Division. The 46th, on the left, with Commandos attached, was to seize Salerno. The 56th, on the right, was to drive inward to take the Montecorvino airfield and then drive southward through Battipaglia and eventually join the Americans at Ponte Sele. On the extreme left, operating directly under 10 Corps Headquarters, Lieutenant Colonel William O. Darby's American Rangers were to seize the heights over the Vietri Pass. The Vietri Pass was a double-edged sword. It was the gateway to Vesuvius and Naples, but it was also a position which, if occupied by German forces, could form a nearly impregnable defensive position.

On the right of the Sele River Valley, Dawley's single division was Major General Fred Walker's 36th,[12] a Texas National Guard unit undergoing its first combat. Behind the 36th, still aboard ship, Clark had a float-

---

12. Walker had commanded a battalion of the 30th Infantry in the 3d Division's epic Second Battle of the Marne in 1918. He had also been Clark's instructor at the Army Command and General Staff School at Fort Leavenworth, Kansas.

ing reserve of two (later three) regimental combat teams from the 45th Infantry Division.[13]

Those were the plans by which Mark W. Clark intended to make the great amphibious landing at Salerno.

The Approach to Salerno

Despite the high risks of the operation, Clark managed to maintain a calm, even somewhat lighthearted appearance to the public. On the voyage between Bizerte and Salerno he had met with the newsmen aboard the *Ancon* to give them a briefing on the plans. Among those present was the noted war correspondent Quentin Reynolds. Reynolds was something of a celebrity, a reporter who lived among the higher echelons, the generals and admirals. He had previously made a trip to Russia and another to the Middle East. At Salerno he had just left Eisenhower's headquarters in Algiers, having borrowed a wristwatch from Ike's naval aide, Lieutenant Commander Harry Butcher. Reynolds saw Clark in the most favorable light, describing him as "lanky and likeable."

As Reynolds described the scene, Clark grinned when he told the correspondents to sit down. He then asked their opinion of the plan. "My God, it's daring," Reynolds blurted out.

Clark agreed with a laugh. "Sure, we're spitting in the lion's mouth. We know it. But we have to do that. We had several alternate plans and we studied them all carefully. This seemed to be the only answer. . . . We may get hurt, but you can't play with fire without the risk of burning your fingers."

After a discussion of the risks, and Clark's frank admission that he was "scared stiff" about what the German Air Force would do, the meeting was over. Reynolds left with satisfaction: "When we left General Clark we felt a little better because of his quiet air of confidence. Clark at forty-six looks thirty-six—if that. He had never commanded large units in combat, but Eisenhower had picked him. General Eisenhower didn't make mistakes—and he was sold on Clark."[14]

One imponderable in Allied planning was the intensity of the resistance that would greet Clark's men when they landed. Perhaps, they hoped,

---

13. A regimental combat team was a task force organization consisting of an infantry regiment, its normal supporting field artillery battalion, some reconnaissance units, and a company of combat engineers. It was under the command of the infantry regimental commander.

14. Quentin Reynolds, *The Curtain Rises*, 281–83.

they would meet none. That evening of September 8, in Admiral Hewitt's cabin aboard the *Ancon*, Clark and Hewitt listened to General Eisenhower's announcement of the Italian surrender to the Allies, which was being beamed over the radio from Algiers. If the Italians, as the Allies hoped, could disarm the greatly outnumbered German forces on their soil, Clark's men might find themselves greeted on the Salerno beaches as liberators. But would the Italians have the will to do that? The Allies had no way to know.

Unfortunately for Clark and his men, the hope of being welcomed as liberators turned out to be a pipe dream. The Germans were also listening to Eisenhower's proclamation, and the high command knew exactly what it would do in such a contingency. The codeword "Axis" was radioed to all commands, and German units in the whole of the Mediterranean "from the Gulf of Lyons to Crete and Rhodes" quickly disarmed the lukewarm Italians.[15] German troops assumed the defense of Italy, and withdrawal orders went out to the two German divisions facing Montgomery in the south. Those two divisions would follow Route 19, which ran just inland from the Gulf of Salerno.

The Germans had taken these actions even before the Allies landed at Salerno.

They had also anticipated Allied strategy. Suspecting a landing at Salerno,[16] they moved the 16th Panzer Division, a relatively fresh unit, into the hills behind the Salerno landing beaches. This had happened two days earlier. The 16th Panzer had thus been afforded two days to survey the area, to place guns in position in the passes, and to mine the beaches. Landing at Salerno would be no pushover for the Fifth Army.

The Landing at Salerno

Clark was still on the bridge of the *Ancon* with Hewitt as the first American troops descended their landing nets into the craft below and began their long journey into the beaches. It was 3:00 A.M. A half hour later reports came in that the first landing craft had reached the beaches. At that point, however, Clark realized that he had made a grievous error in his tactical planning; he had allowed his two corps commanders to use

---

15. Walter Warlimont, *Inside Hitler's Headquarters, 1939–1945*, 381.

16. German intelligence, knowing the effective range of Allied fighter aircraft, had also noticed the Allied habit of refusing to fight without that air cover. That meant a landing at Salerno.

different fire support plans. To the left, on the north, Clark could see "flashes of gunfire . . . where British warships were laying down a barrage in front of X Corps' [sic] first wave." On the south side, however, the American VI Corps was attempting to reach shore by stealth, without fire support. Clark could now see that any attempts at secrecy had been useless. In front of his eyes he saw "flares and the flames of demolition fires." Once the two assault regiments of the 36th Division had landed, Clark records, ". . . a loudspeaker voice on the shore roared out in English, 'Come on in and give up. You're covered.' Flares shot high into the air to illuminate the beaches, and German guns previously sighted on the beaches opened up with a roar."[17]

Still the troops of the 36th made their landing.

Tactical control of the American units in the Salerno land battle that first day was vested in Major General Fred Walker, since his 36th Division was the only major American unit ashore. In that early stage, Walker reported directly to Admiral Hewitt, who was still in overall army-navy command. Clark was still excess baggage aboard the *Ancon,* and Dawley would not have his VI Corps headquarters established for another day. It would be up to Walker to direct his two assault combat teams, the 142d on the left, the 141st on the right, and the 143d in floating reserve.

At 5:00 A.M. Walker and his staff clambered down the rope ladders from the USS *Chase* onto a small craft termed an LCVP.[18] After circling a while to organize the small flotilla, the sailors began the twelve-mile trip into shore. About a half hour later the LCVP was heading eastward to its designated beach. It was an exciting trip. At one point the craft was forced to swerve to avoid a floating mine, a menacing globe about two feet in diameter with six-inch horns jutting out of it.

As they neared the beach, Walker found himself fascinated by a barrage balloon up ahead. It was about a hundred feet high and moored to the ground at a spot about fifty feet from the water's edge. As Walker watched, a German airplane came out of nowhere and began pumping shots into the balloon, causing it to catch fire and collapse. Walker's reverie was broken when he found himself unloaded into waist-deep water, still some seventy-five feet from the shore. The landing craft's steersman was already headed out to sea; the young man had no desire to stay around that beach.

German artillery fire was coming down on the beach as Walker and his

17. Clark, *Calculated Risk,* 188.
18. Landing Craft, Vehicles and Personnel.

staff dashed inland. One detail gave Walker confidence that the 142d Infantry, in whose sector he was, had done a good job of surprising the Germans. Lying on the ground were a couple of German radios still receiving messages from the enemy. Walker was chagrined that none of his group understood German; had they been able, they might have picked up some valuable information. As they continued, Walker noted that they were passing the Temple of Ceres in the ruins of the ancient Greek city of Paestum. That fact gave him the uncomfortable thought that they were "desecrating hallowed ground."[19]

Eventually Walker and his party found the set of buildings he had picked out from aerial photos to be his future command post. It was located not far from Paestum, in what turned out to be a small tobacco factory. The family that owned it came out to greet him wearing their best clothes, delighted that they and their establishment were to be spared. Before long Walker's command post was functioning. "Almost immediately," he later crowed, "the unit commanders began reporting their progress and locations."

By the end of the first day, September 9, nearly all of Clark's troops had secured footholds in their respective sectors. On the extreme left of the line, Darby's American Rangers had reached the heights around Maiori, thereby securing the Vietri Pass. The British 46th and 56th Divisions had landed at points flanking the important Montecorvino Airfield, while elements of the 46th, their British Commandos, were closing in on the town of Salerno. The 56th Division, on the British right, had pushed on toward Battipaglia and was preparing to continue along the north bank of the Sele River toward Ponte Sele. The American 36th Division, after the first stiff resistance on the beaches, had gained control of the plain south of the Sele River and had pushed inland about five miles.

Clark was satisfied at the close of the first day. "By nightfall," he later wrote, "I could feel that we had secured the beaches and were in a position to close the gap between 10 and VI Corps and to start the drive for the dominated mountain heights which we must seize and through which we must pass toward Naples."

---

19. Fred L. Walker, *From Texas to Rome: A General's Journal*, 235. Actually, the Temple was to Athena, though calling it the Temple of Ceres was a common error. Paestum was, incidentally, the northernmost limit of the ancient Greek colonial empire in Italy. See H. W. Hanson, *History of Art* (Englewood Cliffs, N. J.: Prentice Hall, 1962), 91.

CHAPTER 2

THE GERMANS REACT

Though General Clark had declared himself satisfied with the results of the landing on September 9, Field Marshal Albert Kesselring, commanding the German forces in southern Italy, was also highly satisfied. The Allied landing at Salerno had, in fact, relieved his mind of a great deal of uncertainty. He knew that the Allies were planning to invade mainland Italy at some point, but previously he had been forced to guess where they would come ashore—Salerno, Gaeta, Apulia, or even Rome itself. But now, since the Allies had landed in such strength at Salerno, Kesselring was sure that they lacked the resources to mount another invasion anywhere. He could now concentrate on defending that area.

Kesselring's biggest worry had been the prospect of an Allied landing near Rome. Had the Allies been bold enough to risk such a venture, he was not the least bit confident that German forces in the area could have subdued the three Italian divisions on hand. But that fear had now dissipated. Without the stiffening influence of an American or British force near Rome, those Italian divisions, consisting of men who had little stomach for the war, quickly submitted. Kesselring's 2d Parachute Division disarmed them and sent their members home.

As of September 9, the date of the Allied landing, Kesselring had eight divisions in southern Italy. His main force was the Tenth Army, under Colonel General Heinrich von Vietinghoff, which in turn broke down into two corps, the 76th and 14th Panzer Corps. The 76th Panzer Corps consisted of the 29th Panzer Grenadier (PG) Division, the 26th Panzer, and the 3d Parachute Division. Two of them, the 29th PG and the 26th Panzer, were facing Montgomery's Eighth Army in Calabria, and they were in danger of being cut off by the Salerno landing if they did not move northward immediately. (The 3d Parachute, at Apulia, near Taranto, was temporarily

Field Marshal Albert Kesselring, commanding the German Army Group South, defending Rome. National Archives.

out of contact with the enemy.) Fortunately, from Kesselring and Von Vietinghoff's viewpoint, Montgomery was moving so slowly and cautiously that the 26th and 29th German Divisions could break contact easily, leaving only light forces to cover the withdrawal.

Von Vietinghoff's other corps, the 14th Panzer, was the one most immediately concerned with Salerno. It consisted of the 16th Panzer Division, which had been resisting Clark's landing, the Hermann Goering Division,[1] just northeast of Naples, and the 15th Panzer Grenadier, in a defensive position at the Gulf of Gaeta.

Kesselring's command also included, besides the Tenth Army, the 11th Flak Corps, a misnamed outfit consisting of the 3d Panzer Grenadier Division and the 2d Parachute Division, both in the vicinity of Rome. It was the 2d Parachute, as mentioned, that had just disarmed the Italian divisions in the vicinity.[2]

1. The Hermann Goering Division was a peculiar formation, including both panzer and parachute units. It was probably the most powerful of the German divisions.
2. Albert Kesselring, *The Memoirs of Field-Marshal Kesselring,* 182; and *West Point Atlas,*

Colonel General Heinrich von Vietinghoff, commander of the German Tenth Army. National Archives.

What made Kesselring's forces so dangerous to the Allies was the fact that most of his units were capable of moving to the Salerno area within a few days. The 76th Panzer Corps of Vietinghoff's Tenth Army was already moving north, leaving only rear guards. The 14th Panzer Corps was already located in the areas he considered the greatest threat: the Gulf of Salerno and the Gulf of Gaeta.

Aside from the deployment of troops, Kesselring was facing two other problems, one chronic and one acute. The chronic problem entailed his relationships with the German high command, commonly called OKW (*Oberkommandwehrmacht*). It was not OKW in itself that was so troublesome: his real problem was with Hitler himself. Colonel General Alfred Jodl and Field Marshal Wilhelm Keitel, Hitler's lackeys in uniform, could be counted on to follow Hitler's instruction slavishly and without question.

Map #94. Kesselring does not mention the 15th PG Division at the Gulf of Gaeta. In addition to the Tenth Army and the 11th Flak Corps, Kesselring was also responsible for the forces occupying Sardinia and Corsica. On Corsica he had only one brigade, the SS *Reichsfuhrer*. On Sardinia he had the 90th Panzer Grenadier Division with a brigade of fortification troops.

Hitler had long recognized that Kesselring was among his ablest field commanders, but "Smiling Albert" had, by force of circumstances, been overshadowed in Hitler's favor by Kesselring's former subordinate, Erwin Rommel, whose *Afrika Korps* had operated almost independently in North Africa.[3] To make matters worse, Kesselring and Rommel had developed a mutual antagonism based on differing attitudes toward the Italians and accentuated, one suspects, by a certain degree of mutual jealousy. For the moment, at least, Rommel held the advantage. The éclat that surrounded him as the "Desert Fox" had given him an influence with both the German people and with Hitler that now overshadowed his former boss.

In addition to Rommel, Kesselring had other detractors in the officer corps of the German Army. Though he had spent many years as an army officer, he had been assigned to the German Air Force, the *Luftwaffe,* when war approached. Though he had performed brilliantly as a *Luftwaffe* officer in the Polish, French, and Russian campaigns, his duties now, as commander in southern Italy, were far more involved with army matters than with air force. That circumstance had caused regular German Army officers to feel threatened. They derided his nickname of "Smiling Albert" and claimed that his affinity for the Italians had damaged his effectiveness as an officer of the Third Reich.

Kesselring held one trump card in his relations with Hitler: his views on the defense of Italy. Rommel, tired and pessimistic, advocated withdrawing German forces from nearly the entire peninsula and assuming a defensive position in the north, merely settling for guarding the passes to Austria and Germany through the Alps. Kesselring, on the other hand, favored defending Italy as far south as possible. He even deemed it possible to hold Rome throughout 1943 and well into the year 1944. That thinking was close to Hitler's.

Hitler compromised, thereby taking the worst possible course of action. Rather than take sides in the contretemps between his two field marshals, he simply split the German forces in Italy and gave half to each. In the north, he created Army Group B, commanded by Rommel, with eight German divisions. In the south, he designated Kesselring's command as OB South (Oberbefeld South), with like strength.[4] By this arrangement, Hitler unwittingly assured that Rommel's divisions would be unavailable to Kesselring in the latter's desperate fight to stop the Allies from landing and taking Rome. Kesselring felt this loss keenly. As he later wrote,

3. When Rommel had commanded the *Afrika Korps* in Libya and later Tunisia, he had been under Kesselring, in overall command in the Mediterranean.
4. Oberbefeld means "supreme command."

This Italian duumvirate of myself and Rommel, with Hitler's almost obsequious submissiveness to Rommel, was responsible for the rejection of my priority calls for reinforcements. . . . How easily this critical time—"a dramatic week" even according to the English—might have led to a decisive German victory if Hitler had acceded to my very modest demands.[5]

Kesselring was also facing a more acute problem. On September 8, the day before the landing, the Allied Air Forces had bombed and destroyed his headquarters at Frascati, just south of Rome. It was a heavy raid, and communications between OB South and Hitler's headquarters, OKW, were temporarily cut. Such a development had its bright side; it gave Kesselring a certain temporary latitude to fight his own war free of interference from above.

Undeterred by his problems, Kesselring set about to use his 76th Panzer Corps as it came north from Calabria to help destroy the Allied landing at Salerno. The two objectives fit hand in glove. The 26th Panzer and the 29th PG Divisions could easily be included in the immense counterattack Kesselring was planning.

At the same time, Kesselring set about making plans for his subsequent delaying action up the Italian peninsula in case he was unsuccessful in driving Clark into the sea. Two lines south of Rome were obvious. The first was the strong delaying position along the Volturno River north of Naples. The other was the very serious defense line along the Rapido and Garagliano, hinged on the strong position at Cassino.

So on the very night that Clark's Fifth Army made the first major landing in mainland Europe, Kesselring was planning the defenses that would very nearly, in future weeks, prove the invader's nemesis.

5. Kesselring, *Memoirs*, 186.

Battle of the Sele River Valley, 11-14 September 1943

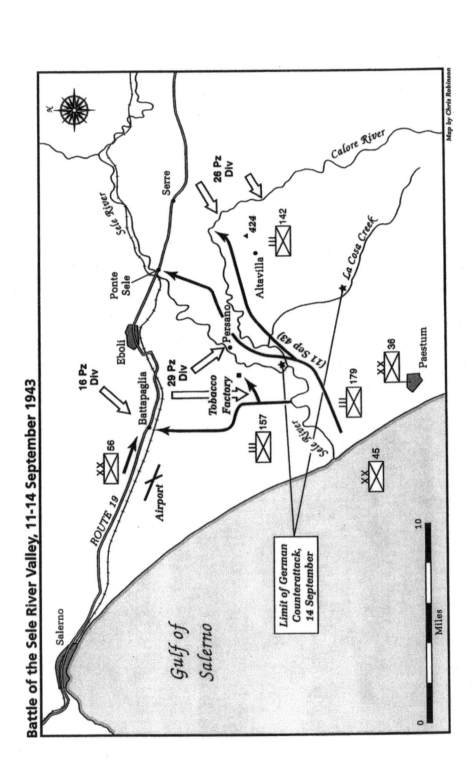

Map by Chris Robinson

CHAPTER 3

ORDEAL OF FIRE IN THE SELE VALLEY

The initial landing at Salerno, and even the day after, had been misleading to the Americans and to Clark. In spite of intelligence reports that presaged heavy fighting ahead, it seemed as if an easy victory was in sight. Part of that optimism stemmed, it seems, from the fact that the Fifth Army was new to battle. Its commander, staff, VI Corps commander, and 36th Division had never seen combat at a high level before.[1]

As a result, the four days following the 10th of September would be doubly difficult for Clark and his men. Their struggle would center around the Sele River Valley, and it would share some aspects with the later Anzio operation. This Fifth Army, however, was not the experienced formation that it would become when the latter invasion was launched. Salerno was therefore a training ground, though a perilous one, for Anzio.

General Clark stayed aboard the *Ancon* during the day of September 9, and during that time he had no command function. The next morning, however, he decided to go ashore and inspect. He was not yet ready to establish his command post on the beach, but he wanted to take a tour of the front. He drove his own jeep, accompanied in the vehicle by three tall MPs.[2] Together they made an impressive group, easily recognizable. The American soldiers cheered them as they drove along the dusty roads.

---

1. The Seventh Army, under General George S. Patton, was preparing in Sicily for the invasion of southern France, which held high priority. Of the divisions that had fought in Sicily, all but the 3d and 45th Infantry Division had been earmarked for transfer to the United Kingdom for Overlord.

2. Hugh Pond, *Salerno,* 122. Clark's custom continued throughout the war, even into the occupation of Austria in 1946. The author, assigned to Clark's headquarters, noticed that all his bodyguards of MPs had to be over six feet tall—but none quite so tall as the commanding general himself.

Clark's first destination was the American sector, where he visited the command post of his old friend and onetime school instructor Fred Walker, commanding the 36th Division. He bypassed Dawley's VI Corps headquarters, because it was not yet established that morning. Furthermore, the VI Corps had only one division committed at that time.

Clark was satisfied with what he saw. Walker's bridgeheads were secure, and it was becoming apparent that the German 16th Panzer Division was stretched. Evidence indicated that the Germans had been forced to move the bulk of their strength to the British front, where lay the greatest threat to Naples. Events of the day confirmed that this was definitely what was happening. As a result, Walker was able to move forward and occupy the entire hill complex to its front. At the end of the day, the 36th front line included the vital Hill 424, on which stood the town of Altavilla. Walker's troops had actually pushed forward to a line a short distance behind the Calore River to its front.

From the American zone, Clark drove over to visit General McCreery's 10 British Corps. Arriving in the early afternoon, he found the situation there much more difficult. The 46th Division had taken Salerno, but German artillery fire from the surrounding hills was preventing their making use of the town's port facilities.[3] The same situation prevailed at the Montecorvino airport, which had been taken by the 56th Division. It too was unusable because of enemy fire.[4]

Matters were even worse at Battipaglia, an important town on Route 19 that had to be taken before the British on the north could join the Americans on the south at Ponte Sele. Sometime earlier, the Royal Fusiliers, of the 56th Division, had secured a foothold in the town but had soon been hit with severe counterattacks, losing many men as prisoners. Heavy and effective naval gunfire had saved the remnants of the Fusiliers from total destruction, but Battipaglia remained in German hands.

On the extreme left of 10 Corps, Clark was told, Darby's American Rangers and the British Commandos were fighting atop the Sorrento Peninsula near Nocera and Vietri. Enemy pressure was strong, but the beleaguered special forces were using their advantageous position to adjust highly effective naval gunfire on their attackers. To back them up, he planned to further reinforce Darby with a battalion from the American 36th Division.

Back in the VI Corps zone, Clark identified two all-important terrain features that he called critical. One, already occupied by Walker, was Hill

3. Ibid., 105.
4. Ibid., 111.

424. The other was the Sele River Valley. Clark quickly concluded that the 36th Division alone lacked the strength to occupy both. He therefore decided to commit the 179th Regimental Combat Team, still in floating reserve, to move up the Sele River Valley.[5] Late on September 10 the 179th disembarked at Paestum, ready to move out. The 157th Infantry Regiment, also from the 45th Division, was to attack abreast of the 179th, though along the north bank, protecting the left flank of the 179th and assisting the British in taking Battipaglia.[6] Dawley's VI Corps command post had been set up near Paestum during the afternoon, and with the addition of the 157th and 179th Regiments of the 45th Division, he now had nearly two divisions with the promise of reinforcements later from the 82d Airborne.

All in all, Clark continued to be optimistic at the end of the day of the 10th, and in the evening he sent a message to General Alexander in Sicily saying that he would soon be ready to attack northward through the Molina Pass above Vietri and capture Naples.[7]

Clark's optimism was premature. On that same evening, General Heinrich von Vietinghoff reported to Kesselring that the 29th Panzer Grenadier Division would be able to attack the Americans as early as the next morning,[8] the same time that the American 179th Infantry would begin its advance up the Sele River Valley. Following the 29th PG would be the 26th Panzer, then the 15th PG and the Hermann Goering.[9]

Vietinghoff, like Clark, recognized that the decisive point in the Salerno beachhead was the Sele River Valley, or, to be more exact, the floodplain that lay between the Sele and the Calore Rivers. These streams join at a point about five miles from the sea.[10] It was at the Sele Valley that

5. The 45th Division's third regiment, the 180th, had been left behind because of shipping shortages.

6. Inadvertently the 157th had been landed in the wrong place. The mistake was nobody's fault. Admiral Hewitt, whose ships were required elsewhere in the Mediterranean, had been forced to land the 157th without checking with Clark. Through no fault of his own, he disembarked them in the VI Corps sector.

7. Pond, *Salerno*, 123.

8. Kesselring, *Memoirs*, 186.

9. Ibid. It is interesting that these were four of the best divisions in the German Army.

10. "The vital ground in the American sector was the flood plain between the Sele and Calore rivers. The plain forms a corridor of low ground at Serre, a village 12 miles inland that nestles at the foot of the hills. The corridor descends gently to the junction of the two rivers, just 5 miles from the sea. This was the obvious line of advance for any defender launching a counterattack against a beachhead, yet its significance did not become apparent until the troops were on the ground. Mark Clark and his Fifth Army staff had largely ignored this feature" (Eric Morris, *Salerno: A Military Fiasco*, 226).

Kesselring and von Vietinghoff could—and nearly did—break through the Allied lines and drive the invaders back into the sea. As a result, the Salerno drama has become associated with the Sele Valley almost to the exclusion of the rest of the action.

Late in the day of September 10, 1943, Colonel Robert B. Hutchins, commanding the 179th Infantry Regimental Combat Team, reported to General Dawley for instructions. His objective, Dawley specified, was Route 19, some thirteen miles inland. On reaching that road, his units were to fan out, sending one force southward to occupy the town of Serre and another force northward to Ponte Sele.[11] There, if all went well, the British 56th Division, driving southward through Battipaglia and Eboli, would join him. That juncture achieved, the Americans and British would be facing Kesselring with a solid front.

This plan was a monument to faulty Allied intelligence and hubris on the part of the American command. Hutchins and his men were to march in the dark for several miles over rough ground that nobody from the regiment had ever laid eyes on. He would have to cross the Calore River at a point about six miles from the Sele River's mouth. The Sele was known to be unfordable, and perhaps the Calore was also.

Hutchins's planned maneuver can be explained only by his assumption that no enemy would be in his way. After his regiment crossed the Calore, the main body would continue along the narrow strip of land between the two rivers, past Persano, to his objective. One battalion, supported by tanks and artillery, was to proceed along the south bank of the Calore, and cross it only when coming within about three miles from Ponte Sele.

Until the 2d Battalion of the 179th crossed the Calore, the two parts of Hutchins's regiment would be split, out of supporting distance from each other. The scheme would have been unthinkable except for the assumption that no German troops lay in the path. Hutchins's plan has been called by one authority an "outrageous defiance of the enemy."[12]

That same afternoon, as Hutchins was leaving Dawley's command post, von Vietinghoff was confidently completing plans. He had concentrated enough troops to hit the British 10 Corps with two divisions—the Hermann Goering Division and the 15th Panzer Grenadier Division—[13]

11. The Italian coastline runs northwest to southeast in the Salerno area, but at the risk of oversimplification, I am presuming that it runs south to north. The Sele River is therefore presumed to run east to west.

12. Morris, *Salerno*, 181.

13. These divisions were under the 14th Panzer Corps.

and he planned to reinforce the 16th Panzer with the 29th PG that evening for his major attack against the American VI Corps. The 26th Panzer and the 1st Parachute Division would not be far behind.

This concentration of force he had accomplished with great difficulty. The roads leading to the bridgehead were restrictive, and Vietinghoff faced vexing supply problems brought about by the need to set up his own supply depots in light of the Italian collapse.[14] By the evening of the 10th of September, however, von Vietinghoff, as he promised Kesselring, was ready to attack.[15]

Hutchins's men moved out promptly at 7:30 P.M. on September 10, and from the first the regiment ran into trouble. The bridge over which they had intended to cross the Calore was in flames,[16] causing a delay of a couple of hours. The crossing complete, the 179th stumbled through the darkness up the narrow neck of land between the Sele and the Calore, Hutchins neglecting, in the process, to occupy the high ground on which the important town of Persano stood.

In spite of the difficulties, the lead company of Hutchins's 3d Battalion reached the high ground overlooking Ponte Sele by dawn of the 11th of September, his troops strung out single file for miles. Further, the regiment was still split.

At the first crack of dawn, elements of the German 16th Panzer and 29th PG hit the lead company of the 179th with machine guns and mortars. German tanks and artillery crossed the Sele from the north and occupied Persano, which was now Hutchins's rear. American tanks and tank destroyers attempting to come to the rescue of the 179th were stopped at the "Burned Bridge." Throughout the day, American efforts to relieve Hutchins with tanks, infantry, and artillery proved fruitless. As evening approached, the two battalions of the 179th were low on water and food. The two batteries of the 160th Field Artillery were down to ten rounds per piece. Even rifle ammunition was low. In desperation, possibly to raise morale, Hutchins passed the order down the line to fix bayonets.[17]

Still there was no thought of giving up. One lieutenant from the Ammunition and Pioneer Platoon of the 179th recorded a vivid vignette:

---

14. The most serious shortage lay in gasoline. The 29th Panzer Grenadier, for example, had been immobilized throughout the period of September 9 and 10 for the simple reason that it had no fuel, Morris, *Salerno*, 162–63.

15. Kesselring, *Memoirs*, 186.

16. The bridge would thenceforward be called the "Burned bridge" by the Americans.

17. Morris, *Salerno*, 228.

That night, the whole battalion was in a circle. When you're gettin' tank fire from four directions, nobody has to tell you the enemy's behind you. We had a young major named Pete Donaldson. He was just a kid, maybe twenty-two years old, but he was a hell of a good Okie. He wanted everybody to know the situation. He went around and told everybody that the situation wasn't too good. His exact words were, "Tonight you're not fightin' for your country, you're fighting for your ass, because they're behind us." We had only one artillery piece with us . . . That's a desperate situation.[18]

Still, the two battalions held on. By the next morning, September 12, they were still there.

Across the Sele River, the 157th Infantry[19] finally began its attack toward Battipaglia. Its immediate objective was a cluster of buildings the Americans called the "Tobacco Factory,"[20] a key feature because it dominated Persano, across the river. This attack against the Tobacco Factory failed, however, because it contained camouflaged antitank weapons. Within moments, German antitank guns knocked out seven American tanks. The rest withdrew.[21] The situation of the 179th at Persano remained precarious.

That Saturday, September 11, 1943, also saw action on the part of the German Air Force, which flew 460 missions against the Allied shipping in the Gulf of Salerno. Two targets received priority. One was the fleet of cruisers whose guns the Allies were using to such great advantage.[22] The other was the *Ancon* itself, which was well known to the Germans as the Allies' primary command vessel. On the morning of the attack, Clark and Hewitt, standing on the bridge, were startled to hear a screeching noise followed by a loud explosion; the cruiser USS *Savannah*, only two hundred yards away from the *Ancon,* had been badly hit. There was no doubt in Clark's mind that the target of the bomb had been the *Ancon,* not the *Savannah*.[23]

18. Ray Williams, interview with author. Flint Whitlock, *The Rock of Anzio: From Sicily to Dachau: The History of the 45th Infantry Division,* 87.

19. Minus the battalion sent to the Sorrento Peninsula to reinforce Darby.

20. Tobacco factories abounded, as with Fred Walker's first command post. However, this is the set of installations the Americans regarded by that name.

21. Morris, *Salerno,* 228–29.

22. On one evening alone, the USS *Philadelphia* fired one thousand six-inch rounds into German tanks and troop formations. Morris, *Salerno,* 232.

23. Clark, *Calculated Risk,* 196.

That evening, the 15th Panzer Grenadier Regiment, of the 29th PG Division, began infiltrating across the Calore River into the positions of the overstretched 142d Infantry, 36th Division, on Hill 424 and Altavilla.

Sunday, September 12, 1943

For four days, from September 11 through September 14, the Allied position was to remain precarious, with every day bringing its crisis. Fortunately, especially for the more endangered Americans, von Vietinghoff's difficulties in bringing up his troops, plus the broken nature of the terrain, made it impossible for him to launch an all-out coordinated attack across the entire front. Each day, therefore, even though some portion of the line would be hard-pressed, the danger would shift from one section of the front to another. Sunday, September 12, 1943, was no exception.

The morning began with a welcome relief for the two endangered battalions of the 179th Infantry bottled up in the Sele River Valley. Brigadier General Raymond S. McLain, the artillery commander of the 45th Division, took matters into his own hands. Loading up a two-and-a-half-ton truck with artillery ammunition, he personally accompanied the vehicle and broke into the position amidst a shower of incoming artillery fire. He was soon followed by a squadron of tank destroyers that added to the firepower of the infantry. Faced with this surprising show of strength the German 29th Panzer Grenadier withdrew up the valley toward Eboli. The siege of the 179th Infantry was raised.[24]

That emergency averted, another sprung up on the front of the 143d Infantry, 36th Division, at Altavilla. At daybreak, just as General McLain was starting on his heroic mission, the German 15th PG Regiment began opening fire from all directions against the battalion holding that position. By mid-afternoon, both Hill 424 and Altavilla were lost. Though General Walker ordered the regimental commander to retake the position, he was unable to do so. The possession of that high ground gave the Germans observation over the entire VI Corps sector of the Salerno bridgehead.[25]

24. Whitlock, *Rock of Anzio,* 90. McLain went on to become a corps commander in the European campaign, the only National Guard officer to attain that high a rank. Tank destroyers were a separate branch of the Army during World War II. The tank destroyers were a single-mission weapon, designed only to destroy tanks. Lightly armored themselves, they carried 90 mm guns, in contrast to the smaller 75 mm guns of the Sherman M-4s. They were, of course, vulnerable to artillery and even small arms themselves.

25. Morris, *Salerno,* 232–33.

At 4:00 P.M., about the time that Altavilla was being lost for good, General Dawley sent for Walker to come to VI Corps command post. On arrival, Walker found General Middleton, commander of the 45th Division, already on hand. Dawley had called his two division commanders to discuss a radical and hardly favorable change of the VI Corps situation. The British were being hard-pressed around Battipaglia, and the gap between the two corps was still wide open. To ease the British situation, therefore, General Clark had ordered VI Corps to sideslip northward and send a regiment from the 45th Division—the much-weakened 179th—across the Sele River. Responsibility for the vital Persano plain between the Sele and Calore Rivers, so recently relieved from German pressure, had to be assumed by the 36th Division. Walker, judging that he could spare only one battalion, sent his reserve, the 2d Battalion of the 142d Infantry. He was apparently unaware of the intensity of the previous fighting in that area. His only warning to the battalion commander was not to "expose his men to enemy observation,"[26] an admonition easier said than done.

Shortly after that meeting ended, Clark arrived at Dawley's headquarters, and it soon became obvious that the two men were thinking differently. Clark was concerned about the Sele River Valley, but Dawley was obsessed with the heights of Altavilla and Hill 424. Neither man seems to have listened very closely to the other.

Whether or not Clark realized it at the time, Dawley had been giving indications of battle fatigue. With lack of sleep, a conscientious nature, and an anomalous position in the command structure, his nerves were becoming frayed. Earlier in the day he was reported to have been badly shaken by the sight of American corpses piled up near Paestum. "Take them away," he had shouted. "I can't stand them." Other witnesses, including doctors and staff officers, reported that Dawley was "going wild," "zonked," or "cracking."[27] If that was the case, however, Clark did not notice any irregularity in Dawley's condition.

The meeting, however, resulted only in further confusion. Whatever the viewpoints of the two men, Dawley ignored Clark's order to send all units in the 45th Infantry Division across the Sele and continued the battle for Altavilla. His rationale, it was reported, was that "his army commander had only disagreed, not forbidden."[28]

At the end of the day, Clark happily made his move from the *Ancon* to the beachhead itself. His headquarters commandant, seeking nothing but

26. Walker, *Texas to Rome*, 244.
27. Des Hickey and Gus Smith, *Operation Avalanche: The Salerno Landings, 1943,* 189.
28. Morris, *Salerno*, 235.

the best for his chief, chose a villa called the Bellili Palace, a comfortable, lavish mansion, but very close to the front lines. Clark prudently declined to occupy it personally, preferring to stay in his own trailer away from the staff and at some distance. His staff, however, were delighted with the comforts of a villa after days cramped aboard ship, and they occupied the building. They soon left in a hurry. As General Walker later wrote, with apparent satisfaction, "They had no business being there . . . In their enthusiasm for comfort, they overlooked the tactical situation."[29]

Other developments gave increased hope that the emergency might soon end. From Sicily, General Alexander informed Clark that the 82d Airborne Division, previously taken from him, was now restored.[30] And to further bolster Clark's spirits, he learned that the 157th Infantry, 45th Division, which was inching its way toward Battipaglia, had taken the Tobacco Factory.

That evening, September 12, Kesselring visited von Vietinghoff at Salerno. Both were satisfied with the way things were going. The Germans, despite the limited Italian road net, were bringing reinforcements to the bridgehead far faster than could the Allies, with their limited shipping, and it still appeared possible that the Allies might be driven into the sea. Though Kesselring later wrote that both men were "skeptical" about this prospect, von Vietinghoff was highly optimistic. His intelligence had detected Allied convoys coming into the beaches, and he surmised that the ships were there to evacuate rather than to reinforce.[31] One thing was certain: the Allies were not going to be spared every effort that Kesselring and von Vietinghoff could exert to remove them.

Monday, September 13, 1943

From the Allied point of view, September 13 was to represent the crisis of the Sele River Valley campaign. So touchy was the situation that it has often been referred to as "Black Monday."

It was Walker's 36th Division that would bear the brunt of the danger. The division was badly understrength, estimated as equivalent to only seven weak battalions,[32] and holding a front of about twenty-two miles.

29. Walker, *Texas to Rome*, 249.
30. This was Clark's claim. Morris, *Salerno*, 241, claims that Clark was informed three days earlier.
31. Kesselring, *Memoirs*, 186; Morris, *Salerno*, 239–40.
32. Morris, *Salerno*, 236.

Still Walker attempted to retake Altavilla. The 1st Battalion of Colonel Martin's 143d Infantry gained a foothold in the town but was soon driven out. The episode did, however, provide one of the war's legends. When Company K left Altavilla, Technical Sergeant Charles E. Kelly stayed behind. Using all the weapons at hand—rifles, machine guns, and even mortar rounds, which he dropped from a third-story building as hand grenades, he held out alone, finally making his escape. His exploits earned him both a Congressional Medal of Honor and the nickname "Commando Kelly."[33]

It was on Walker's left flank, however, that the Germans came closest to destroying the bridgehead. Von Vietinghoff, having determined that the weak point in the Allied lines was the Persano corridor, hit the 2d Battalion, 143d Infantry, from all sides. The battalion, unaware of the danger, had, like its predecessor, neglected to occupy the high ground around Persano. Soon the battalion was overrun, its commander captured. The way seemed open for a German drive to the sea.

At that point Dawley called Clark for orders. "What," Clark asked, "are you going to do about it. What can you do?"

"Nothing," Dawley replied. "I have no reserves. All I have is a prayer."[34] Clark determined to go forward to see for himself, remarking that "It would have been agreed by any military expert that we didn't have much to stop [von Vietinghoff]."[35]

At that point, Clark personally witnessed the action that saved the day. Two field artillery battalions from the 45th Division, the 158th and the 189th, commanded by alert men,[36] formed their own defense south of the Calore River. First they stripped down the crews of their artillery pieces and sent the extra members down to the bank to fight as infantry. They stopped all passing vehicles and pressed the drivers into action. Artillerymen, mechanics, and truck drivers manned the front lines. At one point, according to Clark's estimate, the two artillery battalions were firing at the rate of eight rounds a minute per gun. By dusk the two battalions had fired over 3,600 rounds. The Germans wavered and fell back, and soon further reinforcements joined the two artillery battalions.[37]

Still, Clark remained concerned. A renewed German attack in that same area, he feared, could still split the bridgehead. In the late afternoon, he met with Dawley and the two division commanders to discuss his tenta-

33. Ibid., 243.
34. Clark, *Calculated Risk*, 200.
35. Ibid., 201.
36. Lieutenant Colonels Hal L. Muldrow, Jr., and Russel D. Funk.
37. Clark, *Calculated Risk*, 202.

tive plans. Clark never intended, he wrote later, to evacuate the entire bridgehead; his idea was to consolidate the two corps on one or the other side of the Sele River. One corps would be evacuated by the navy and moved over to the area of the adjacent corps.

In the meantime, General Middleton, who had set up his command post beneath a fig tree near Paestum, called his staff together to outline his plan for the defense of the area north of the Sele. One witness, a junior staff officer, watched intently as the general placed a large map, with a plywood backing, up against a tree and began his explanation. Hardly had the meeting begun when a jeep pulled up and General Clark dismounted from the front seat.

Clark immediately took over. It might be necessary, he said, to evacuate half of the Salerno bridgehead, either the 10 Corps or VI Corps zone. Once Clark had started his presentation, however, Middleton interrupted him and motioned him aside. The two generals then moved away from the crowd a "few trees away" and began a serious talk. Using another map propped against a tree, Middleton was doing most of the talking, using gestures so violent as to stick his finger in Clark's chest. After a short while the two returned to the waiting staff and Clark issued a set of formal instructions. They were identical to the concept that Middleton had been expounding before Clark's arrival.[38]

Nothing more came of the incident, because it was merely a discussion of contingency planning. Middleton, however, had no intention of withdrawing from his position, come what may. As soon as he returned to the 45th Division sector he issued an order: "Put food and ammunition behind the Forty-fifth. We are going to stay."[39]

What was otherwise a dismal day ended on an optimistic note for Mark Clark. Just as he was meeting with his corps and division commanders, the 504th Parachute Infantry, of the 82d Airborne Division, was flying overhead to parachute into the rear of the 36th Division sector.

At his advanced command post at Carthage, General Eisenhower, who had been keeping in close touch with the details of the Salerno battle, reported to the Combined Chiefs of Staff in Washington that the situation at Salerno was "unfavorable." He told of the British repulse at Battipaglia, of German infiltration in the north, and of the uselessness of the Montecorvino airport. He made a diplomatic nod to Montgomery's Eighth

38. General Michael S. Davison, interview with author, July 24, 2003.

39. Whitlock, *Rock of Anzio,* 92. British General McCreery, when he learned indirectly of Clark's plans, was furious. For a while he planned to go to Clark's headquarters for a confrontation. Morris, *Salerno,* 250.

Army "striving to push forward." On the optimistic side, he advised that the British 7th Armoured Division was beginning to arrive on the 10 Corps front. As for his own actions, he advised that he was using the additional landing craft recently allocated to him to move the American 3d Infantry Division to the bridgehead as a matter of top priority. In summary, he wrote that

> . . . the present situation is tense but not unexpected. Everything de-
> pends upon our ability to build up our forces more rapidly than the
> enemy and this again depends on transportation and the effect of our
> air force upon enemy ground units and communications. The next
> several days will be critical but everybody is working at top speed
> and if the job can be done we will do it.[40]

The next day Eisenhower wrote to General Marshall telling about the depletion in the Mediterranean air force and advising that "unless reme-dial measures are taken at once, I feel that our air strength will drop below that essential for conduct of operations." He protested again the planned transfer of B-17's, B-26's, B-25's, and P-38's. He concluded with a plea: "I urge that you most seriously consider this matter to the end of securing correction at the earliest possible date."[41]

When he wrote those words, Eisenhower had no way of knowing that the worst of the Salerno crisis had passed. By the evening of Tuesday, September 12, the 180th Infantry Regiment, of the 45th Division, had un-loaded, and elements of the British 7th Armoured Division were landing in the 10 Corps sector. Through the day of the 14th the Germans contin-ued to make heavy attacks against the Tobacco Factory, and General Clark announced pontifically that "We don't give another inch. This is it." But the Salerno crisis was already over.

The Salerno landing was a true crisis of World War II. An Allied failure would been devastating to the Allied cause.[42] As it was, the psycho-logical impact of the "near-run thing," as Wellington called Waterloo, was great. Eisenhower would remember it as the time he had been forced to negotiate to attain the air power he needed to ensure its survival. He de-termined that he would never be placed in that position again.

---

40. Eisenhower to the CCS, Sept. 13, 1943, *The Papers of Dwight David Eisenhower: The War Years*, 3:1414.

41. Eisenhower to Marshall, Sept. 14, 1943, *Papers*, 3:1417.

42. In an interview with General Michael Davison, cited above, the author asked if Davison had ever feared that the Allies would evacuate Salerno. He had not.

Clark, on the other hand, seems to have been most affected in his attitude toward the British. Having fought a bloody, precarious battle for several days, Clark was perturbed to receive guidance from General Alexander's 15th Army Group regarding any releases to be given to the Allied press: "First, play up the [British] Eighth Army progress henceforth. Second, the Fifth Army is pushing the enemy back on his [the Germans'] right flank. Americans may be mentioned. There should be no suggestion that the enemy has made good his getaway."

Clark exploded: "When men have just been through a bruising battle such as the Fifth Army had just experienced, it is difficult for them to understand the reasons, if there are any, for instructions to play down their activities and play up the operations of someone else."[43]

The Salerno battle over, General Mark Clark assessed the performances of his subordinates and found Dawley wanting. He and Alexander had already agreed that a change in command of VI Corps was necessary. Clark had already installed General Matthew Ridgway as deputy to Dawley, and when General Eisenhower came to Salerno a couple of days later, he concurred that a change would be in the best interest of all concerned. He would relieve Dawley, he said, and replace him with Major General John P. Lucas.[44] On September 20 Clark informed Dawley of the situation, relieved him of command, and directed him to report to Eisenhower.[45]

The battle for Salerno had been bloody and difficult. Few of the participants would look back on it with pleasure. But it had been a necessary beginning. All Allied troops had gained vital experience for the days ahead.

Even more important, the Allies were established on the mainland of Europe, even though the Alps lay between them and Germany. The battle for Italy had begun.

---

43. Clark, *Calculated Risk*, 209–10.
44. Eisenhower turned down Clark's request for Ridgway, however.
45. Clark, *Calculated Risk*, 208.

The Fall of Naples, 1 October 1943

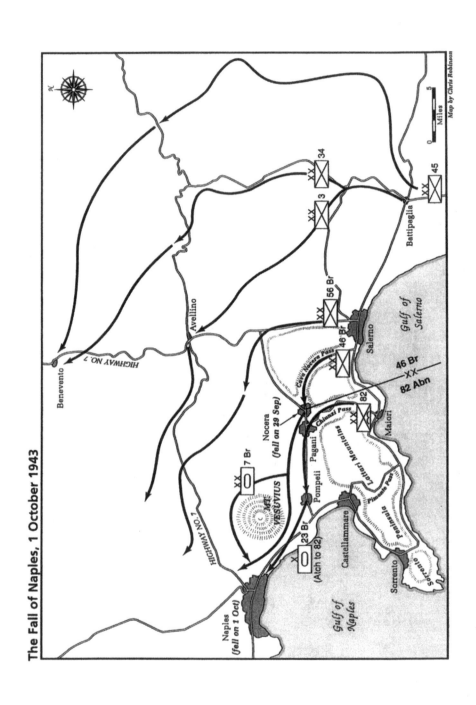

Map by Chris Robinson

CHAPTER 4

SALERNO TO NAPLES IN TEN DAYS

On September 20, 1943, General Sir Bernard Law Montgomery strode into Fifth Army Headquarters for his first official visit with Clark. It was a strange meeting. Monty was flushed with pride over the feat of the British Eighth Army in pushing the 150 miles over winding roads from Calabria in what he considered the creditable time of seventeen days. Clark, who had been hanging on to the Salerno bridgehead almost literally by his fingertips, was not impressed.

Clark, however, put his feelings aside. He listened without comment as Monty described his troubles with supply and his intention to set up a base at Bari, on the Adriatic, across the Italian boot from Salerno. Clark assumed the role of the student. "The Fifth Army is just a young outfit trying to get along, while your Eighth Army is a battle-tried veteran," he said. "We would appreciate having you teach us some of your tricks." Monty beamed, and their relationship started on an auspicious note.

The extent to which Monty was mesmerized by Clark and his suave manner showed itself when the cocky little Irishman prepared to leave. As he climbed into his jeep, he asked, "Do you know Alexander well?"

"No," replied Clark.

"Well, I do. From time to time you will get instructions from Alex that you won't understand. When you do, just tell him to go to hell."

"I have a better idea, General," said Clark. "If I have that trouble, I'll tell you about it and let you tell Alex for me."[1]

The meeting had delighted Montgomery, and Clark felt satisfied. Like it or not, he would have to work with both Alex and Monty, and he wanted to get off on the right foot.

---

1. Clark, *Calculated Risk,* 210–11, passim.

Though the meeting afforded the two men an opportunity to get acquainted, they had no tactical problems to coordinate. Monty's future axis of advance would be parallel to Clark's, up the peninsula on the Adriatic coast. The immediate thrust of his Eighth Army's attack would therefore be eastward, from Calabria to Apulia, in other words, from the toe of the Italian boot toward the heel. There he would join up with the British 1st Airborne Division, which had landed at Taranto on September 9. The British 5 Corps Headquarters had come ashore and would soon be joined by the British 78th Division and the Indian 8th. That force had, in fact, moved far enough along the road to Foggia as to be abreast with Clark's Fifth Army.[2]

Clark's main route from Salerno to Naples ran across the Sorrento Peninsula, beneath Monte Vesuvius, and directly into the city. To execute this maneuver, the British 10 Corps, already established in the Sorrento mountains, would make the main effort. That scheme, however, would require adjustments in the battle line to turn the 46th and 56th British Divisions ninety degrees to the left. Without waiting for the 10 Corps to attack, therefore, Clark sent VI Corps forward. It was to make a wide sweeping movement to the left and bypass Naples on its way to the Volturno River. Since von Vietinghoff's Tenth German Army had definitely left the Salerno area by the evening of September 18, Clark expected to encounter only delaying tactics.

The key terrain feature in the VI Corps zone was the town of Avellino, about twenty miles north of Salerno. Its value lay in the fact that it was situated on Route 7, the main avenue into Naples from the east. If 10 Corps got into trouble in approaching Naples directly, VI Corps might envelope it along that route. The main attack toward Avellino would be made by General Lucian Truscott's 3d Infantry Division, which had entered the line at Battipaglia, on the left of Middleton's 45th. The 45th would make a wide sweep with a mission to take Benevento, a town about forty miles ahead, where it would make contact with Montgomery's Eighth Army. Walker's 36th Division was to be held in reserve, refitting after its depletion at Salerno.

The arrival of the 3d Division was a significant addition to the VI Corps, both for its high state of training and for the fighting qualities of its commander, Major General Lucian K. Truscott, Jr. Truscott was a remarkable soldier, of whom few spoke in terms other than superlatives. He did not look the part of a great warrior. Of average size, stooped, with a shock of brindle hair and bulging blue eyes, he suffered periodically from some

---

2. Martin Blumenson, *Salerno to Cassino,* 154–55.

sort of throat condition that made his voice a rasp, almost a whisper. In manner he was humorless and unpretending. His pride in the 3d Division could only be described as ferocious. Yet, despite his personal drive, he had a generous nature. Unlike George Patton, who could pick a quarrel with anyone, especially sailors, airmen, and anyone British, Truscott had a way of making fast friends with everyone regardless of service or nationality. They all liked him because he respected them and regarded them as comrades. One of the army's champion polo players in peacetime, he was physically fearless.

Truscott and his men had arrived at Salerno too late to take part in the battle for the bridgehead. The first elements of the 3d Division arrived on the morning of September 17, and by the 20th the last elements had closed in north of the Sele River, where it relieved the British 56th Division at Battipaglia. The British 56th would then join the other units of 10 Corps on the right of the 46th in their drive up the coast to the Volturno.

On the evening of September 19, 1943, Truscott was summoned to VI Corps Headquarters, which was now located in the noted Tobacco Factory. Since the building had so many large windows that could not be covered, the room was kept in darkness to avoid presenting a target for German air attack. General Dawley, who was still in command of VI Corps, issued his orders using only a small, pencil-sized flashlight to illuminate a map leaning up against a wall. Truscott remarked that, despite the activities of German aircraft over the beachhead, "danger from air attack at night hardly seemed sufficient to warrant such extreme protective measures as to preclude normal and efficient functioning of command and staff."[3]

On the next morning VI Corps began its move northward from Battipaglia and the Sele River. Though the distance from Battipaglia to Avellino was not great, the Germans' delaying tactics were masterful, and their use of terrain and demolitions made for slow going indeed. A blown bridge in such precipitate mountain terrain could delay a unit for hours, even days. Fortunately for Truscott and his men, the terrain was not unlike what they had encountered when they had fought their way across the north coast of Sicily in July. Based on that experience, the 3d Division had developed pack trains of mules to provide the infantry in mountainous terrain and even to bring supplies of ammunition to the artillery. But Truscott's speed was dependent on his engineers, and he called their feats "epic." He described them vividly,

3. Lucian K. Truscott, Jr., *Command Missions*, 255.

> Building bridges, constructing by-passes, building roads and trails,
> sweeping roads and bivouac areas for mines, removing mine-fields,
> constructing landing strips for artillery observation airplanes, operat-
> ing water-points, providing the engineers supplies for troops, and oc-
> casionally taking their weapons in hand and fighting as infantry: those
> were the missions performed by the 10th Engineer Battalion and the
> Corps of Engineers which supported them. There was no weapon
> more valuable than the engineer bulldozer, no soldiers more effective
> than the engineers who moved us forward.[4]

As if the precipitous slopes, narrow road, and devilish German demolitions were not enough, the men of the VI Corps began facing another
formidable obstacle to the advance. Downpours of rain began on September 26, washing out road repairs and making movement of vehicles off
the roads virtually impossible. With the delays, it was the night of September 29 before the 3d Division could get into position to seize Avellino.
Truscott's recollections of the moment when Avellino was taken were
vivid:

> . . . there was a sea of fog above which the sun shone brightly and dis-
> tant mountains were clearly visible. And from this vast sea of fog,
> there were the sounds of firing, of scattered actions in a dozen places—
> rifles, machine guns, mortars, and the characteristic sound of the
> German machine pistol, occasional salvos of artillery. Our infantry
> battalions, moving through darkness and fog, had bypassed enemy
> resistance and had so completely infiltrated German defenses that
> small fights were in progress in a wide area as the German delaying
> forces tried desperately to escape . . . I waited while the sounds of fir-
> ing grew less and less, and finally none at all. I knew then that Avellino
> was in our hands.[5]

It was September 30, 1943.
  While the 3d Division was closing in on Avellino, other units of the VI
Corps also had their hands full. The 333d Infantry Regiment, of the newly
arrived 34th Division, had been attached to the 45th, and this fresh regiment took Benevento. The rest of the 45th Division, meanwhile, made contact with the British Eighth Army on its right.
  In that mountainous terrain, operations of the various divisions had to
be decentralized, each unit operating fairly independently. The new corps

  4. Ibid., 259.
  5. Ibid., 260–61.

Major General John P. Lucas, commanding VI Corps, September 1943–February 1944. U.S. Army, Eisenhower Library.

commander, John P. Lucas, was quite accepting of that arrangement. His three division commanders, Truscott, Middleton, and Charles Ryder (commanding the 34th) were men of considerable experience and all of them reliable.

Lucas himself was new to command at a high level. Though wounded while serving in the artillery of the 33d Division in the First World War, his assignments in the Second World War had been largely confined to training and staff. In the spring of 1943 he had been assigned to Allied Force Headquarters, where General Eisenhower considered him as a sort of deputy for the American command, serving as Ike's own "eyes and ears." Though without immediate command responsibilities, Lucas had observed the entire Sicily campaign from up front.

At the time of his unexpected assignment to take command of VI Corps from the luckless Dawley, Lucas had just assumed command of II Corps in Sicily. A good-humored, articulate, even lovable man, he looked older than his fifty-four years. Though Lucas's diary reflected some frustration during this campaign, he comported himself well in the eyes of both Clark and Alexander. He had passed his first test as a commander.

While VI Corps was fighting its way inch by inch through the mountains, the British 10 Corps, on the Sorrento Ridge, was stymied. Von Vietinghoff, realizing that Naples lay on his main line of retreat, was resisting fiercely. Even more difficult than Vietinghoff's troops, however, was the terrain, with mountains rising precipitously to heights of four thousand feet straight from the Gulf of Salerno.

The Sorrento Ridge stretches about twenty miles due west from the town of Salerno, ending at the town of Sorrento, with the Isle of Capri only about four miles off the tip. Though three passes cut through the hill mass, the two closest to Salerno were the Vietri-Nocera Pass, which heads north from a point just west of Salerno, and the smaller Chiunzi Pass, farther west, which joins Maiori and Pagani. General McCreery much preferred the Vietri Pass, and his plan called for it to be taken by the 46th Division, followed up by the British 7th Armoured Division once the infantry had broken through the mountains onto the Naples Plain.

The Chiunzi Pass, however, presented another possibility, and it had been held by Lieutenant Colonel William O. Darby's three American Ranger battalions from the day of the Salerno landing on September 9. Since then Darby's command had been augmented by a glider infantry battalion and enough artillery and signal troops to bring his strength up to 8,500 men, a whopping command for an officer of such modest rank.

McCreery, with his mind set on sending the 46th Division through the Nocera Pass, decided to send Darby through the Chiunzi Pass with the idea of seizing the town of Pagani, a suburb of Nocera, before the arrival of the 7th Armoured Division. In that mountainous terrain, however, with supply so difficult, it was all Darby could do to hold on to his position, much less advance down to the plain. Seizing Pagani was, for the moment at least, out of the question.

On September 26th, therefore, Clark attached Ridgway's 82d Airborne Division to McCreery for the purpose of taking over Darby's mission. Ridgway, appreciating the worth of Darby and his men, assigned the right half of the 82d Airborne sector to the Rangers and the left sector, above the Amalfi Drive, to the 505th Parachute Infantry Regiment under Colonel James Gavin. That was the day the rains hit, and even Ridgway could do very little. His problem was not the German resistance, which was spotty: it was the terrain, the four thousand-foot hills that were crossed only by footpaths. "It was a terrific task to get ammunition and water up to the fighting men," Ridgway later wrote, "and to bring down a wounded man took six able-bodied troopers out of the fight."[6]

6. Ridgway, *Soldier,* 87.

Ridgway then resorted to the same device that Truscott used, animal transport. He set about to scour the countryside for mules and men who knew how to handle them. That effort, however, failed:

> The idea was probably sound, but it didn't work out worth a damn. We got the animals all right . . . but most of the animals were big, clumsy, heavy-footed horses, and they were no good at all on those steep, winding twisting mountain trails. So we abandoned this plan and recruited a few hundred native mountaineers who could carry heavy loads on their backs.[7]

All this took three days. On September 29, with the weather clearing temporarily, Darby's men took Pagani and the 46th Division took Nocera. The next day Avellino fell to the 3d Division, and von Vietinghoff, realizing that Route 7 was untenable as far as Naples, withdrew rapidly.

Naples was now open, and on the 29th of September the 7th Armoured Division passed through Nocera and joined up with the British 23d Armoured Brigade, attached to Ridgway. The 7th Armoured turned north, and the 23d Brigade drove on through and entered Naples.

The 82d was assigned to occupy and consolidate Naples, but the rest of Fifth Army, both 10 Corps and VI Corps, bypassed the city in order to drive on to the Volturno. Once the town of Castellammare was taken, on the north side of the Sorrento Ridge, Ridgway found no enemy resistance in front of him. The going was slow, however, because the people in the string of towns and villages poured out of their homes to greet their liberators. "In every little village," Ridgway later wrote, "[the people] thronged the streets, shouting and throwing flowers, overwhelmed with joy to see the Germans running and the Americans coming in . . . You can't just run a truck over a delegation that wants to make a speech, or present you with some flowers, and I know of no soldier who won't pause for a moment when a pretty girl throws her arms around his neck and offers him a glass of wine."[8] Ridgway had to do something to break up the carnival.

About five or six miles short of Naples, Ridgway halted his division and sent for the city chief of police. A couple of hours later, when the official arrived, Ridgway gave him his instructions. He wanted the streets of Naples completely cleared, warning that when his men came in, they would come in fast, and anybody in the way, regardless of nationality,

7. Ibid.
8. Ibid., 87.

was in danger of being hurt. The chief of police, accustomed to taking orders from the Germans, carried out Ridgway's instructions explicitly.[9]

On October 1, General Mark W. Clark was preparing to savor the victory of Salerno and Naples. At the moment he had General Alphonse Juin, the commander of the French Expeditionary Corps, as his guest. The two men decided to take a tour of the front, hoping to see a little of the action. On reaching the southern outskirts, however, they discovered that the city had been taken by the 23d Armoured Brigade. At about that time they encountered Ridgway, who was about to enter Naples.

Clark had a touchy matter of protocol on his hands. Juin was his guest, but that privileged position took second place to Clark's grand entrance to the city. Clark, sensitive to the matter of appearances, quickly decided that his American and British troops would resent his entering Naples in the company of the commander of the French, who had not participated in its capture. So Clark took leave of Juin and climbed into an armored car with Ridgway for his public entrance.

Along the streets the two generals were impressed by the wreckage, created not only by the recent fighting but also by the methodical German demolitions. As they drove through the streets, however, Clark was surprised by their sheer emptiness. "There was something besides the wreckage that impressed me," he later wrote. "I felt that I was riding through ghostly streets in a city of ghosts. We didn't see a soul. . . . There was simply nobody in the streets with the exception of a few *Carabinieri*."[10] It seems strange that Clark never mentioned the lack of welcoming crowds to Ridgway. Ridgway, apparently, did not volunteer his instructions to the chief of police.

The 82d Airborne occupied and organized the City of Naples for a little over a month. It was to be the last assignment for the paratroopers and their glider comrades. The "All-Americans" were among those divisions earmarked for transfer to London to play a key role in Operation Overlord.

One privileged group that was allowed a little time to relax in Naples was Darby's Ranger Force. Nobody begrudged the Rangers a little rest, and they took full advantage of it.

Darby himself was a rare type of man, who was personally convinced that he was a man of destiny. Nothing he ever did was without purpose.

9. Ibid., 87–88.
10. Clark, *Calculated Risk*, 214.

Colonel William O. Darby, commanding the 1st, 3d, and 4th Ranger Battalions.

A West Pointer from the Class of 1933, he was only thirty-three years of age at the time. He was courageous, even fearless, and he was always at the very forefront of his unit when fighting was going on. He was not, however, "one of the boys." He retained a certain aloofness from his enlisted men. They held him more in awe than affection. "El Darbo" they might call him when he was not present, but they were correct to his face.

Darby, however, was capable of relaxing a bit when alone with his officers, and one evening in Naples a group of them, including Darby, went to a beer garden. This was not the first time; a humorous routine had been worked out whereby Darby was a "stooge" for the singing of "Ach Du Lieber." On the evening in question, they were going through the routine.

All of a sudden the door burst open. Darby and his officers stared in amazement to see a group of American paratroops from the 82d Airborne confronting them with guns. The paratroopers had believed, from the German singing, that they had achieved a dream: they had captured a German command post.

Darby looked at their leader. He was a man Darby had known at West Point—"overly zealous and conscientious" Darby called him. Everyone roared except the conscientious leader, who saw no humor in the situation. The Rangers invited their captors to have a beer, however.[11] It added zest to an evening of relaxation.

On October 3, the day after Naples fell, Clark visited Lucas at his command post in Avellino. The weary Lucas, who at one point in his diary described himself as a "poor working girl," nevertheless had a keen interest in what Clark had to tell him. Mellowed by the fresh vegetables and frying chickens that Lucas's men had been able to scrounge in the mountains, Clark expansively approved the plans his corps commander had drawn up.

Clark then gave his concept of future operations. He expected to lose McCreery's 10 Corps, which had been assigned to him primarily so that Britain and America might share equally in the dangers of the risky landing at Salerno. In McCreery's place, Clark went on, he planned to insert General Geoffrey Keyes's II Corps on the left of the line. That meant that Lucas would stay in the mountains. "You know how to fight in the mountains," Clark said.

"Maybe I do," Lucas later recorded in his diary, "But I have had a bellyful of it." He was only partially placated by Clark's professed intention that VI Corps would eventually take Rome.[12]

Lucas continued to have his frustrations, which he wryly recorded in his diary, but his troops fought well, closing in on the left bank of the Volturno River by October 7. At that point, Operation Avalanche, which had included the seizure of Naples by way of the Salerno landing, was officially complete. The cost had been heavy: more than 12,000 British and American casualties, of which 2,000 were killed, 7,000 wounded, and 3,500 missing.[13] Notably, the British casualties had been considerably higher than the American despite the critical nature of the Sele River action, higher even in proportion to the number of troops involved.[14]

The jobs of clearing out Naples and reestablishing a working port began the moment the Allies entered the city. They were separate and distinct tasks. To govern the city, therefore, Clark had designated Brigadier

11. William O. Darby and William H. Baumer, *Darby's Rangers: We Led the Way*, 222–23.
12. John P. Lucas diary, 170.
13. Blumenson, *Salerno to Cassino*, 166.
14. There were more British troops than American at Salerno, it will be recalled.

General Edgar E. Hume, a medical officer, as chief of the Allied military government, and to restore the port he named Brigadier General Arthur W. Pence, an engineer officer, to command the Fifth Army Base Section.

Hume's task was difficult, even though about half of the city population had fled. It took his men three months to restore normal life to Naples.

As expected, the Germans had done great damage to the port facilities. They had

> . . . destroyed or removed all transportation facilities, blasted communications installations, knocked out power and water systems, and broken open sewer mains. They had demolished bridges, mined buildings, fired stockpiles of coal, burned hotels and university buildings, looted the city, ripped up the port railroads and choked the harbor with the wreckage of sunken ships. . . .[15]

Nevertheless the extent of the damage might have been worse. General Pence and many of his officers had spent much of their careers in river and harbor work, so they did not consider their task to be impossible.

Pence's men worked around the clock at feverish pace. They resorted to unconventional devices. They did not, for example, bother to remove all the sunken ships; they simply used their hulls to serve as piling for the docks they were building. Within seventy-two hours after the Allied entry into Naples, the first landing points for lighters had been provided, together with exit routes. The next day a berth for a Liberty Ship was cleared. Supplies were coming in within a week, and soon Naples was bringing in 20,000 tons of cargo daily.[16]

The first stage of the invasion of Italy was complete, the landing and consolidation, including the capture of Naples.

That, however, was only one of the objectives that the Combined Chiefs of Staff had assigned to General Eisenhower at Quebec in August 1943. The other was to "contain the maximum number of German divisions."[17] What this involved depended largely upon German intentions. Would Kesselring elect to fight in southern Italy to protect Rome, or would he voluntarily withdraw to the north and settle for defending a strong line to protect the Po Valley?

Kesselring's course of action was important to Allied thinking because it affected the amount of force that would have to be committed to Italy. Given

15. Blumenson, *Salerno to Cassino,* 166. See also 168.
16. Clark, *Calculated Risk,* 217.
17. Blumenson, *Salerno to Cassino,* 175.

46THE ROAD TO THE RAPIDO

the abominable rains that drench southern Italy in the autumn of the year, added to the ideal defensive terrain, it was possible that a painful advance up the boot of Italy could tie down more Allied divisions than German.

The decision, however, had already been made by the overriding importance of the city of Rome. From a military viewpoint, Rome was not worth a major campaign, despite its excellent airfields and road net. These military advantages were dwarfed by Rome's overwhelming importance to the Allies from a political viewpoint. Winston Churchill, now the generalissimo of the Mediterranean Theater of War, had Rome constantly on his mind.

Churchill had good reason for his obsession. The Allied objectives in World War II were symbolized by the three capitals: Berlin, Rome, and Tokyo. Rome would be the first of the three to topple. Even General Marshall, no proponent of operations in the Mediterranean, automatically assumed that Rome was a major objective. On September 23, 1943, in his message critiquing Eisenhower's conduct of the campaign, Marshall had warned that if Eisenhower took time to develop the port of Naples, "the Germans would have time to prepare their defenses, thus making the road to Rome a long and difficult one."[18]

Of some influence, though less important, was the intelligence that both Eisenhower's and Alexander's headquarters had been receiving. Both believed that the Germans would withdraw to northern Italy without fighting for Rome. On September 26, therefore, even before the Fifth Army took Naples, Allied Force Headquarters in Algiers issued the order that the campaign would continue across the Volturno River without delay.

By October 7, 1943, the Fifth and Eighth Armies were drawn up along the Volturno, getting into position for a crossing. The front of the Fifth Army extended about sixty miles, from the Tyrrhenian Sea on the west to a point just north of Benevento on the east. The Eighth Army held a similar line from Benevento to the Adriatic. The Fifth Army's front was being manned by two corps of four divisions each. The British 10 Corps, which was still with Clark, consisted of the 46th Infantry Division, then the 7th Armoured, with the 56th Infantry Division held closely behind. VI Corps on the right was being held by Truscott's 3d Infantry Division and Middleton's 45th Infantry Division on its right. The 34th Infantry Division was in reserve. The 36th, badly mauled in the Salerno fighting, was still in the rear refitting.

By October 12, the day specified for the crossing, Clark committed the

18. Eisenhower, *Papers,* 3:1474.

third division of each corps. Thus each corps was making the assault with three divisions abreast. The ground across from 10 Corps, the Campanian Plain, was generally low, so the key terrain would be the high ground facing VI Corps.[19] It was rugged country, described as "barren and rocky peaks several thousand feet high, with deep gorges, jagged ridges, and overhanging cliffs."[20]

Facing the Allies, General von Vietinghoff's Tenth Army consisted of about sixty thousand men. Opposite the Fifth Army was the XIV Panzer Corps, with about thirty-five thousand troops, consisting of the 15th Panzer Grenadier Division, the Hermann Goering Division, and the 3d Panzer Grenadier Division.[21] These were all good divisions; the crossing would not be easy.

Preparations were being made under the disadvantage of adverse weather conditions. Truscott, of the 3d Division, complained about "incessant rains" that had created "appalling road conditions along the entire front."[22] And the rain affected more than the troops; it affected the high command as well. At about this time, a discouraged John Lucas, VI Corps commander, was writing in his diary,

> Rain, rain, rain. Military operations are always conducted in the rain. The roads are so deep in mud that moving troops and supplies forward is a terrific job. Enemy resistance is not nearly as great as Mother Nature, who certain [sic] seems to be fighting on the side of the German. I feel pretty old this morning, but will be younger, I hope, later on.[23]

In the early morning hours of October 10, just shortly after midnight, the artillery began its barrage all along the Volturno River. Truscott and General Geoffrey Keyes went to an observation post in an old monastery. The two men could see little amid the bursting of shells, even though the night was clear. Then came word that the infantry battalions were crossing. Soon thereafter, however, came word that the British 56th Division, on Truscott's left, had failed to get across the river. Truscott was not surprised. If the British had been serious about that crossing, he reasoned, they would have used more force. He therefore protected his flank with artillery and by noon he was able to attack the critical high point at Triflisco.

---

19. The 34th had been inserted in the line between the 3d and 45th.
20. Blumenson, *Salerno to Cassino*, 188.
21. Ibid., 190.
22. Truscott, *Command Missions*, 266.
23. Lucas diary, 177.

That cleared, he could begin work on building the all-important thirty-ton bridge. By October 14, the crossing over the Volturno was safe. The VI Corps boundary was changed to give the British the road leading from Capua.

Both sides were satisfied when the Fifth Army had completed its crossing of the Volturno. Unbeknownst to Clark, October 12 was the date that Kesselring had set as a target for delaying the Allies. The Volturno was only an intermediate position, albeit a formidable one.

CHAPTER 5

THE OTHER SIDE OF THE HILL

Frido von Senger and the Gustav Line

On October 8, 1943, as Mark Clark's Fifth Army was preparing to cross the Volturno River, General der Panzertruppen Frido von Senger und Etterlin assumed command of the German XIV Panzer Corps, part of von Vietinghoff's Tenth German Army. Kesselring and von Vietinghoff were preparing to defend Italy south of Rome at Cassino, and they had chosen von Senger to command this all-important sector.

Von Senger had been selected for this responsible post sheerly on merit; he was no favorite of Hitler's. Nor was he the picture of a German commander. He was slim, bony-faced, with a high forehead and an extraordinarily high-bridged nose, and drooping eyelids. A casual observer could well have taken him for a waiter in a Bavarian hotel rather than a prominent general. But if his physical attributes were not impressive, his intellect was.

Senger was, in fact, a complicated man. He was not a member of the German General Staff, and he had joined the German Army almost by chance. As a youth he had been an Anglophile, and in 1912 he had attended St. John's College, Oxford, as a Rhodes Scholar. As a loyal German, however, he had returned to his home country and been drafted into the army during the First World War. Economic conditions in Germany had caused him to sign up with the regulars, and he had spent the years between world wars in the horse cavalry. But like his counterpart George Patton in the United States, he had converted to the mechanized forces when war came a second time. He never, however, considered the tank as an end in itself; he recognized the primacy of the infantry in battle.

On the personal side, Senger was a devout Catholic, a lay member of the Benedictine Order. His unpopularity with the Nazis resulted, as one historian put it, in his being "an officer whose known anti-Nazi feelings

Lieutenant General Frido von Senger und Etterlin, commanding the German 14th Panzer Corps, defending Cassino.

resulted in his contributions to the defence of Cassino being played down by German authorities."[1]

The unconventional aspects of von Senger's military career did not, however, mean that he would perform his military duties halfheartedly. He was a professional soldier, a tough adversary, who fought for Germany, not the Nazis. Years later, on his death in 1963, a friend wrote his wife trying to explain Senger's absorption in his career. "Anyone who knows he has a talent for leadership at a high level," he wrote, "will find exactly its challenge fascinating. To be denied it is to feel like the left-behind hunter who paws at the loose-box door as his stable-mates are led out for the day." His friend did not believe that Senger's enthusiasm for battle command had anything to do with militarism. His conclusion made some sense: "War provides the challenge. Despite its senselessness and the hopelessness of the strategy in which it is conceived and the inescapability of the fateful outcome, one is bound by its challenge to be an exponent of battle."[2]

It is not surprising, then, that Senger was happy to receive the command of the XIV Panzer Corps. For one thing, the post came as a great re-

1. Fred Majdalany, *Cassino: Portrait of a Battle*, 46–47.
2. "Senger," by Stephan von Senger und Etterlin, in *Hitler's Generals*, edited by Correlli Barnett, 388.

lief, because he had just finished a series of assignments that he had found highly distasteful. In the previous June, Hitler had personally sent him to Sicily in a completely anomalous capacity. Technically, his title was simply liaison officer to General Alfredo Guzzoni, the commander of the Italian Army defending Sicily against Allied attack. At the same time Senger was unofficially being held responsible for overseeing the employment of the German forces augmenting the Italian Army. Those forces had consisted of only two German divisions, the Hermann Goering Parachute Division and the 15th Panzer Grenadier Division, and Senger had no real control over them. Further, he was hampered in his role as "liaison officer" to Guzzoni, in that he had been provided with no staff worthy of mention. Furthermore, he even lacked his own communications with his titular chief, Kesselring.

Admittedly, the Italian commander was cooperative, even obsequious, in his dealings with the Germans. He was, however, facing an impossible task in the light of the amount of force the Allies were able to land in Sicily on July 10 of that year, 1943. To make matters worse, Kesselring demonstrated an annoying propensity to send "suggestions" for Guzzoni's deployment of troops.

One of Kesselring's orders made no military sense whatsoever. He insisted that the Hermann Goering Parachute Division be assigned to the defense of the major threat to Messina, the corridor along the east coast of Sicily under Monte Etna.[3] The 15th Panzer Grenadier was stronger and better suited for this difficult task. Senger surmised that Kesselring, who had to play a certain degree of politics, was under pressure from Berlin to give the Hermann Goering the place of honor. Reichsmarschall Hermann Goering took an inordinate pride in the division that he once commanded and still bore his name.

Senger had left Sicily before its fall to the Allies on August 19, but he had then been sent to perform the same indefinite mission with the Italian forces in Sardinia and Corsica. It was soon obvious, however, that Allied naval and air power would make it impossible for the German forces to remain in the islands. So the German troops in Sardinia were soon evacuated to Corsica, whence they would be evacuated to Italy. At this point Senger had been given some real authority. Following the Italian surrender to the Allies, he was ordered to evacuate the thirty thousand or more German troops to the mainland. Aided to some extent by tepid coopera-

---

3. The Hermann Goering, once a bodyguard regiment for Goering, was officially a *Luftwaffe* unit, though at this time it was both a parachute and a panzer grenadier unit. Senger was also partial to the 15th Panzer Grenadier.

tion from the Italians,[4] Senger had concentrated most of the German forces at two airfields, supervising the evacuation at the rate of three thousand men per day. The rest escaped, with equipment, by ship out of various ports.

To Senger, the most memorable incident in this operation was the dilemma he faced in deciding to disobey orders from Hitler himself. While withdrawal of the German forces from Corsica was in progress, Senger received instructions to execute all Italian officers on Corsica who had failed to cooperate with Germans after the announcement of the Italian surrender to the Allies on September 8. As Senger later wrote,

> [It was] now perfectly clear that the moment had come to disobey a di-
> rect order. I spoke at once to Field-Marshal Kesselring on the radio
> link to his headquarters and told him that I refused to carry out the
> order. The Field-Marshal listened to my news without comment and
> then said he would say exactly the same to OKW in Berlin. I arranged
> for the officers concerned to be shipped to the mainland where they
> were at least safe from the gallows. I owe a debt to Kesselring that he
> entirely accepted my refusal to obey orders and let the matter rest.[5]

Senger had performed well in the "island campaigns," and he was now back into the regular chain of command, where he felt comfortable. But his influence on the forthcoming campaign was very much circumscribed. By the time he arrived at his headquarters at Roccasecca, in the Liri Valley, Kesselring, with Hitler's approval, had already undertaken to defend Italy on a line as far south of Rome as possible. His major defense line was to be at Cassino. The Gustav Line, as he called this position, ran across the Italian peninsula about halfway between Naples and Rome. It was an extremely strong position, laid out behind unfordable rivers with strong currents, now flooded with the heavy autumn rains. To the east, it ran behind the Moro River, on which stood the towns of Orsogna and Ortona, in the zone of the Eighth Army.[6]

Senger's first preoccupation was to assess the team with which he would be working. By this time he was familiar with Kesselring, and though he disagreed with some of the field marshal's policies and actions, he felt a gratitude toward him for his unflagging support in the incident with the Italian commanders on Corsica. He much admired Kesselring's

4. Corsica had a strong French resistance that was so fierce that the Italians much preferred to be taken prisoner by the Germans than by the French.
5. General Frido von Senger und Etterlin, *Neither Fear nor Hope*, 164.
6. Morris, *Circles of Hell*, 224.

chief of staff, Lieutenant General Siegfried Westphal, whom he described as "one of the best horses in the stable."[7] Between Kesselring's Army Group C and Senger's XIV Panzer Corps was Colonel General Heinrich von Vietinghoff's Tenth Army, the headquarters that Senger would work with most closely. Senger viewed von Vietinghoff with respect, calling him "competent, sure of himself, and adaptable." Vietinghoff's relations with his troops were not close, in Senger's view, but the old Prussian infantryman would serve as an ideal buffer between the fighting troops and high command. On the whole, Senger regarded von Vietinghoff's Tenth Army staff as "the best I ever encountered during this war."[8]

Senger was generally satisfied with his own staff. Some of its members were familiar, as they had been with him in Sicily the previous summer. He had doubts, however, about his chief of staff, Colonel von Bonin. That officer was a devoted disciple of Erwin Rommel, and Senger feared he might perform with less zeal than Senger would like. Von Bonin had obviously absorbed some of Rommel's pessimism about trying to defend southern Italy.[9]

With that team, Senger set about to defend the sector that had been assigned to him. The XIV Panzer Corps was to defend the right (west) half of the Gustav Line, that portion facing Mark Clark's Fifth Army. But the American Fifth Army had not yet reached the Gustav Line, so for the moment Senger was to delay as long as possible along a series of strong points out ahead known collectively by the Germans as the Bernhardt Line and by the Allies as the Winter Line.[10]

Though the Gustav was to be the main German position, the Winter Line was also strong. On the right, it began behind the Garigliano River, as did the Gustav, but in the center it pushed out about ten miles ahead (east) of the Gustav to include a series of rugged hills, the most prominent of which were the Monte Camino complex and Monte Sammucro. The low ground between Camino and Sammucro was known as the Mignano Gap, through which ran Route 6, the main artery between Naples and Rome. Senger and his superiors considered this area to be the greatest threat, as it was the only place where the Allies could commit their armor. In a country where the

---

7. Senger, *Neither Fear nor Hope,* 181. Senger's evaluation of Westphal took on a special significance in the German Army, because, unlike the practice in the American Army, a commander's chief of staff was appointed by the high command to balance out the commander's strengths and weaknesses. The commander may have been able to make requests, but the decision as to the selection of his principal assistant was not in his hands.

8. Ibid.

9. Ibid., 179–80.

10. For convenience, I will call the line the Winter, the term used by the Americans and British.

mountains were precipitous and roads extremely scarce, Route 6 (and the valleys through which it ran) practically dictated the avenue the Allies would be forced to take. Admittedly, there were other mountains between the Mignano Gap and the Gustav Line, most notably Monte Croce, but the Mignano was considered the key to the Winter Line.

The Gustav Line, at Cassino, had been established in an area of breathtaking beauty. According to the historian Fred Majdalany, the valley of the Rapido, behind which the line was established, was three miles wide, beyond which, viewed from the Allied side presented

> a great wall of mountains which . . . extends limitlessly to the right and to the rear into main mountain mass of the Abruzzi, but it ends with an almost artificial abruptness. . . . To the left of [the wall of mountains] there is an open space, indicating the entrance to another and wider valley, the valley of the River Liri which is a tributary of the Rapido. So sudden, so theatrical is the appearance of this mountain barrier three miles across the valley, that one has the impression that it reaches out to the road for the sole purpose of menacing it.[11]

Atop this cliff sat the Monte Cassino Abbey, a Benedictine monastery dating back to the sixth century, and in the valley behind the Rapido River lay the town of the same name, known to the Romans in the 4th century B.C. as Casinum. For some reason, the fact that this Rapido River line was to be Kesselring's main defensive position had escaped the eyes of Allied intelligence. Nothing like the struggles that lay ahead were anticipated.

When Senger took over there were four divisions along the Winter Line—two infantry and two panzer grenadier. By and large they were well deployed. The German 94th Infantry Division, on the right, had been assigned a long front, its length justified by the fact that it was somewhat protected by the Tyrrhenian Sea in its right half and the Garigliano in its left. On the extreme left of XIV Panzer Corps was the 305th Infantry Division, well led but weak in tanks and antitank defenses.

In the center of Senger's line, the area of greatest threat, were two panzer grenadier divisions, whose mixture of infantry and tanks made them ideally organized in Senger's mind. But though similarly organized, the two divisions were of different quality. On the right, next to the 94th Infantry Division, was the 15th Panzer Grenadier, with which Senger was familiar from the operation in Sicily. Its commander, General Rodt, was reliable, and an inspection convinced Senger that its subordinate commanders were also reliable. The 3d Panzer Grenadier was a much weaker

11. Majdalany, *Cassino*, 3.

division. Its commander was a good soldier, but many of the men had been recruited from the German-occupied portions of Poland and were serving in the German Army on probation. Many of these men had been receiving letters from home telling of the abuses their families had been suffering at the hands of the German party officials. That division, which had a high desertion rate, would be of concern.[12]

When Senger took over his part of the Winter Line, fighting was already well under way. But in the six weeks of fighting that took place between his assumption of command and the end of November 1943, he could report optimistically that, though he had lost some hill positions and the town of Mignano, he had kept both Monte Sammucro and Monte Cassino. Further, he welcomed the arrival of two experienced divisions. As a result, the morale of the whole corps had been raised. "The troops had regained confidence."[13]

While Frido von Senger was conducting his skillful defense along the Winter Line, Adolf Hitler, in his *Wolfschanze* (Wolf's Lair) in East Prussia, was finally coming to grips with the awkward command arrangement in Italy. He took a long time in making his decision. In all probability, he was torn between his admiration for Erwin Rommel and the fact that Kesselring, Rommel's rival, held views on Italian defense closer to his own. Hitler, in keeping with those commanders who act on impulse, always tended to side with the last man who had come to see him—until the next one came in, of course.

In early October, Hitler seemed to vacillate almost on an hourly basis. At first he was hopeful of defending south of Rome, but then after the Allies crossed the Volturno he summoned Rommel to his headquarters for a conference. Rommel was negative. He pointed out the vulnerability of the west coast of Italy to amphibious assault and said there was a danger that the whole German Tenth Army might be trapped. In that case, he went on, he "would not wish to answer for this risk."[14] Hitler, convinced, directed his staff to prepare a draft order putting Rommel in command of all German forces in Italy, replacing Kesselring. When Rommel returned to his headquarters, however, he found that the order had not arrived. A few days later Colonel General Alfred Jodl, of OKW, informed Rommel's chief of staff that the decision was being delayed.

Hitler then sent for Kesselring, and the conversation took a different turn. Kesselring, always optimistic, said that he could hold the Allies from

12. Senger, *Neither Fear nor Hope,* 183.
13. Ibid., 186. The mountains are about five miles beyond Mignano.
14. General Siegfried Westphal, *The German Army in the West,* 154.

reaching northern Italy for six to nine months. Hitler was apparently convinced. A few days later he ordered his staff to draw up another order, this time placing Kesselring in charge.

The matter was settled for good on November 5, when Rommel was called back to East Prussia. Hitler had assigned the position of Supreme Commander, Italy, to Kesselring, and Rommel was to go to northwest France to supervise the construction of coastline defenses in anticipation of the expected Allied crossing of the English Channel. Hitler's shilly-shallying had caused untold damage to the German defense, but the problem had been resolved. As Westphal later put it, "The duality that had long bedeviled the German leadership in Italy was now ended. It was immaterial who the commander was; now at last there was a single commander who had all the forces at his disposal."[15]

In the meantime, German troops, especially engineers, were busy at fortifying the Gustav Line. As the articulate Fred Majdalany so aptly describes the process, "From the beginning of December the Rapido, Cassino, Monastery hill and the adjacent heights were no longer respectively a river, a town, and a spur of the Abruzzi. They were the raw material of a conspiracy between man and nature aimed at devising a perfect and impregnable defensive system."[16]

No stone—literally in places—was left unturned. Mortar positions were placed in strategic locations such as the Monte Venere, a hill just below the Abbey. More remarkable, the Germans found natural caves in the mountainside, caves that could provide shelter for, say, a platoon of troops while a machine gun guarded the entrance. Some caves housed command posts. Stone houses scattered throughout the area were organized into small fortresses. In one location the Germans made use of a small fort built by the Italians as far back as 1820.[17] Down in the valley, the Germans drew on their experiences in Russia: destroyed cities made better defensive positions than intact cities. They therefore wrecked the town of Cassino by demolitions to make the streets impassable for tanks. South of Cassino, on the Liri, Rapido, Gari, and Garigliano Rivers, they destroyed the bridges and cleared fields of fire. They destroyed dams over these rivers to make the approaches become swamps. As described by Hapgood and Richardson, "By the time the Germans had finished building the Gustav Line, there was no way the Allies could go that would not encounter formidable natural and manmade defenses."[18]

15. Ibid. See also Blumenson, *Salerno to Cassino,* 243–46, from which much of this account has been drawn.
16. Majdalany, *Cassino,* 53.
17. David Hapgood and David Richardson, *Monte Cassino,* 75.
18. Ibid., 75.

One matter that caused the Germans much concern was the existence of the Monte Cassino Abbey, which dominated the area, at one time the strategic location but at the same time the point of greatest sensitivity. No matter how much the two sides in this conflict disagreed on everything else, neither wanted to see the venerable building destroyed. For this was no ordinary abbey. Built only about a century after the fall of Rome, it had been the site where St. Benedict himself had founded the world-famed Benedictine Order, of which von Senger himself was a member. But Senger was busy fighting the Allies on the Winter Line; it would fall to others to see to the preservation of this shrine, or at least of its treasures.

On October 15, 1943, as the Fifth Army was consolidating its crossing of the Volturno, two German officers from the Hermann Goering Division arrived at the Monte Cassino Abbey for a serious conference with the abbot, Gregorio Diamare. All three knew the purpose of the visit; in fact the two officers had come to see the abbot independently the day before. The two Germans were there to recommend most strongly—issue a veiled order, in fact—that the abbot consent to evacuating the Abbey, its archives, its art treasures, and most of its monks to a spot north of Rome. Only by evacuation could the abbot avoid the destruction that would inevitably befall when the British and Americans should arrive. It now appeared that they would do so in a matter of weeks.

It was not a matter of Allied intentions, actually. Though the Germans could not be sure, they believed that the Allies might spare the venerable Abbey. But even if the Allies demonstrated the best of intentions, they were nearing the Gustav Line in great force. Bitter, bloody fighting was inevitable. Stray bombs might—almost certainly would—hit the Abbey. Both the abbot and the Germans had convincing evidence of Allied power. Only four days earlier, the enemy air forces had hit the town of Cassino, down in the valley below, and the destruction that a single raid could wreak on any stone construction was obvious.

The two German officers made a strange pair, with little in common. One, Maximilian J. Becker, was a captain of the Medical Corps, and the other was a lieutenant colonel of the Transportation Corps, Julius Schlegel. Becker was a strong anti-Nazi; Schlegel, an Austrian, was devoted to Hitler. He did, in fact, claim to have been one of the original members of the Austrian Nazi movement before that country's annexation to Germany five years before. Each felt some resentment toward the other. Becker, in fact, was suspicious that Schlegel was toying with the idea of sending one of the wooden sculptures from the Abbey to Goering himself, the patron of their division.

The two, however, shared a genuine passion to preserve the archives and art treasures of the Abbey. Schlegel was the man who held the cards.

As a transportation officer, he controlled the trucks that would be necessary to move the contents of the Abbey, and he was much higher ranking in the division. But Becker had something to offer also: experience. Some weeks before, he had managed to remove the books from the monastery of Teano, a town halfway between Naples and Cassino. Though the two German officers disliked each other, they worked harmoniously.

Not surprisingly, Abbot Diamare was both reluctant and suspicious. At age seventy-seven, with many years of peaceful administration behind him, he could not bring himself to believe that the Allies would destroy such a venerated edifice as the Abbey. He had been assured by Field Marshal Kesselring that the Germans would not use the Abbey for military purposes. The Germans had declared that they would allow no soldiers to approach closer than three hundred meters from the Abbey's gates. As for the Allies, the abbot trusted that the thousands of American and English visitors who had come to the Abbey throughout the years would be in a position to prevent such a "crime against civilization" as to destroy the building.[19]

The abbot, however, was a practical man as well as an influential religious leader. He knew that time was running out, because the Allies had crossed the Volturno within the last forty-eight hours. And the air raid on Cassino four days earlier had destroyed the funicular that brought visitors up from the town of Cassino to the Abbey, thus bringing the war close to home. The Abbey was already without telephone and electricity. More serious was the problem of the refugees, terrified people who had crowded into the Abbey's walls to escape the war outside. The monks, by sacred tradition, could not deny them hospitality, but the number had swollen to a thousand, and that many people, added to the monks and nuns, far exceeded the Abbey's supply of food and water. Something had to be done.[20]

The Abbey would be evacuated. The treasures within its walls, along with most of the monks, would be sent to the Benedictine monasteries in the vicinity of Rome. Such of the building's contents that belonged to the Italian government—archives stored in the Abbey along with artworks previously removed from Naples—would be sent to the supply depot of the Hermann Goering Division located at Spoleto, a town seventy miles north of Rome. Though warned of the danger, Abbot Diamare refused evacuation himself. "I will remain here," he declared.[21]

During the next two days, both the Germans and the Benedictines made preparations for the removal. Schlegel secured the official permis-

19. Ibid., 9.
20. Ibid., 10.
21. Ibid., 17–18.

sion of the commander of the Hermann Goering Division[22] to use trucks that had brought supplies from the north and were returning empty, and Abbot Diamare, in a solemn conference, informed his monks, many of whom had spent their entire adult lives within the Abbey's walls, that they were to leave.

The abbot and his monks and nuns had little to lift their despondent spirits during this traumatic episode except for one thing: it solved the emergency the Abbey was encountering with the dirty, hungry, and in some cases diseased refugees who had flocked through the gates seeking safety. Schlegel absolved the abbot from his rigid obligation to those people by interceding with them personally. Those who stayed in the Abbey, he declared, would have to work in packing and crating the archives and art. The rest of the refugees would have to leave. Cruel as the move appeared, it was necessary. Most of the refugees departed, but Schlegel and Diamare made use of the talents of those who stayed.

For those days in late October, the halls of the Abbey echoed with the sounds of saws and hammers, intermingled with those of heavy boots. The people working were an odd mixture of soldiers, monks, and refugees. Schlegel, as a transportation expert, oversaw the activities. So efficient were they that less than a week after the original meeting between Becker, Schlegel, and the abbot, the first German trucks were loaded up and ready to leave Monte Cassino. Diamare, Schlegel, and a small group saw them off, destined for Rome and Spoleto. The job of evacuating the Monte Cassino Abbey was completed in the first days of November. But Abbot Diamare, true to his word, stayed behind with a group of diehard monks.[23]

Frido von Senger, though highly approving of these measures to protect the treasures of Monte Cassino Abbey, had played no direct role in them. But he showed his devotion in an unconventional way. On Christmas Eve 1943, he violated the three hundred-meter restricted area around the Abbey by donning civilian clothes and going alone to attend midnight mass with Abbot Diamare and the monks who had stayed behind with him.

22. General Paul Conrath. It seems incredible that Schlegel could have taken so much initiative on himself without some tacit approval of Conrath himself.

23. This account comes largely from Hapgood and Richardson, *Monte Cassino*. For an absorbing and detailed account of the removal, see pages 3–37.

Alexander's Plan, 8 November 1943

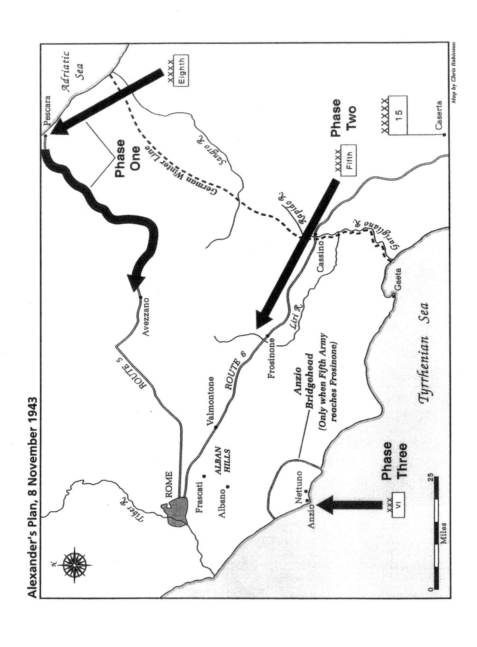

Map by Chris Robinson

CHAPTER 6

PURPLE HEART VALLEY

San Pietro

At 15th Army Group Headquarters in the Palace of Caserta, General Sir Harold R. L. G. Alexander and his staff spent the last weeks of October 1943 making plans for the capture of Rome. Unfortunately for the Allied cause, few options were available.

Alexander was a distinguished soldier, a veteran of the First World War and of several campaigns of the Second. In June 1940, he had commanded a division at the Dunkirk evacuation, and he later commanded British forces in Burma. In late 1942, he was Montgomery's superior as Commander, Eastern Mediterranean Theater, at the Battle of El Alamein. When the Eighth Army, under him, reached the Western Mediterranean Theater, he had come under Eisenhower, whose territory it was. Officially designated as Eisenhower's deputy, his main function was to command the 15th Army Group. In that capacity he had conducted day-to-day ground operations in Tunisia, Sicily, and Italy, with generally creditable results.

Alexander was an enigmatic man, mysterious behind his personal reserve. Because of his modest demeanor and unfailing courtesy, he was a favorite of the Americans, who never tired of contrasting him favorably with his colorful subordinate, Montgomery. Lucian Truscott, a man who was often critical of his peers and superiors, was a strong admirer.

And yet Alexander had his critics. Americans often sensed that he secretly held a low opinion of the Yanks and their officers, considering them too inexperienced to be trusted with difficult assignments. As the Tunisian campaign was ending in May 1943, General Eisenhower, who rarely interfered with Alexander's conduct of operations, felt forced to give Alexander a direct order to move the American II Corps from a quiet front to a position from which they could participate in the last phase, necessary for American morale. And in Sicily, many Americans believed that

First Attack on San Pietro, 8-9 December 1943

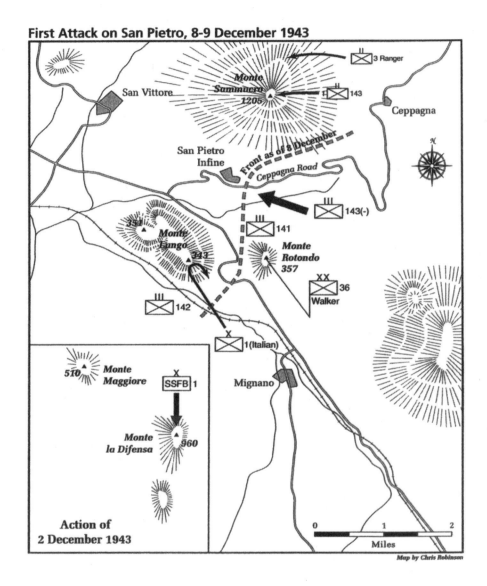

Map by Chris Robinson

Second Attack on San Pietro, 15-17 December 1943

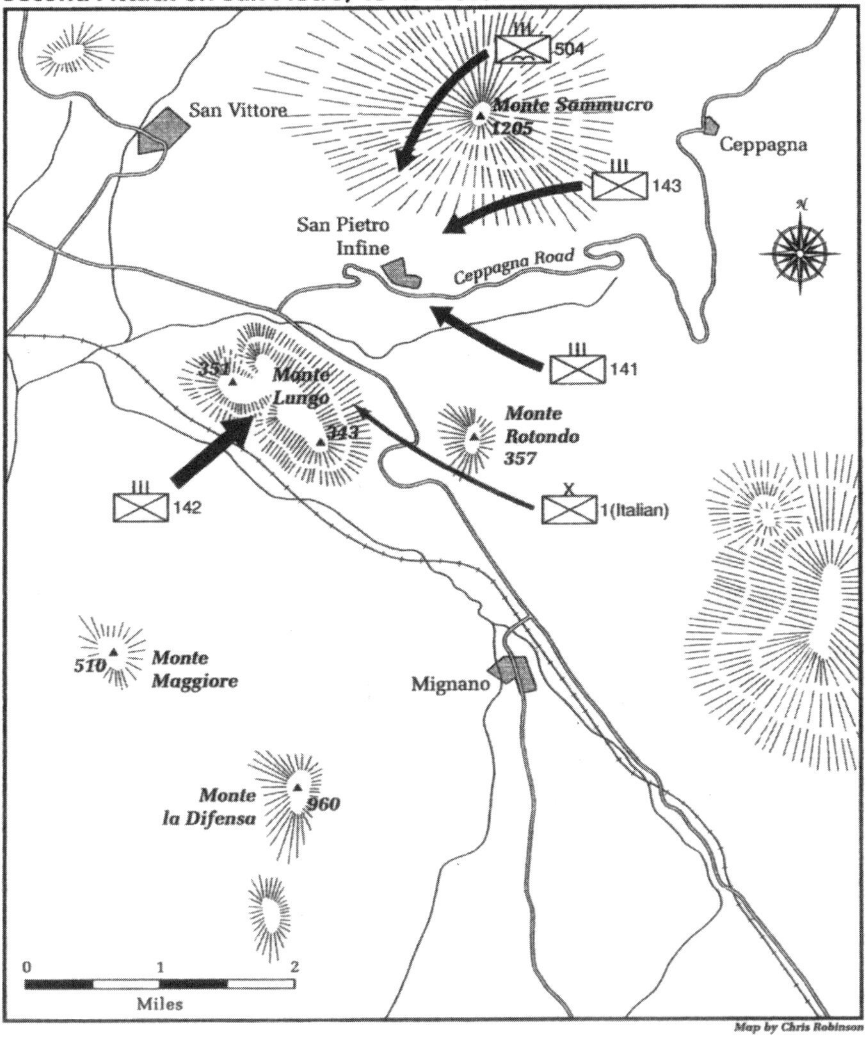

San Vittore

Monte Sammucro
1205

504

143

Ceppagna

San Pietro
Infine

Ceppagna Road

141

251
Monte
Lungo

343

Monte
Rotondo
357

142

1 (Italian)

510
Monte
Maggiore

Mignano

Monte
la Difensa

960

0   1   2

Miles

Map by Chris Robinson

Alexander, in the allocation of roads, had so favored Montgomery's Eighth Army over Patton's Seventh that the victory had been less decisive than it might have been.

Some of Alexander's British colleagues also had reservations, but based on a different theme. He was too reticent, they contended, to exert his authority in his dealings with his American subordinates. His command style bore much resemblance to that of the American Confederate general Robert E. Lee, whose gentle way of commanding has often been blamed for the disaster that befell the Confederate army at Gettysburg in July of 1863. Be all that as it may, Alexander remained generally and deservedly popular.

On November 2, 1943, Alexander flew to Algiers to confer with Eisenhower on the plans he had drawn up for a fall campaign. With Ike's approval, Alexander's headquarters on November 8 issued a directive visualizing a general offensive broken into three phases. The first phase was to consist of an attack by Montgomery's Eighth Army up the Adriatic coast to take the town of Pescara, an important point because it was located on Highway 5, a major route that led directly to Rome. The second phase was to begin once Monty had secured Pescara and then taken Avezzano, about fifty miles from Rome. At that point, the Fifth Army, on the Winter Line, would jump off, crossing the Rapido and driving up the Liri Valley on Route 6. The bulk of the air support would switch from the support of Eighth Army to Fifth Army at that time.[1]

The third phase was to begin when elements of the Fifth Army reached Frosinone, in the Liri Valley near Rome. An amphibious landing of one division would be made somewhere in the vicinity of Rome, probably at Anzio-Nettuno. Everyone agreed, however, that any amphibious landing would have to be within a day's reach of the main force; nobody wanted a repetition of the situation at Salerno, where Montgomery's Eighth Army had been out of supporting distance of Clark. Besides, a single division could not survive long by itself.

As scheduled, Montgomery's Eighth Army attacked across the Sangro River on November 28, 1943, employing 13 Corps with a British and a Canadian division on the left, and 5 Corps, with a British, an Indian, and a New Zealand division on the right. Things went well at first, and Montgomery himself declaimed to the press, "My troops have won the battle as they always do," he exulted. "The road to Rome is open."[2]

1. Blumenson, 257. According to Eric Morris, Alexander and Montgomery, unbeknownst to Clark, considered it possible that Eighth Army, along this route, could reach Rome before the Fifth Army, Morris, *Circles*, 222.

2. Morris, *Circles*, 223.

Lieutenant General Mark W. Clark, Fifth Army; General Sir
Harold R. L. Alexander, commanding the 15th Army Group;
and Lieutenant General Sir Richard McCreery, commanding
the British Eighth Army. Photo taken after McCreery had
replaced General Oliver Leese in command of the Eighth
Army. National Archives.

That was Monty's last moment of triumph in Italy. What he apparently
failed to realize was that the position on the Sangro, formidable though
the river was, represented only an outpost. The extension of the Gustav
Line lay along the Moro River, a few miles further on. As a result,
Montgomery's attack went no further, and the cost was tremendous. One
New Zealand battalion, for example, had been reduced from a normal
component of some eight hundred men to eighteen.[3] With the frustration
of the Eighth Army's attack, the task of moving toward Rome fell almost
exclusively to Clark's Fifth Army.[4]

Unfortunately for the Allied cause, the Americans were nearly as exhausted as the British; both needed rest. For even though the German high
command had emphasized certain "lines" for special fortification, they

3. Fourteen men refused to make a predawn attack, and the authorities showed no compassion. They were all tried by court-martial and sentenced to two years' imprisonment.
Morris, *Circles*, 224.

4. Ibid., 212. Montgomery was fighting with one hand tied behind his back. The seaport
supporting Eighth Army was Bari, on the Adriatic near the heel of the boot. Perhaps necessary in the wide strategy but detrimental to the Sangro River attack was the fact that a
great amount of the tonnage of Bari was being sent to the Allied air forces. The airfields at
Foggia constituted one of the main justifications for the Italian campaign, and the Allies

had not conceded an inch of ground between those lines without a fight. Every hill in the path of the Allies was defended with wire, booby traps, mortars and machine guns. Those man-made obstacles had to be over-come under miserable conditions. The mud, which varied between ankle-deep and knee-deep, made progress all the slower. By the time Clark's men had reached the outer reaches of the Winter Line, they could go no farther without time to refit and regroup.

On the whole, Clark was served by a well-qualified group of subordi-nate commanders. John P. Lucas, commander of VI Corps, had performed well in the mountains, despite his chronic pessimism. Clark had also re-ceived the II Corps, under Major General Geoffrey Keyes. Keyes was a quiet, unassuming man, so unassuming that General Eisenhower, in ap-pointing him, had suggested that he be more outgoing in encouraging his subordinates. But Keyes had come highly recommended by General Patton, and he was welcome.[5] As to Clark's divisions, Truscott was still with the 3d, as was Charles Ryder with the 34th. The 45th, however, had lost its outstanding commander, Troy Middleton, who had not returned from the hospital after incurring a knee injury.[6] Middleton's replacement was Major General William W. Eagles, former assistant division com-mander in the 3d Division under Truscott. Eagles was an able soldier, "one of our most accomplished soldiers" according to Lucas,[7] but he lacked the warmth that had so endeared Middleton to the "Thunderbirds."

The one unhappy relationship was that between Clark and the com-mander of the British 10 Corps, Richard McCreery. Clark had attempted to have 10 Corps replaced by an American corps, but so far had been un-successful.

Clark would have welcomed more American units, because the Fifth Army was quite adequately supported by the port of Naples. Allied strate-gic planning, however, called for the transfer of units away from Italy, not

---

had made sure that that advantage was exploited. Within three weeks after the British had seized Foggia, the Allies had opened up ten fully equipped airfields, manned by 35,000 air-men, at the cost of 300,000 tons of shipping, enough to supply twenty divisions for a month. (The general rule of thumb for supplying a division in the Second World War was 500 tons a day.) Add to that the miserable downpours, the cold, and the fact that an air raid on the port of Bari, which occurred four days after Montgomery's attack, caused more death and damage than any since the Japanese raid on Pearl Harbor in December 1941.

5. See Eisenhower letter to Keyes, Sept. 27, 1943, *Papers*, 3:1465–67.

6. Middleton, after extended hospitalization, left the Mediterranean for London, where he was promoted to command VIII U.S. Corps for Overlord. He had expected to return to the 45th, and the members of the division accused Clark of engineering his removal. Interview with General Michael Davison, July 24, 2003.

7. Blumenson, *Salerno*, 252.

toward it. But he was losing only one division in the transfer of seven divisions from the Mediterranean to the United Kingdom, the 82d Airborne. Even that loss aggrieved him.[8] As great as the loss of the division itself was the departure of its dynamic commander, Matthew Ridgway, on whom Clark had come to rely. Clark would miss Ridgway mightily.[9]

To replace the 82d Airborne, Clark was receiving other units. One of these was the 2d French Moroccan Division, the first of several that would later become the French Expeditionary Corps. Another highly welcome addition would be the 1st Special Service Force, the bland name of which would soon be replaced in everyone's mind by the Germans' nickname for it, the "Devil's Brigade." This was a bizarre unit, its enlisted strength being half American and half Canadian, for a total of about 1,500 officers and men. It was specially trained for mountain fighting. Its commander, Colonel Robert T. Frederick, would later be listed among those whom Lucian Truscott considered the outstanding battle leaders of the war.

Finally Fifth Army would receive the 1st Italian Motorized Brigade, commanded by Brigadier General Vincenzo Dapino. The addition of this last unit presented Clark with certain problems. It was the first Italian unit to fight the Germans since the surrender of Italy on September 8 and its subsequent joining of the Allies. Clark and his superiors therefore deemed it absolutely necessary for it to be successful in its first action.

Those were the tools with which Clark began his effort to cross the Rapido into the Liri Valley.

The Battle of San Pietro

By mid-November 1943, even before the British offensive had halted, Clark was ready, and he chose not to wait. The specter of Montgomery's taking Rome loomed too large in his mind. He therefore began his push into the Winter Line, an operation he aptly code-named Operation Raincoat. The location of his attack could not be a secret; Frido von Senger had predicted that it would occur in the Mignano Gap, often loosely termed the Liri Valley.[10] Before long, the American troops would

---

8. He managed to retain one of its regiments, the 504th Parachute Infantry, but for only a limited time.

9. The other American divisions were the 1st Infantry, the 9th Infantry, and the 1st Armored Divisions. None of these had fought in Italy, however, so Clark did not feel their loss.

10. The Mignano Gap was indeed an extension of the Liri Valley, but the Liri River flowed into the Rapido, up ahead, from the west, that is from the direction of Rome. Much similarity exists between this terrain and that of the final front of the Korean War, which

wryly call the gap "Purple Heart Valley" because of the number of dead and wounded that the fighting there would produce.

To execute the attack through the Mignano Gap, Clark chose the 36th Infantry Division, his only "rested" unit, which had been refitting since Salerno. General Fred Walker, its commander, had needed every minute of that time to rebuild it.[11] The 36th began relieving the exhausted 3d Division at the town of Mignano on November 15, as always amid drenching downpours. Immediately upon assuming command of the Mignano sector, Walker began a program of aggressive patrolling to familiarize his officers and men with its new sector and to capture German prisoners. In the meantime, he began laying plans to seize the division's first objective, the American portion of the Monte Camino complex, which dominated the main axis, Route 6, from the south (left).[12]

Monte Camino was one of two major complexes that dominated the Mignano Valley. The other was the Monte Sammucro on the north. But there were other critical points. Nestled at the foot of Monte Sammucro, north of the valley, was the small town of San Pietro, a place of only 1,400 souls. It was an old town, and its buildings had thick stone walls, making it easy for the Germans to make it into a fortress. It was worth holding, so located that the level ground to the south of it was covered by deadly fire. An American commander would usually bypass such a strongpoint, but in this instance, such was impossible, for Highway 6 in front of it was unusable so long as San Pietro remained in enemy hands. So Walker's task could not be accomplished without the reduction of that home of frightened Italian civilians.

In the cave that he used as his command post, Walker spent the last couple of weeks of November 1943, rechecking his plans, based on information from his patrols. His was an odd situation. Keyes's II Corps had been inserted between Lucas's VI Corps and McCreery's 10 British Corps, but the II Corps front was being held by only one division, Walker's. With it all, Walker remained optimistic.

---

ended a little more than a decade after the events described here. The Chorwon Valley in Korea cut through the mountains as did the Liri-Mignano, making it the obvious, almost the only approach for large-scale operations.

11. New replacements had to be processed and trained. Eric Morris has noted that the division was no longer a "Texas" division. That is only partly so. Its high-ranking officers who set the tone were all, except for Walker himself, part of the original Texas National Guard command structure.

12. In this part of Italy, the front lines ran nearly north-south. The Allies were therefore attacking always due westward.

Walker's later account of the period reads largely as a list of complaints. He growled, for example, over the hordes of visitors who were beating a path to his door to take a look at the front. More important, however, was his consciousness that he was older and far more experienced in combat than nearly all his superiors. He viewed the high command, in fact, with a remarkable degree of disdain. He was convinced, with more than a grain of truth, that the corps and army commanders lacked a true appreciation of the hardships his men were going through in the cold, the wet, and the wind. Yet, even if he was often critical of the instructions he was receiving, Walker does not seem to have complained very much to those who had issued them.

Despite his formidable appearance—erect posture and piercing black eyes—Walker was almost tender in his feelings for his men. He had joined the 36th in the fall of 1941, when General Marshall, well aware that the division was in dire need of new leadership, assigned his most experienced commander to it. Walker had problems at first. He was replacing a popular Texas National Guard division commander, and therefore his welcome was cold. However, he had soon become accepted by the bulk of the National Guard officers, and he had become their most ardent partisan. That characteristic would prove to be a source of both strength and weakness in his performance during the Italian campaign.

It was well that Walker was a strong, hands-on division commander, because the attack on San Pietro, like many others in the campaign, called for a command method that might be called micromanagement. Each of the German defensive lines was, in truth, a series of isolated strongpoints that had to be taken one at a time, and that circumstance made coordination between his infantry battalions nearly impossible. As a division commander, therefore, Walker was forced to think in terms of ten infantry battalions[13] instead of three regiments. It made for a complicated battle plan, but in the mountains of southern Italy, he had no other choice.

The attack to take San Pietro and the Mignano Gap was to be carried out in two phases. The first phase, on which the second depended, was the reduction of the Monte Camino hill mass on the left, which included several peaks almost as high as Monte Camino itself.[14] Because of the size of

13. The nine battalions of the 36th Division proper, with the 3d Ranger Battalion attached. This summation does not include the five thousand–man Special Service Force or the 1st Italian Motorized Infantry Brigade.

14. The town of S. Pietro Infine lay like a cork in a bottle and was the key to the approaches to the Liri Valley—on the way to Rome. The village itself nestled along the bottom

the hill mass, Clark had split responsibility for its reduction between the British 10 Corps on the left and the American II Corps on the right. The division immediately to Walker's left was the British 56th.

The second phase of his attack, the main phase, involved taking San Pietro and Monte Sammucro above it. It was tentatively scheduled to jump off on December 8, six days after the Camino attack. By then, Walker expected the Camino mass to be cleared of German defenders.

One terrain feature that everyone, even Walker, appeared to underestimate was Monte Lungo, a smaller hill that lay between Camino on the left and Sammucro on the right. Compared with the other two ranges, Lungo seemed insignificant. Its elevation was only 351 meters, dwarfed by Camino (963 meters) and Sammucro (1,250 meters). Its importance, however, lay in its location. It stood between the Rome-Naples railway line on the southwest and Route 6 on the northeast, and it afforded the Germans excellent observation over the town of San Pietro. Everyone, including Walker, seemed to regard Monte Lungo as a minor objective. (As a matter of fact, Senger had placed a whole battalion from the 15th Panzer Grenadier on Lungo.)

As a result of his underestimating German intentions to hold Lungo, Walker assigned its capture to the 1st Italian Motorized Infantry Brigade. He was unimpressed by its commander, Brigadier General Vincenzo Dapino, but he knew that for political reasons, Clark desired to employ it.[15] Since the Motorized Brigade was being assigned what Walker believed would be an easily attainable objective, all well and good.

Walker's optimism seems to have gripped all echelons of the American high command. When Alexander visited Mark Clark in mid-November, he warned Clark that so far the Fifth Army had met only delaying positions, not serious defense lines. The Germans, he cautioned, would defend the Winter Line with great determination. Clark, according to one witness, answered, "Oh, don't worry. I'll get through the Winter Line all right and push the Germans out."[16] Everyone's eyes were focused on

---

of the steep western slopes of Sammucro which towered some four thousand feet to the northeast, while in front of San Pietro to the southwest was a narrow defile extending perhaps a mile until blocked by Monte Lungo which lay astride the entrance to the pass (Mignano Gap). Beyond Monte Lungo on the west was Monte Maggiore and somewhat south and west of it the higher peaks of Monte de la Difensa (Hill 960) and the adjoining Monte Camino (Hill 963). This area was known collectively as the Camino Hill Mass. Robert L. Wagner, *The Texas Army: A History of the 36th Division in the Italian Campaign,* 64–65.

15. Walker, *Texas to Rome,* 282.

16. Dr. Sidney T. Mathews, interview with General Alexander, Jan. 10–15, 1949. Cited in Blumenson, 265.

Cassino and the Rapido River up ahead. San Pietro, they thought, would only be another delaying position.

The optimism was not unrealistic. Up to November, Kesselring had planned to hold the gap only lightly until overridden by orders from Hitler.[17]

As of December 1, 1943, the 36th Division, on a five-mile front, was disposed with all three infantry regiments on the line. On the left, occupying a foothold on the south end of Monte Lungo, was the 142d Infantry, under Colonel George E. Lynch. In the center, stretching across the gap in front of Monte Rotondo, was the 141st Infantry, under Colonel Richard J. Werner. On the right, facing San Pietro and across the base of Monte Sammucro, was the 143d Infantry under Colonel William H. Martin.

Of the three, the 142d was expected to face the greatest challenge. It was to attack westward from the base of Monte Lungo and take the eastern portion of the Monte Camino complex, specifically Monte La Difensa and Monte Maggiore, both of which overlooked Lungo. Because of the difficulty of that task, Walker had attached Frederick's newly arrived Devil's Brigade to the 142d. To the 143d, which also faced a tough assignment, he attached the 3d Ranger Battalion.

On the night of December 2, the attack began on all fronts. The British 10 Corps, heavily supported by Allied airpower, launched its very difficult attack on Monte Camino.[18] It was a steep climb to the crest, which stood at 963 meters. Nevertheless, the 56th Division reached the top by the morning of December 3d, only to be pushed off by violent German counterattacks. A seesaw battle resulted, but the British 56th, despite certain previous misgivings of General Walker, finally secured Monte Camino by the evening of December 6.

The reinforced 142d Infantry, starting from the base of Lungo, attacked the eastern side of the Camino hill mass concurrently. The first of the two American objectives was La Difensa, assigned to Frederick's Devil's Brigade. To the ordinary observer, this hill appeared to be impossible to scale. The only roads up the south side of the hill were narrow dirt paths, exposed to German observation and artillery fire. The north side was such a steep cliff as to appear utterly impenetrable. On studying the ground, however, Frederick quickly decided that his force of mountain troops could go up the north side, which the Germans had not considered necessary to defend.

17. Blumenson, 273.
18. The British replacement system was faltering. Britain had simply reached the end of its manpower supply. This was the fourth effort of the 56th Division.

Brigadier General Robert A.
Frederick, commanding the 1st
Special Service Force (Devil's
Brigade). U.S. Army.

During the night of December 2, Frederick's force of Canadians and Americans clambered up the "impassable" cliff despite the rainy, sloppy conditions and the lack of trails. They reached the summit by daybreak and took the German defenders by complete surprise. From then on, amid cold, wet, and a series of German counterattacks, the Devil's Brigade held out despite Frederick's frequent requests for relief. During the eight days they stayed up on the mountain, they lost about two-thirds of their ranks. It is easy to see why. It required eight men ten hours to bring a wounded man down from the top to the base.[19] The men of the Devil's Brigade had paid a price: 73 dead, 9 missing, 313 wounded, and 116 hospitalized for exhaustion.[20]

With the Camino hill mass secure, Walker and Keyes set the time for the attack on San Pietro for the early morning of December 8. During the previous evening the troops would be moving into position, some of them, such as those on Monte Sammucro, from some distance away.

Still convinced that the Germans would not make a stand at San Pietro, Walker had designed his plan for quick exploitation against light resistance, not for heavy fighting. Colonel Martin's 143d Infantry Regiment was to attack the town with two battalions and Monte Sammucro with his

19. Adelman, 123–24.
20. Blumenson, 267.

other two. The only other action was to be the seizure of Monte Lungo by the Italian Motorized Brigade, on Martin's left.[21]

On the evening of December 7, the 1st Battalion, 143d Infantry, followed by the 3d Ranger Battalion, moved to the base of Monte Sammucro and began ascending the steep, slippery slopes to the summit of Hill 1205.[22] Favored by surprise, the "T-Patchers" seized the height by early morning and then withstood the inevitable, heavy German counterattacks. The 1st Battalion held, but the 3d Ranger Battalion on the right was less fortunate. The German counterattacks were so strong that the Rangers were forced to abandon the position. It took them several days of seesaw fighting before their position on Hill 950 was secured. These attacks were the most successful of the 36th Division's first effort. But the cost had been great. The 1st Battalion lost half its strength, with the battalion commander wounded and two company commanders out of three killed.[23]

On that same evening of December 7, the Italian Motorized Brigade moved up in trucks to a position where they could pass through the 141st Infantry and begin their assault on Monte Lungo the next morning. They had made no reconnaissance of the ground, and the one security patrol they had sent out on their left flank during the evening had failed to return.[24] Though the American troops preparing the assault expected little resistance, the Italians went much further in their optimism. They acted, in fact, as if they were on a pleasure trip. By chance, a doctor in the Eleventh Field Hospital described them:

> Truck load after truck load went by, all the troops whooping and hollering, waving Italian flags and singing at the top of their lungs. One would think that they were bound for a glorious holiday rather than going into the front lines. The contrast between these troops and the Americans is startling. The Americans all sit quietly, grim-faced and serious.[25]

---

21. The 141st Infantry would not participate in the assault, occupying the foot of Monte Lungo and Monte Rotondo, behind it. The 142d Infantry was still on Monte Maggiore mopping up.

22. The hills are often designated by their height. Thus this hill stood 1,205 meters above sea level. Care must be taken to ensure whether the heights are being counted in meters or feet. Hill 1205 is often referred to as 4,000 feet, which is remarkably close.

23. Blumenson, 277. One of those killed was Captain Henry G. Waskow, commanding Company B. Waskow was immortalized by Ernie Pyle, who described the scene with great poignance in his acclaimed book *Brave Men*.

24. Blumenson, 276.

25. Luther Wolff MD, *Forward Surgeon*, 51, cited in Morris, *Circles of Hell*, 227.

The Italian attack on Lungo seemed to begin favorably. After a thirty-minute artillery preparation, General Dapino's men jumped off, two battalions abreast,[26] and attacked through the mist to the top of Lungo. Having reached their objective at the top of the hill, they pressed on beyond in their enthusiasm. They did not go far. Caught in a barrage of German machine gun and mortar fire, they stopped, held their position for three hours, then broke. The artillery battalion supporting them ran out of ammunition, and the other divisional batteries were too far away to help them. The men lost all organization and poured down the hill, finally taking refuge behind the 141st Infantry at the foot of the hill. The effective strength of the Italian brigade was now down to the equivalent of a battalion, 700 men out of an original 1,600.[27] Most of the missing men returned, however, and General Dapino had his own solution to the problem of what had gone wrong: he asked the Italian Army to provide him with an additional battalion.

Across Route 6, Walker's main attack on San Pietro, that of the 2d and 3d Battalions, 143d Infantry, was conducted with the men advancing single file because of the narrowness of the gap. Starting out from a point only a mile from the town of San Pietro, the lead battalion was caught up in heavy German machine gun, mortar, and artillery fire. Martin attempted to develop the situation by committing one company around the left and the rest around to the right. Still they made no progress. The plan had gone awry because it depended on the help of the other two battalions up on Monte Sammucro, which had been stalled.

With that, the first attack on San Pietro ended.

Walker's plan for the second attack was really a continuation of the first, except that he was using more force. The main objectives were Monte Lungo on the left and Monte Sammucro on the right. On Lungo, he would employ the 142d Infantry, which was now free to leave Camino, assigning the Italians a small objective on the near side, to be attacked only when the hill was essentially secured. On the right flank, what was left of the 1st Battalion, 143d Infantry, was to push ahead of the crest (1205) and take three smaller peaks farther down the hill mass.

Walker was well aware of the weakened state of both the infantry and the Ranger battalions up on Monte Sammucro. He accordingly asked for, and received, the 504th Parachute Infantry, from the 82d Airborne, to protect their right flank. The 504th was then to continue the attack of the

26. Though designated as a brigade, Dapino's force was actually of regimental size.
27. Blumenson, 276.

Major General Fred Walker, commanding the 36th Infantry Division. Note the "T" in the shoulder patch, which stood for Texas. From it came the nickname "T-Patchers."

Rangers on the right. In Purple Heart Valley, three battalions were to resume the assault from the southeast.[28]

It was here that Walker planned to use his tanks to support the infantry in taking San Pietro. Two platoons, of five tanks each, were to move westward on the Ceppagna road until they reached a point where a small trail branches off to the right and makes its way up across terraces of olive groves, toward the town. The two platoons would split at that junction, one proceeding westward to turn and take the town generally from that direction, and the other, as mentioned, to follow the dirt road to the town. In order to coordinate the action of the two platoons, the tank commander interlaced them, every other tank in the column coming from each platoon. Smoke would be laid down on both Lungo and Sammucro to protect all troops, infantry and tanks, from enemy observation. That scheme turned into a fiasco.

The attack on Monte Sammucro remained stalled for a time. The mountain was totally devoid of concealment, and German artillery was still punishing the 1st Battalion unmercifully. The 504th Parachute Infantry, on the right, also ran into trouble some five hundred yards short of its ob-

28. They were, on the left, the 2d Battalion, 141st Infantry, and the two battalions from the 143d that had paid so dearly a week earlier.

jective and moved edgewise, occupying Hill 1205, on top of the mountain. Finally, Walker relieved the exhausted and depleted 1st Battalion, and in its place he sent the 1st Battalion, 141st Infantry. Soon the T-Patchers were closing in and threatening San Pietro from the north.

In the valley, the 141st Infantry made progress but could not get into town despite heavy losses. One battalion had been reduced to an effective strength of 130 men and was returned to the rear to rest and reorganize.[29]

The critical action came when the western base of Monte Lungo was taken. During the night of December 15, the 142d Infantry was able to cross Route 6 and join in the attack of the 143d. When closed in upon from both Lungo and Sammucro, the German defenders of San Pietro pulled out.

Only about a hundred Germans, well supported, had actually been in San Pietro, though Monte Lungo and Sammucro had each had a panzer grenadier battalion.[30] As the price to take the Mignano Gap, the Americans had paid heavily. The 36th Division alone had suffered about 1,200 casualties, including about 150 killed and 800 wounded. The 504th Parachute Infantry had lost nearly 300. These figures do not include the losses of the attached units—the 3d Ranger Battalion, the 753d Tank Battalion, or the attached engineers. Nor do they include the heavy losses of the 56th British Division on Camino.[31]

The 36th did not pause at San Pietro after its liberation. It immediately continued two miles to San Vittore, hoping that the German defenses had crumbled. They had not. San Vittore would have to be reduced in the same tedious way as San Pietro. This was an encapsulation of the story of the Italian campaign.

29. Blumenson, 284.
30. Ibid., 272.
31. Ibid., 285.

BOOK TWO

THE PLANNING FOR
SHINGLE

CHAPTER 7

THE INCEPTION OF SHINGLE

*The decision for Anzio gestated for two months,
a period of time marked by false labor.*

Lucian Truscott never forgot the date November 13, 1943, for that was the day when he first learned of plans for the Anzio landing, code-named Shingle. Summoned to General Clark's headquarters for a conference, his mind had not been on future plans. His exhausted and depleted 3d Infantry Division was even then being relieved on Monte Lungo by Walker's 36th Division, which had just been selected to seize the Mignano Gap. Truscott's thoughts that morning had been concentrated on the impending relief.

Upon arrival in Clark's office, however, Truscott could see that the army commander had an important matter on his mind. For also present were Lucas and the other two division commanders of VI Corps—Middleton,[1] of the 45th Division, and Charles E. Ryder of the 34th.

After the usual, brief formalities, Clark reviewed the essence of the recent meeting between General Alexander and General Eisenhower at Algiers and the resulting directive that Alexander had issued on November 8. He described the three phases of the forthcoming offensive to take Rome: the attack by the Eighth Army to seize Pescara, the subsequent attack by the Fifth Army to cross the Rapido and drive up the Liri Valley, and finally the amphibious landing designed to place a division-sized force ashore in the vicinity of Anzio-Nettuno concurrently with the arrival of the Fifth Army at Frosinone. That plan, if it worked, would put the Fifth Army within about a day's distance from the Anzio force. The planners presumed that the enemy would be in full retreat by the time that point had been reached.

1. Troy Middleton had not yet left the Mediterranean Theater for the United Kingdom.

Major General (later General) Lucian K. Truscott, Jr., commanding the 3d Infantry Division. National Archives.

Truscott heard no more of the plan for about a month. Nor did he give it much thought. There was much to do at 3d Division—refitting, absorbing new replacements, and training. Clark, however, continued to plan for Shingle, though the lack of landing craft available made the prospect seem remote. On December 10, as the first attack on San Pietro was winding down, he received word that the Combined Chiefs in Washington had approved General Eisenhower's request to retain sixty-eight LSTs, previously scheduled to sail for England on December 15, for a month, to January 15, 1944. That change made it possible, Clark saw, to execute the amphibious landing.

But time was now short. Two days after the first message, on December 12, Clark received another from Bedell Smith,[2] chief of staff at Allied Force Headquarters, reminding him of the need for an all-out effort. It took some six weeks to prepare for an amphibious landing, Smith remarked, and Clark must notify higher headquarters soon if he planned to make it.

The next day, on December 13, Clark summoned Truscott once more to his headquarters. Alexander's plan, Clark now told him, had been changed. Instead of waiting for II Corps to reach Frosinone before launching the amphibious attack, the plan now called for a much earlier date for the landing,

2. Lieutenant General Walter Bedell Smith, known as Bedell or Beetle.

which was to be executed while the rest of Fifth Army was still in the Cassino area. Instead of serving as an adjunct to a successful drive by the Fifth Army up the Liri Valley, the beachhead was now seen as a threat to cause the Germans to withdraw from Cassino. This was an entirely different mission from the one Clark had presented a month earlier.

As Truscott listened to this new concept, he quickly detected its obvious flaw. There was no chance, in his view, that the Fifth Army could cross the Rapido River, drive up the Liri Valley to Frosinone, and join up with the beachhead within a week. Nevertheless, the plan called for the invading force to take only a week's supply, on which it would have to subsist until the linkup, because the landing craft necessary for resupply of the beachhead were scheduled for removal to the United Kingdom. Though Truscott could see that this plan meant the sacrifice of the division so assigned, he held his tongue for the moment. He returned to 3d Division Headquarters and set his staff to work on the plan.

Truscott did not feel free to share his misgivings with his staff, "It will be our task to find ways to do the operation," he said, "not reasons why it should not be done."[3] His staff, which he noted was more experienced than either the corps or army staffs above them, then set to work. First they sought to substitute light weapons for those assigned by the tables of organization—light machine guns for heavy machine guns, mortars for artillery, and other innovations. They worked on ways to increase the carrying capacity of their vehicles. When they were finished, Truscott knew that, despite the fine work the staff had done, its members saw through the basic flaw of the plan. They were far too wise and experienced to be fooled.

Once more at Caserta, Truscott presented his doubts calmly—at first. Drawing on his extensive experience in Sicily, he pointed out that under more favorable conditions—better troops and lighter German resistance— the 3d Division had been able to advance only about two miles a day. German demolitions alone could slow the movement of supplies, tanks, and artillery.

Finally, however, Truscott could restrain himself no longer. "We are perfectly willing to undertake the operation if we are ordered to and will maintain ourselves to the last round of ammunition," he said, "but if we do undertake it, you are going to destroy the best damn division in the United States Army for there will be no survivors."[4] Truscott would consent to undergo such a sacrifice, he continued, but he felt that he and his

3. Truscott, *Command Missions,* 292.
4. Ibid., 292.

division "deserved a better fate." Clark responded that they would have to wait and see.

Clark thought the matter over. He had not yet launched his second attack to take the Mignano Gap and San Pietro. That being the case, he realized that Truscott was right. On December 18, therefore, he sent a message to Alexander at 15th Army Group recommending that all plans for Shingle be abandoned.

The Anzio landing, as far as Clark and Truscott were concerned, had been canceled.

CHAPTER 8

CHRISTMAS AT CARTHAGE, 1943

Winston S. Churchill, Prime Minister of Great Britain, seemed oddly out of place as the last days of 1943 came to a close. Far from his native England, he was laid up in what he mournfully referred to as the "ruins of Carthage," recovering from a dangerous bout with pneumonia. Everything possible was being done to provide for Churchill's comfort and quick recovery. Lord Moran, his personal physician, had sent to England for Churchill's wife, Clementine, to join him—one of his daughters, Sarah, was already on hand—and his host, General Dwight D. Eisenhower, was the soul of solicitude.

Churchill was occupying Ike's villa, La Maison Blanche, which was a comfortable place, described as "an attractive white structure with a beckoning terrace, a view of Cape Bon across the Bay of Tunis, and steps right down to the water."[1] But he was restless even when his sickness was at its height. Never noted for his stoicism, Churchill complained in a letter to President Roosevelt, "All your people are doing everything possible, but I do not pretend I am enjoying myself."[2]

Churchill had arrived at el Alouina Airport, Tunis, on December 11, 1943, expecting to spend only a night with Eisenhower and then fly from Tunisia to Italy the next day to inspect British fighting troops. But the exhausting schedule he had kept the previous month was telling on him. Lord Moran later claimed he knew Churchill was "riding for a fall,"[3] and Churchill was also aware of his condition. During the car trip from the airport to Eisenhower's villa, he said to his host, "I am afraid I shall have

1. Kay Summersby, *Eisenhower Was My Boss*, 75.
2. Churchill to Roosevelt, Dec. 15, 1943, cited in Winston S. Churchill, *Closing the Ring*, 422.
3. Lord Moran, *Churchill, Taken from the Diaries of Lord Moran*, 159.

to stay with you longer than I had planned. I am completely at the end of my tether, and I cannot go on to the front until I have recovered some strength." He slept all day, but the damage was done; fever soon set in, and his pneumonia symptoms appeared at the base of his lung.[4]

The last two months had been exceedingly difficult for the aging British leader. The first symptoms of his lengthy bout with respiratory troubles had appeared as early as mid-November, when he was resting at Malta preparing for his forthcoming meeting with President Franklin Roosevelt at Cairo. The frustrations he had suffered at Cairo and later at the Tehran meeting were no help.[5] When the Big Three had met at Tehran in the closing days of November, Churchill fumed when told that Roosevelt had met several times with Stalin while avoiding any such huddles with him. In the plenary meetings Roosevelt and Stalin had confronted Churchill together, jointly insisting on a date of May 1, 1944, for the launching of Overlord, the great Anglo-American invasion of northwest Germany. They also insisted on a secondary landing at Marseilles with troops drawn from Churchill's beloved Mediterranean Theater.

But Churchill had not lost all his battles in his discussions with Roosevelt and Stalin. Intent on keeping Britain's status and prestige on a par with that of the United States, he had categorically vetoed an American effort to combine the Mediterranean Theater of war with that of the future theater in northwest Europe, thus creating one single generalissimo for all Western forces fighting Hitler.[6] He had successfully insisted that the Western Mediterranean, previously under the command of an American, would now be combined with the former British Middle East Command into a consolidated Mediterranean command, under a British general. Since the British military chiefs were more amenable to close supervision than were the Americans, Churchill, as British defence minister, would be able to control operations in the Mediterranean as if it were his own British lake. That development was eminently satisfactory to the controlling Churchill.

As the future proprietor of the Mediterranean Theater, Churchill took close interest in the details of military operations. He asked probing questions even from his sickbed. He worried about the slow progress of the

4. Churchill, *Ring*, 421.

5. See Arthur Bryant, *Triumph in the West, 1943–1946: Based on the Diaries and Autobiographical Notes of Field Marshal the Viscount Alanbrooke*, 71.

6. "I cannot accept the combination of the two Commands under one Commander-in-Chief. . . . This will not occur while I hold my present office. You may at your discretion impart the above to Mr. Hopkins." Churchill to Admiral William Leahy, Nov. 8, 1932, cited in Churchill, *Ring*, 305. He quotes Leahy, on receipt of this letter, as saying, "If that is the opinion of the Prime Minister, there is nothing more to be said about it."

British and Americans as they fought their way up the Italian boot; as his body grew stronger, his mind focused ever more on the problem at hand.

Churchill reviewed means by which Rome might be taken soon. An airborne assault was out of the question. Though the Allies had gained air superiority over Italy, they had not completely swept the skies of German aircraft. German Field Marshal Albert Kesselring, a *Luftwaffe* officer himself, was still capable of making effective air raids against American and British ground troops. But on the seas the Allies reigned supreme. The German surface navy was nearly nonexistent, and three months earlier, when representatives of the Italian government under Marshal Badoglio had traveled to Eisenhower's headquarters, to sign an instrument of surrender, the Italian Navy had sailed out of the ports of La Spezia and Taranto and sailed to the British base at Malta.[7] The Allies, therefore, could go anywhere they wished in the Mediterranean and its subsidiary, the Tyrrhenian Sea, and deliver troops anywhere in the area.

That being the case, Churchill reasoned, the Allies should make an amphibious landing somewhere up the coast of Italy, probably at the port of Anzio-Nettuno, only thirty miles away from Rome. He had always, as he put it, been a partisan of the "end run," as the Americans called it, or "catclaw," which was "my term."[8] He was well aware, of course, that Alexander's plan of November 8 had included an amphibious assault, which had been dropped as too dangerous. But a two-division assault, sufficiently supplied, might prove decisive. That was the idea Churchill intended to sell to the British generals and, with more difficulty, to the Americans.

Before broaching the proposal to the Americans, therefore, Churchill set out to assure himself of solid support from his own generals and admirals. His chance to do that came when Chief of the Imperial General Staff Sir Alan Brooke dropped by Carthage on his way to visit Alexander in Italy. Brooke, a sardonic man but a solid soldier, usually played the role of balance wheel to the imaginative but impulsive Churchill. When the two agreed on any plan, or at least on a policy, Churchill had cleared a

7. "[The Italian Navy] did not wish to be the victims of another Scapa Flow. Therefore the Navy's heavy units would shortly make a major surprise sortie from La Spezia to steam around the western cape of Sicily to seek an engagement with the British fleet, which would end either in victory or on the sea's bed. This move must remain secret until the very last minute, and the German liaison party would therefore be taken aboard a short while before weighing anchor. The emotion with which [Count] de Courten made his statement, his tears and his invocation of the Germanre blood that flowed in his veins from his mother's side, did not fail to make a deep impression. Neither to Kesselring or to myself did the thought occur that this was most probably all a ruse to lull German suspicions of the impending cruise of the Italian fleet to internment in Malta" (Westphal, *German Army,* 148).

8. Churchill, *Ring,* 127.

large hurdle.[9] Churchill also sent a message to the Chiefs of Staff in Britain asking for a full list of all landing craft types in the Mediterranean. His letter was as much an argument as a request for information. He called the present stagnation "scandalous," and noted that none of the landing craft available had been used for assault purposes for three months—that is, since the Salerno landing.[10] But time was important. Many of the available landing craft would soon be leaving the Mediterranean. In fact, of the one hundred or so LSTs available at the moment, all but thirty-six would be gone by the middle of January. It would require eighty-eight such vessels to carry the two divisions Churchill had in mind for the assault.[11]

On Christmas Day, Churchill held a meeting in La Maison Blanche that included the key officers in the Mediterranean. Three of them—by no coincidence all British—would be directly involved in the operation Churchill had in mind. One was General Sir Henry Maitland Wilson, newly named Supreme Commander, Mediterranean Theater, and the others were General Sir Harold Alexander, commanding the Allied Forces in Italy, and Admiral Sir John Cunningham, Commander of Naval Forces in the Mediterranean. Three others, all on the eve of departing the Mediterranean for London, were General Dwight D. Eisenhower, the designated Supreme Commander for Overlord,[12] Air Marshal Sir Arthur Tedder, Eisenhower's future deputy, and Lieutenant General Walter Bedell Smith, Eisenhower's chief of staff.

Strangely, it was the departing Eisenhower to whom everyone looked. Though only a week remained before Ike officially turned over command to "Jumbo" Wilson, he was central to this discussion because, as future Supreme Commander of Overlord, he controlled the landing ships that Churchill needed to conduct his prospective amphibious landing. Churchill could never ask President Roosevelt to delay redeployment of these LSTs, all American ships, without Eisenhower's concurrence.

When Churchill outlined his plans and asked Eisenhower's help in securing the needed delay, Eisenhower was reluctant. He was not concerned so much because of his own need for the vessels as hesitant regarding the operation itself. He was dubious about Churchill's plan to land only two divi-

---

9. Bryant, *Triumph in the West,* makes no mention of Brooke's conversation with Churchill about an amphibious landing. Brooke's main interest at the time was the new command setup occasioned by Eisenhower's departure from the Mediterranean to command Overlord.

10. Churchill, *Ring,* 430–31.

11. Fifteen more were arriving from the Indian Ocean. Churchill, *Ring,* 431.

12. Though Churchill's host, Eisenhower came and went while the Prime Minister was convalescing. On Christmas he had just returned from his last trip to Italy before leaving for the United Kingdom.

sions at Anzio, a hundred miles beyond the Allied front lines. It would be a risky affair, Eisenhower believed, and he questioned Churchill's premise that the attack would cause the Germans automatically to withdraw from their extremely strong position on the Rapido River. As Eisenhower later recollected the meeting, he warned that war should not be compared too closely to chess; "a threatened king in chess must be protected; in war he may choose to fight." He pointed out that the Germans had not automatically pulled out in two previous campaigns, Tunisia and Sicily, just because their flanks were threatened. He believed that the Anzio landing would have to comprise "several strong divisions" to bring about decisive results.

Having made these arguments, Eisenhower acceded to Churchill's request. Churchill, he could see, was determined on the operation, and since he (Eisenhower) had no responsibility for the operation, the American promised to do what he could to arrange a delay of the necessary landing craft in their inevitable and vital transfer to Britain.[13]

The Prime Minister, though he listened to Eisenhower's arguments politely, had no real interest in his strategic views. All he wanted was Eisenhower's concurrence regarding the delay of landing craft transfer.[14] Having attained that assurance, he lost no time, once the meeting ended, in cabling the President to report on his conference:

> General Alexander is prepared to execute the landing at Anzio about January 20 if he can get a lift of two divisions. This should decide the battle for Rome, and possibly achieve the destruction of a substantial part of the enemy's army. To strike with less than two divisions would be to court disaster . . .
>
> For this purpose eighty-eight LSTs are required. These can only be obtained by delaying the return home [Britain] of fifty-six LSTs due to leave the Mediterranean from January 15 onward . . . nothing less than this will suffice. The fifteen LSTs from India cannot arrive in time, though they would be invaluable to replace casualties and for the buildup of Anvil.[15]

13. Eisenhower, *Crusade in Europe*, 212–13.

14. "At the Tunis conference on Christmas Day, the decision already had been made, at Churchill's insistence, as I understood it, before the Prime Minister turned to the chief of intelligence of Allied Force Headquarters and said, 'Now we will hear the seamy side of the question.' The G-2 of AFHQ, Brigadier Kenneth Strong, was skeptical of the advisability of the operation, because he knew the political importance of Rome to Hitler; he knew there were German divisions in France and Yugoslavia not too busily engaged during this winter period [that he could move] to Italy if they were needed . . . Churchill was ready to accept the obvious hazards . . ." (Clark, *Calculated Risk*, 284).

15. Anvil was the code name for the dispatch of several divisions from Italy to land in Southern France concurrently with the Overlord landing. It was always a bone of contention between the British and the Americans and was undoubtedly thrown out as bait.

Churchill's message then turned to his strategic arguments. It would be dangerous, he insisted, to let the Italian battle stagnate (which most Americans were willing to do), claiming that it would be leaving a half-finished job. He finished with a final plea for approval of a three-week delay in the transfer of the fifty-six LSTs to Britain. He also added that "orders have been issued to General Alexander to prepare accordingly."[16]

By this time Churchill's retinue was becoming uneasy about his extended stay at Carthage. He had been there long enough for German intelligence to have discovered his presence, and that fact increased the chance of an air raid. In addition, the bay overlooked by La Villa Maison Blanche was, for precautionary purposes, being patrolled by numerous ships from the Royal Navy that could be used elsewhere. So on December 27, 1943, Churchill took leave of Eisenhower and boarded a plane for Marrakech. There, still the guest of the U.S. Army, he could stay once more in the same villa that he and President Roosevelt had enjoyed so much the previous year after the historic Casablanca Conference. Marrakech had also been one of Churchill's favorite spots during the years before the Second World War.

The next day Churchill received a message from President Roosevelt approving the retention of the fifty-six LSTs he had requested. Gratefully, Churchill answered, "I thank God for this fine decision, which engages us once again in wholehearted unity upon a great enterprise."[17]

Two days later he was still ecstatic:

> . . . . The sun is shining today, but nothing did me the same good as your telegram showing how easily our minds work together on the grimly simple issues of this vast war. Alexander reports he has arranged satisfactory plans with [General Mark W.] Clark for Anzio. He is using the British 1st and the American 3d Divisions, with paratroops and armour. I am glad of this. It is fitting that we should share equally in suffering, risk, and honour.[18]

An enthusiastic and willful Prime Minister had single-handedly assured an Allied landing at Anzio for January 20, 1944.

16. Churchill, *Ring*, 436–37.
17. Ibid., 441.
18. Ibid., 445.

CHAPTER 9

PLANNING SHINGLE ON A SHOESTRING

Despite the apparent finality of the actions taken by Churchill and the staff at Carthage, there was still much to be done to make Shingle a reality. Practical difficulties remained unsolved. During the Second World War, both Churchill and Roosevelt were often justified in considering their admirals and generals too pessimistic. Often the military subordinates could accomplish more than they had believed possible. But not always.

The American general who most keenly felt the difference between concept and reality was Major General John P. Lucas, whose American VI Corps had been selected to execute the operation. Lucas certainly had much on his side; anyone would have felt the burden. In his case, however, the anxiety was exacerbated by his personal nature. He was not an aggressive, driving leader of troops. He was professionally competent, intelligent, and popular among his contemporaries, but lacking the basic optimism so necessary to command. That weakness had not yet become apparent, however. The VI Corps had fought well in the mountains between Avellino and Venafro, and only Lucas knew how much he had taken the hardships of his men to heart. He may have believed, but he could not practice, the motto of General George Patton, "Never take counsel of your fears." Johnny Lucas did his duty to the best of his abilities, but his fears haunted him.[1]

In late December 1943, Lucas received orders at VI Corps Headquarters near Prata to report to General Clark at Caserta. There was, as he conjectured, a "new chicken in the pot," but the nature of the "chicken" was still

---

1. The less respectful of the VI Corps staff sometimes referred to Lucas as "Foxy Grandpa" behind his back. Truscott, *Command Missions*, 320.

being kept highly secret. He was curious as he hastened to see his boss, as ordered.

Lucas's diary claims that this was the first time he had heard of Operation Shingle, even though Clark had discussed it with Truscott two weeks earlier. The reason for Clark's leaving Lucas in the dark certainly carried no adverse implications regarding Lucas himself. Clark had probably avoided bothering him because the VI Corps had been fighting hard in the Venafro area, and Lucas was also occupied with accommodating to the arrival of a new French division, the 2d Moroccan. Truscott's 3d Infantry Division was in reserve, so he had been more readily available.

What Lucas learned at Caserta that day was only a general outline of the new plan. His VI Corps was to be withdrawn from the front shortly after the turn of the year, its mission assumed by the French Expeditionary Corps under French general Juin, even then arriving in Italy. VI Corps would then begin making preparations for an amphibious landing at Anzio-Nettuno between January 20 and January 25, 1944. The force would consist of two divisions, reinforced by Rangers, Commandos, the 504th Parachute Infantry Regiment, and some tanks from the 1st Armored Division. One of the two divisions was to be Truscott's 3d, but the other had not yet been specified. Intriguing though that news must have been, Lucas had to return to his headquarters to continue the battle. It would still be a few days before his release from his current responsibilities.

To avoid loss of time in planning, Lucas sent a group of staff officers to Fifth Army Headquarters in the Palace of Caserta to begin work alongside their counterparts from Fifth Army and 3d Division. In the interim he would be able to visit them periodically by hopping down to Caserta in a Cub airplane.[2] Three weeks to organize such an expedition was incredibly short, he fretted, noting that the plans for an amphibious operation are "more intricate than for any other type with which I am familiar, [and] take months to develop."[3]

On January 3, 1944, Lucas's VI Corps relinquished command of the sector to Juin. The ceremony was unusually elaborate under the circumstances, but it represented the entry of a new nation, France, into the Italian campaign. The bands of the two nations played both of their national anthems—each with its own first, of course. "It seems strange not

2. The Piper Cub was a small, sixty-five-horsepower, canvas plane used by the artillery for adjustment of fires. It was a real workhorse, designated the L-4, and it served as convenient command transportation, being under complete control of the local headquarters and able to land in short fields.

3. Lucas diary, 281.

to hear the guns and to feel no responsibility for what goes on at the front," Lucas recorded. "Strange and a bit depressing."[4] He then threw himself into planning for Operation Shingle.

By now General Alexander had chosen the division that was to land alongside the 3d, the 1st British Infantry Division, commanded by Major General W. R. C. Penney. Like any Yankee, Lucas would have much preferred another American division, if for no other reason than the complications a force of mixed nationality would encounter in the matter of supply. Clark assured him, however, that the problems would be minimized. The British would eat American rations and use American motor vehicles for replacements. The only difference would be in the types of ammunition the two national forces would use. Lucas, however, was doubtful, and he felt little satisfaction at being proven correct when it later turned out that his doubts had been justified. When the going got tough, he later wrote, "the only types of supplies common to both units would be oil and gasoline."[5]

Lucas's mood was not always gloomy, however. At the first opportunity, on January 8, he paid a visit to General Penney's 1st Division, which was then located in an assembly area between Naples and Salerno. He liked what he saw, and he could not help feeling flattered by the royal treatment he received when he had lunch with the 24th Guards Brigade.[6] In his elation, he described the 1st Division as "The British Army at its best," noting that the men were in good hard physical condition and showed pride in their faces. The Irish Guards Battalion of the brigade were all tall—no man was accepted in that unit unless he stood at least 5 feet, 10 and ½ inches. The equipment—guns, and trucks—appeared to be clean, lubricated and well kept. It "filled my heart with joy." Lucas ignored the fact that the 1st Division had not seen action since the bloodless invasion of Pantelleria the previous June.[7]

Lucas was also delighted with the chance to develop a close relationship with his counterparts in the navy. The commander of the Joint British–American Naval Task Force was Admiral Frank J. Lowry, USN,

4. Ibid., 284.
5. Ibid., 285.
6. The 24th Guards Brigade consisted of a battalion from the Grenadier Guards, the Scots Guards, and the Irish Guards. The other brigade of the division was the 3d Infantry Brigade, which consisted of a battalion each from the Duke of Wellington's regiment, the Sherwood Foresters, and the King's Shropshire Light Infantry. These brigades were supported by the 2d Royal Field Artillery regiment, Lucas diary, 293.
7. Ibid. Pantelleria was a small, heavily fortified island in the Mediterranean between Tunisia and Sicily. It succumbed to Allied Air Forces on June 11, 1943, thus sparing the assault troops from any fighting.

who had graduated from the Naval Academy in 1911, the same year that Lucas had graduated from West Point. Lucas was lavish in his praise of his counterpart. "No stronger, more capable man could have been found, and his presence by my side was a great comfort," Lucas wrote.[8]

Lowry, in overall naval command, "wore two hats." Besides commanding the entire task force, he also commanded the VIII Amphibious Task Force, the formation charged with landing the 3d Division. Lowry's British counterpart in that capacity, the officer responsible for landing the British 1st Division, was Rear Admiral Thomas H. Troubridge, a large and talkative man. Troubridge's humorous comments in casual conversation were hardly those of a conventional British officer. "Now that you [Americans] are to be the dominant nation of the world for a while," Troubridge once said, "can't we give you India? A bally nuisance, you know." Lucas was quick to answer politely but in the negative.[9] Obviously, his personal relations with the members of the two sister services would be the least of his problems, despite the fact that most of the difficulties in the Anzio landing would involve naval matters.

The shipping arrangements were always vexing, partly because the number of landing craft to be made available was always changing, and partly because so little was known about the beaches and the capacities of the ports of Anzio and Nettuno. Reconnaissance parties and aerial photos had, at a cost, come up with some sketchy information.[10] Two possible landing beaches existed, one on either side of Anzio. South of the town the beach was three thousand yards long, but it was uncertain what size ship could reach it because of a sandbar offshore. If a channel through the sandbar existed, then ships of all sizes could be used; if not, they would have to depend on smaller craft. The other beach, north of Anzio, was even more problematical. At that early stage of planning, Lowry doubted that anything other than DUKWs and small craft could use that beach. Due to the shallow gradient of the beaches, each LST would be restricted to a payload of only 350 tons and LCTs (Landing Craft, Tank) would be limited to 140 tons.[11]

Lucas decided to assign Truscott's 3d Division to the larger, southern beach, which he named "X-Ray." The northern beach he called "Peter,"

8. Ibid., 289.
9. Ibid., 291.
10. "On the night of December 30, 1943, Ensign E. K. Howe and Ensign C. F. Pirro were sent to make a silhouette and landmark reconnaissance of the beaches. They never returned. The Royal Navy lost two officers on a similar mission" (Samuel Eliot Morison, *History of United States Naval Operations in World War II*, vol. 9, *Sicily–Salerno–Anzio*, 329N).
11. Lucas diary, 289.

and assigned it to Penney's 1st Division. He would send Darby's Rangers across a small beach at Anzio itself, which he called "Yellow" beach.[12]

The tonnage requirements and the number of days' supplies to be landed were matters of prime importance. On this issue, Lucas was adamant: he needed 1,500 tons of supplies per day, most of which would consist of ammunition. Since experience indicated that only two days a week could be counted on for decent landing weather, the problem was exacerbated.[13] On one other issue, everyone agreed. Nobody—not Clark, not Lucas, not Truscott—would stand for landing the VI Corps at Anzio with only seven days' supplies, counting on a juncture with the rest of Fifth Army a week after the troops came ashore.

In early January Lucas learned that a very high-level conference had been called by Prime Minister Churchill at Marrakech the next day to work out the details for Shingle. Surprisingly, none of the commanders involved was invited to attend—neither Lucas, Lowry, nor Clark. The restricted attendance was obviously calculated, for Lucas was instructed to send two staff officers to present his views. Lucas chose his operations officer and logistics officer, respectively, Colonel William H. Hill and Colonel E. J. O'Neill.

Fortunately, both Hill and O'Neill were strong officers and familiar with Lucas's requirements. They were imbued with Lucas's insistence on being provided 1,500 tons of supplies per day. Second, maintenance must be continued after the landing. And third, the operation must be given the opportunity for a rehearsal before the expedition sailed from Naples. Armed with those instructions, Hill and O'Neill left for Marrakech, arriving on January 7, 1944.

Hill and O'Neill would need all the intestinal fortitude they had, because in the next couple of days they would be faced with some very high-ranking civilian and military officials. On their arrival at the Hotel Mamounia, where Winston Churchill had spent many an hour painting between world wars, they were summoned to preparatory meetings. First they met with Alexander and later with Admiral Sir John Cunningham, the naval commander in the Mediterranean. It did not take the two Americans long to realize how far apart they and the British had been in their basic assumptions. Alexander, for example, was surprised at the

12. "Peter" and "X-Ray" were the phonetic terms for "P" and "X," respectively.

13. Lucas diary, 289–90. As noted previously, the amount of supply required to support an infantry division in the Second World War was generally assumed to be five hundred tons per division per day.

demand for 1,500 tons of supply per day, though he eventually accepted it. He needed no convincing, however, that Shingle would have to be supplied on a continuing basis; a Fifth Army drive up the Liri Valley to Frosinone and beyond would take far more than seven days.

The next day Hill and O'Neill were summoned to the Villa Taylor, the sumptuous residence that Churchill and Roosevelt had enjoyed together a year earlier after the Casablanca Conference. Here the assemblage was formidable. The Prime Minister, who presided over the meeting, was accompanied by Lord Beaverbrook, the British Lord Privy Seal and Churchill's close adviser. On the military side there was General Sir Henry Maitland Wilson, Supreme Commander, Mediterranean, and his deputy, American Lieutenant General Jacob L. Devers. Both Alexander and Cunningham were also present, as was Lieutenant General Walter B. ("Bedell") Smith, General Eisenhower's chief of staff, who was soon to leave for the United Kingdom. The American colonels stood practically alone; of the other Americans, Devers had just arrived, and Smith was not scheduled to be a participant in the actual operation.

The Prime Minister, the Americans soon discovered, was going to be their most formidable opponent in his zeal to brush difficulties aside. First he demanded an explanation why continued maintenance for the beachhead was necessary. He had assumed that plans called for only seven days' supplies. Here Alexander chimed in to support the Americans by confirming that a linkup immediately after the landing would be out of the question. Churchill then insisted that the landing must be made by January 20. The two American colonels held out for January 25 in order to allow time for a rehearsal. A rehearsal, the Prime Minister insisted, was unnecessary. After all, both the 3d and 1st Divisions had made amphibious landings before. The Americans then pointed out that since the landings in Sicily, the 3d Division had experienced a turnover of 115 percent in infantry lieutenants, the men who would actually lead the troops. Churchill countered by asserting that one experienced officer or non-commissioned officer per platoon would suffice.

One disagreement was difficult to explain. Colonel O'Neill, in presenting his plan for unloading supplies in a hurry, said that he intended to put the 2½-ton trucks on the LSTs loaded to their realistic capabilities of 5 tons each, and unloading them at Anzio. The LSTs would not have to wait. Other, previously emptied trucks would be waiting for the immediate return trip to Naples. Loading and unloading an LST was a laborious job, they said, and this device would drastically reduce the amount of time a ship would have to remain at Anzio. Churchill, possibly to minimize the number of vehicles at Anzio, demurred, backed up by all the authorities present, including even Bedell Smith.[14]

That evening a "working" group gathered at the Hotel Mamounia. Without Churchill, Beaverbrook, and Wilson, the professionals, unfettered, worked out the knotty questions satisfactorily. With Bedell Smith presiding, the group decided that Lucas would be given between eighty and eighty-eight LSTs for the initial landing operation and that those ships would remain available until February 3, nearly two weeks. The number would then be reduced to twenty-five from the 3d of February to the 13th, and fourteen would remain as long as needed. The daily supply level of 1,500 tons was agreed to, and the date of the landing was set at January 22, a date that would allow for a rehearsal—barely.

The next morning the entire party reassembled at the Villa Taylor and the conclusions of the evening before were presented to Churchill. The Prime Minister was satisfied, especially with the compromise date of January 22. The meeting then broke up.[15]

When his staff officers reported the results of the Marrakech meeting to Lucas, he was disturbed to hear accounts of the British optimism, which was described as "effusive." Churchill, he was told, had been so elated as to declare, "It will astonish the world. . . . It will certainly frighten Kesselring."

Lucas felt no such elation. Always conscious of the fact that the responsibility for the operation lay on his own shoulders, he attempted to protest some of the decisions made at the meeting. It was to no avail. "I felt like a lamb being led to slaughter," he wrote in his diary.[16]

At least one other officer agreed. When General George Patton flew from Palermo to Caserta to wish Lucas Godspeed, he was concerned with what he saw of the plan. "John," he said earnestly, "there is no one in the Army I hate to see killed as much as you, but you can't get out of this thing alive." Then, on second thought, he added, "Of course, you might be only badly wounded. No one ever blames a wounded general for anything." When Lucas summoned what optimism he could muster, Patton simply advised him strongly to read the Bible.

---

14. Lucas later disobeyed that order, definite though it was. He and others claimed that the combat loading and return of empty trucks were all that saved the supply system at Anzio.

15. This account comes from the report of O'Neill and Hill, cited in full in Truscott, *Command Missions*, 298–301.

16. Lucas diary, 295.

Patton went further. Turning to one of Lucas's aides, he said, "Look here, if things get too bad, shoot the old man in the back end, but don't you dare kill the old bastard."

Lucas claimed that from that day on, he was afraid to turn his back on that particular aide.[17]

Logistical support for Shingle was now established. Whether it would provide all that Lucas wanted was another matter; the operation was now considered feasible.

While the debates were going on about such matters as LSTs, the staffs at all echelons were making studies of the terrain to plan the tactical maneuver. Those studies were unanimous in one respect: the hill mass called the Colli Laziali, or Alban Hills, was the prime objective to be taken. General Clark has described its importance lucidly:

> Some fifteen miles south of Rome a high hill mass called Colli Laziali but better known as the Alban Hills, stands like a rugged, broad-shouldered guardian of the two main approaches to the Italian capital. In January of 1944 these hills became the key by which we hoped to unlock the German defenses in the Gustav Line.
>
> The two main highways by which the Gustav Line could be supplied were Routes No. 6 and No. 7. By the same token they were the main avenues of retreat—although there were several secondary roads available to the east—for enemy forces opposing the Fifth Army in the bitter battle for Cassino. No. 6 runs from Cassino along the Liri Valley, passing north of the Alban Hills; while No. 7 swings along the coast from Formia, near the Garigliano River mouth, to Terracina, and thence inland, passing south of the Alban Hills. The two roads then join at Rome. If we could seize the Alban Hills, we would threaten the Gustav Line defenders from the rear and might force the enemy to give up his powerful defense line in order to avoid entrapment.[18]

One imponderable remained concerning the seizure of the Alban Hills, and it was a big one. When could they be taken? Did VI Corps have enough power to land at Anzio and drive on to the Alban Hills without stopping to consolidate the landing?

General Lucas thought no. Intelligence indicated that Kesselring was holding four German divisions in the vicinity of Rome, and that those divisions could easily chop off and destroy any force Lucas might send up those twenty miles to seize them.

17. Ibid., 305.
18. Clark, *Calculated Risk*, 283.

Alexander, on the other hand, said it could be done, at least in his public utterances. But those statements, possibly with an ear cocked toward Churchill, are open to question, for Alexander later admitted in private that a push to the Alban Hills would be "somewhat in the nature of a bluff.[19] Such doubts were not reflected in his Operations Order 34, issued ten days before the landing, which specified the mission as to "cut the enemy's main communications in the Colli Laziali area southeast of Rome, and to threaten the [German] rear."[20]

Clark tended to agree with Lucas. The Fifth Army intelligence officer, Brigadier General Edwin Howard, believed that the two German divisions in the vicinity of Rome had been reinforced by paratroopers and tanks.[21] Besides, Clark was still smarting from his near-disaster at Salerno. In his directive, which was issued the same day as Alexander's, Clark termed the mission differently. After securing a beachhead, it said, Lucas was to "advance *on* Colli Laziali, not *to* Colli Laziali."[22] The difference in wording may seem trivial, but Clark was giving Lucas latitude to judge the situation on the spot. Lucas took this seriously, his caution reinforced by word from Clark, who warned, "Don't take chances, Johnny. I did at Salerno and I was almost cut off."[23]

The direct road from Anzio to the Alban Hills ran due north through the town of Albano Laziale, but the Allies expected the Germans to defend that road bitterly. A less risky route for Lucas to take would be indirect, northeastward to the town of Cisterna di Latina, situated about fifteen miles northeast of X-Ray Beach. The seizure of Cisterna, admittedly, would not cut Highway 6, which was the main route up the Liri Valley, but it would cut Route 7, known historically as the Appian Way. There was also a chance that an attack in that direction might move faster than one toward Albano, because it might not be defended by the Germans with quite the same determination. If the attack toward Cisterna went well, then a further push northeastward to Valmontone would cut Route 6. But that decision would have to await developments.

The attack toward Cisterna carried an additional appeal to Lucas; it would be executed by the experienced 3d Infantry Division, which Lucas favored for the hard fighting. He had great confidence in Truscott, and he also knew that the British replacement system could not keep up with the

19. Matthews interview with Alexander, cited in Morris, *Circles of Hell,* 259.
20. 15th Army Group OI 34, the Battle for Rome, Jan. 12, 1944, cited in Blumenson, *Salerno to Cassino,* 353.
21. Ibid.
22. Fifth Army FO 5, Jan. 12, 1944, cited in Blumenson, *Salerno to Cassino,* 354.
23. Robert H. Adelman and George Walton, *The Devil's Brigade,* 159.

projected casualties. Brave as the British troops were, their numbers were bound to dwindle for lack of reinforcements.

A final attraction for the drive toward Cisterna was the fact that the 3d Division's right flank would be covered by the Mussolini Canal, a formidable obstacle that could be defended eventually by Robert Frederick's Devil's Brigade. Beyond the Mussolini Canal lay the Pontine Marshes, flooded at the moment, which provided additional flank protection. But the immediate problem was to get ashore. Only when that was accomplished could the exploitation of the bridgehead be addressed.

On January 18, 1944, only three days before the VI Corps was scheduled to sail from Naples to Anzio, a full-scale rehearsal of the landing proved that much needed to be done in a short time.

On the night of January 17, 1943, the eleven LSTs assigned to the rehearsal loaded elements of the 3d Division in the ports of Naples and Pozzuoli and headed out to sea. During the early morning hours, before daylight, the troops were to be unloaded from the ships into the DUKWs and headed into shore. The night was completely dark.

Aboard his command ship, an LCI, Lucian Truscott was unhappy to be separated from his naval counterpart, Admiral Lowry. There may have been advantages to Lowry's dual position as naval commander for the entire corps operation and commander of the component charged with landing the 3d Division, but to Truscott the arrangement was frustrating. In his overall command capacity, Lowry would be located on the *Biscayne,* along with Lucas. But that left no room for Truscott and his staff, nor should it have. It was risky enough for both the senior army and navy commanders to be on one ship in any case. To make matters worse, Truscott's communications with Lowry from his LCI were tenuous at best. His protests, however, had fallen on deaf ears, and all Truscott could do was shrug and note, "There the matter stood."[24]

As it turned out, Lucas chose not to observe the landing from the *Biscayne.* Instead the corps commander decided to witness the landing of the 3d Division and the British 2d Brigade from the beaches. Lucas's and Truscott's observations of the exercise, however, were about the same.

Most of the faults in what turned out to be a disastrous rehearsal lay with the navy. Not quite sure where they were in the darkness, the ships disgorged their passengers at daybreak a full twelve miles from the shore. It took the DUKWs three hours to reach the beaches through rough waters. It

---

24. Truscott, *Command Missions,* 302. Lucas estimated the distance at fifteen miles.

added up to a grim experience for the troops who had been cramped up in those conditions.

When Truscott received reports that the troops had crossed the beaches, he landed and followed in their footsteps. The infantry battalions, he quickly learned, had arrived behind schedule, but their experienced commanders, once ashore, had organized them and moved them inland to their objectives. The artillery and tanks, however, were a different matter. As Lucas later recorded it, forty DUKWs had been upset in the choppy seas with the loss of much communication equipment and nineteen 105 mm howitzers.[25]

Lucas and Truscott did not meet on the beaches. When Truscott tried to locate the corps commander, he learned that Lucas had left to report to General Clark in Caserta. Truscott therefore returned to his own command post to write a scathing report to Clark giving chapter and verse as to what had gone wrong.

Lucas, for his part, had indeed gone to Caserta where, in his own words, he "impressed on [Clark] something that he already knew—that the Navy had failed to put his troops on the beach in the proper order and the proper time." That ended the matter as far as Lucas was concerned, because he was told that Admiral Lowry had called a meeting of his naval commanders and had put them straight.[26]

Truscott, however, was not so easily mollified. In his report, which he admitted was being written with incomplete information, he was devastating:

> I recounted all that had gone wrong in the rehearsal—no battalion landed on time or in proper formation or even on its proper beach; no artillery, tanks, or tank destroyers ashore by daylight; loss of DUKW's with much of the Division artillery; lack of communications; obvious lack of control and training on the Naval side as well as lack of Naval preparation. I remarked that to land my Division at Anzio as it was landed during the rehearsal would invite disaster if the Germans counterattacked with tanks soon after daylight.[27]

Based on all that, Truscott urgently recommended another rehearsal. Having sent in his report, Truscott sought out Lucas and found that their observations had been essentially the same. On that basis, Truscott

25. Lucas diary, 321. Truscott, *Command Missions,* 303, estimated that "twenty or more" DUKW's had swamped and sunk, resulting in the loss of "artillery pieces and communications equipment of perhaps two battalions."

26. Lucas diary, 321.

27. Truscott, *Command Missions,* 303.

suggested that the two of them go together to confront Clark. Lucas, however, was unwilling, pleading that he was in a "difficult position" with
the army commander. He expressed no objection, however, to Truscott's
doing so.[28]

At Caserta, Truscott found that Clark had already received his alarming report. Though Clark agreed that things were bad, he could not, as
Truscott practically demanded, delay the Anzio landing to permit a second rehearsal. On that matter his hands were tied, the timing of the landing having been set in concrete at the "highest levels." Clark did, however,
promise to replace the equipment lost during the rehearsal, declaring that
he would obtain the equipment from other divisions. That was all he
could do. It had, indeed, been difficult enough for him to arrange for even
one rehearsal; the higher authorities had expected the Anzio landing to be
executed without even the one they had just finished.

When Truscott left Clark, he went to visit Lowry. The admiral, Truscott
later recorded, was "in very low spirits," especially as reports came in ver-
ifying the losses. Lowry assured Truscott, however, that he would do his
utmost to set matters straight.

Somewhat reassured, Truscott returned to his command post at Pozzuoli to await the departure on the afternoon of January 21, 1944.

28. Ibid., 304.

CHAPTER 10

GRIM FOREBODING

Tragedy at the Rapido

Although Operation Shingle was holding center stage in the early days of January 1944, it was never meant to stand on its own; it was seen as a supplement to the main attack on the Gustav Line in the Cassino area. The Americans and British viewed it somewhat differently. Churchill hoped, perhaps expected, that the Anzio landing might cause Kesselring to give up the Gustav Line and retreat north of Rome, but few Americans believed that the German field marshal would do so. They would settle for the removal of a few German divisions from the Cassino area.

The two efforts—Anzio and Cassino—were to be coordinated. To draw German divisions away from Anzio, Alexander and Clark had agreed that the attack at Cassino should precede Shingle by five days. On January 17, 1944, therefore, the British 10 Corps was to cross the Garigliano River, near the Tyrrhenian coast, and then, after establishing a bridgehead, turn right, threatening the Liri Valley from the south.

Three days later, on the 20th of January, the plan called for the American II Corps, with the 36th Division making the main effort, to force a crossing of the Rapido at Sant' Angelo Lodigiano, five miles south of Cassino. If that was successful, as expected, the Liri Valley would be wide-open. The 34th, in a secondary effort, was to cross the Rapido north of Cassino, and the French Expeditionary Corps, which had replaced Lucas's VI Corps, would make another secondary attack on the extreme right.

These attacks were designed to break the Gustav Line and allow II Corps to begin its decisive drive up the Liri Valley. Failing that, Alexander and Clark hoped that they would at least divert German attention from the Anzio area, where VI Corps would land on January 22, 1944.

Though nobody expected this elaborate scheme to be easy, the general atmosphere among the British and American higher headquarters was

Attempted Crossing of the Rapido, 17-22 January 1944

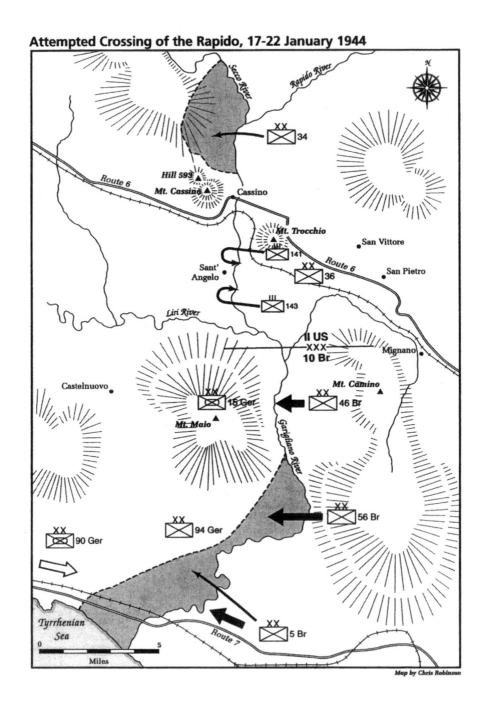

Map by Chris Robinson

optimistic. Allied intelligence predicted some difficulties in the crossing of the Rapido and Garigliano Rivers, but nobody in the upper Allied echelons seemed aware of the extent of the formidable German defensive preparations. The staffs of the lower units, however, were decidedly more realistic, The division commanders designated to make the crossings viewed the prospect with varying degrees of alarm.

During late December 1943, and early January 1944, the progress of the Fifth Army up the Mignano Gap toward Cassino was slower than had been expected. It was only on Sunday, January 16, therefore, that General Fred Walker, of the 36th Division, was formally assigned the task of crossing the Rapido River. Walker had been anticipating this development, however, and he had begun preliminary planning long before. As a man experienced in river-crossing operations, he was able to make an evaluation with authority.[1]

Walker regarded the prospect of crossing the Rapido at Sant' Angelo with grave misgivings, even defeatism. Sometime earlier, when he had been conferring with Clark on the possibility, he had urged that the Rapido be crossed at a point north of Cassino, where the river was fordable, rather than south of the town, where it definitely was not.[2] The approaches to the Rapido at Sant' Angelo, Walker pointed out, were restricted to an open floodplain, swollen by recent rains and devoid of cover and concealment. Scouts had advised him that the river was forty feet wide, from eight to twelve feet deep, with banks of three to four feet on both sides. The current was about four miles per hour, nearly twice the speed of a man walking. The temperature of the water was just above freezing. There were no bridges.

To make matters worse, Walker argued, the Germans had established a main line of resistance on a series of high points ranging from three hundred to eight hundred yards from the riverbank. German strong points were heavily manned by riflemen, machine gunners, mortar crews, antitank crews, and tankers.[3]

Walker was also worried about the equipment he would have available to make the crossing.

1. In the First World War, Walker had commanded the 1st Battalion of the 30th Infantry in its heroic and successful defense of the Marne River east of Chateau Thierry, on July 15, 1918. As he recalled, his battalion, defending behind the river, repulsed the German 10th Infantry Division of ten thousand men. His battalion of twelve hundred men had "turned the Germans back, disorganized them, confused them, and slaughtered them." It was his battalion's first battle, and the German 10th Division was a veteran outfit. He attributed his success to the great advantage that accrued to a unit defending behind an unfordable river, Walker, *Texas to Rome*, 302.
2. Blumenson, *Salerno to Cassino*, 325.
3. Walker, *Texas to Rome*, 298.

> The improvised footbridges—planks lashed to rubber boats—will be
> heavy and clumsy to carry by hand to the river. They will easily be
> punctured by shell fire and will be difficult to launch and use as fer-
> ries because of the high banks and swift current. The wooden boats are
> heavier than the large rubber boats and more difficult to launch in the
> swirling water.

Walker finally noted that his men had been afforded no opportunity to
practice handling this clumsy equipment, which they would be forced to
do under the fire of German artillery. The shortage of time precluded the
engineers from doing a thorough job of clearing out the numerous minefields the Germans had planted on the near side of the river.[4] For that important step, he requested further delay.

Clark rejected Walker's request out of hand; the decision as to timing
had been made at a higher echelon and was not negotiable. Walker, now
faced with the inevitable, decided to cross the Rapido at night to minimize losses due to observed enemy artillery fire. He calculated that it
would take his men four hours, from 4:00 to 8:00 P.M., to move the boats
and footbridges across the marshland to the banks of the river.[5] After that
he would have about eleven hours of darkness, which should enable him
to cross before daylight. He planned to send his two regiments abreast—
Lieutenant Colonel Aaron Wyatt's 141st Infantry on the right and Colonel
William Martin's 143d Infantry on the left. His third regiment, the 142d,
was being held in II Corps reserve, unavailable.

On Tuesday, January 18, Walker was summoned to II Corps Headquarters to give Clark and Keyes a final briefing on his plans for the crossing. He explained the difficulties, he later recorded, but for some reason he
failed to convey the depth of his concern. In so failing, he was probably in-
hibited by the concept, so prevalent in the army, of the "good soldier." He
was anxious to convey to his bosses that he was "doing everything possible
to succeed."[6] Therein Walker committed a major error. So optimistic did he
sound that Keyes, who had previously recommended that the attack be
made farther to the south across the Garigliano, declared himself to be
"heartened."[7]

As planned, McCreery's British 10 Corps crossed the Garigliano on
Monday, January 17, 1944. On the left, the newly arrived 5th Infantry

4. Ibid., 300–301.
5. Clark had originally planned to assign Walker twelve DUKWs, but the losses in the 3d
Division's rehearsal had forced him to transfer them to Truscott. Blumenson, *Salerno*, 330.
6. Walker, *Texas to Rome*, 306.
7. Blumenson, *Salerno*, 326–27.

Division and the 56th Infantry Division made substantial crossings, driving about six miles into the German position, and establishing a substantial bridgehead in the mountains. On the north flank of 10 Corps, however, adjacent to the zone of the American 36th Division, the 46th Division failed to cross and take the vital town of Sant' Ambrogio. German retention of the high ground on his left flank made Walker even more despondent.

The 10 Corps attack, however, produced an unexpected benefit by causing the enemy to overreact. It had hit the German 94th Division, which was still holding the right anchor of the German Gustav Line. General von Senger was now worried that the division was spread out over much too wide a front. Furthermore, it lacked tanks. The British, if they drove on with spirit, could turn the south flank of the German position. In Senger's words, "the entire German front would have been rolled up from the south."[8]

Senger immediately took action. From the headquarters of the 94th Division, he placed a call directly to Field Marshal Kesselring. Would Kesselring release the 29th and 90th Panzer Grenadier Divisions he was holding in reserve near Rome? After considering the situation for a moment, Kesselring agreed. The divisions were on their way.[9]

The attack of the British 10 Corps had already accomplished at least the minimum Allied objective. It had drawn two powerful panzer grenadier divisions down to the Garigliano, away from the vicinity of Rome and Anzio.

In his command post at Monte Rotondo, Fred Walker spent the few hours before the attack reviewing the situation of his division. Nothing had happened to allay his misgivings. "We have done everything we can," he wrote in his diary, "but I do not see how we can succeed." He harked back to his own studies of military history: "I do not know of a single case . . . where an attempt to cross an unfordable river that is incorporated into the enemy's main line of resistance has succeeded. . . . The mission should never have been assigned to any troops and, especially, when both flanks will be exposed when we get across."[10]

Shortly before 6:00 P.M., January 20, the 1st Battalion, 141st Infantry crawled out of its concealed area at the base of Monte Trocchio and headed for its assembly area. There the T-Patchers found that several of

---

8. Senger, *Neither Fear nor Hope,* 190.
9. Ibid., 192.
10. Walker, *Texas to Rome,* 305.

their pre-positioned assault boats had already been destroyed by enemy gunfire—they had never been completely out of the range of German observation. The men picked up what boats they could and began the long portage—between one and two miles—across the open, soggy ground to the river. Soon friendly artillery, sixteen battalions in all, began its preparation against German positions.[11] German artillery responded long before the infantry battalion reached the riverbank. One volley hit Company "C," 141st Infantry and took out the company commander, the executive officer, and thirty men.[12]

The difficulties multiplied. Although the engineers had cleared safe-lanes through the minefields as best they could, incoming artillery had destroyed many of the white tapes they had laid to identify them. In the darkness, many units became disorganized. Coordination between infantry and engineers was bad, especially since so many of the men of the 36th Division were replacements who scarcely even knew the names of their own commanders. Nevertheless, despite these heartbreaking difficulties, a few men of "C" Company, 141st Infantry made it across the Rapido River as early as 9:00 P.M., January 20.[13]

Behind the small bridgeheads seized by the infantry of the 1st Battalion, the engineers tried to erect the four footbridges allotted to that sector. It was a hopeless job. One of the bridges had been destroyed by enemy artillery fire as it was being carried to the riverbank. Another was defective. Two were hit by artillery at the bank. The engineers were resourceful, however, and by cannibalizing the four destroyed bridges, they were able to construct one footbridge by 4:00 A.M., January 21. The infantry support bridge, over which heavy equipment would pass, never came into being, however. It depended on trucks that could never make it across the soggy fields to the construction site.

That was the extent of the advance of the 141st Infantry, across the river but well short of the German line of resistance. General William H. Wilbur, assistant division commander, ordered the 3d Battalion, scheduled to follow the 1st, to take cover in preparation for a crossing. He got a message across the river for the troops to hold on, awaiting reinforcements. Colonel

11. Blumenson, *Salerno to Cassino*, 333.
12. Ibid.
13. Ibid., 334. Fred Majdalany, *Cassino*, 62, has this to say about a narrow river such as the Rapido: "Paradoxically, it is easier to carry out a [river crossing] over a wide river. If the river is wide, the vulnerable period of launching can be disposed of farther from the enemy. The width of the river will make it possible for the attacker's artillery to plaster the enemy bank during launching, and even for a part of the journey across. And it will be less easy for the enemy to detect what is going on and precisely where. The assembly of the boats can be much nearer the river."

Wyatt, however, was unaware of Wilbur's order, and he authorized the 1st Battalion to return to the east bank. Few men were able to follow that order; the majority dug in where they were and waited.[14]

On the left of the 36th Division attack, events turned out much the same. A platoon of "C" Company, 143d Infantry, crossed the Rapido unopposed south of Sant' Angelo, as early as 9:45 P.M. It was soon isolated, however, when incoming artillery destroyed the boats before they could return to the friendly side. So effective was the German artillery fire that it began inflicting casualties on the Americans on both sides of the river. Soon Colonel Martin, the regimental commander, arrived on the scene and personally routed out "B" Company, which had taken cover. He sent them over, with some engineers, in five boats. Amazingly, the entire 1st Battalion, 143d, was across the Rapido by 5:00 A.M., January 21.

That was as far as the 143d went. Trapped by German tanks and artillery fire, the battalion commander found his position so precarious that he requested permission to withdraw. Martin called General Walker, who refused to authorize any such withdrawal. Too late; the battalion commander, on his own, had decided to pull back. With daylight, any movement was becoming ever more precarious, but by 10:00 A.M., the exhausted remnants of the 1st Battalion were back on the east bank of the Rapido.[15]

At 10:00 A.M. of January 21, Major General Geoffrey Keyes, with some of his II Corps staff, arrived at Walker's headquarters. By now all were tired and edgy, and a confrontation resulted.

Keyes and Walker held different interpretations of what had transpired during that previous fourteen hours. To Keyes, the fact that 36th Division troops were across the river meant success, which should be exploited. Walker disagreed. From his point of view, which he forcefully conveyed to Keyes, there had been no success whatsoever with either regiment. But though he held little hope, he had ordered a renewal of the attack for 9:00 P.M.

Keyes would have none of Walker's methodical plans. He ordered Walker to attack by noon, only two hours away. Some of the 141st Infantry were across the river, he said, and there was no reason why their success should not be "augmented." The attack failed.

Similar situations continued throughout the next two days. When the effort was abandoned on the 22nd, the 141st had lost about 400 men killed and wounded, but they later reported a whopping 641 men missing, presumably prisoners.[16]

14. Blumenson, *Salerno to Cassino,* 334–35.
15. Ibid., 336–37.
16. Walker, *Texas to Rome,* 312.

One more controversy was left to be played out. On January 22, Keyes had not yet given up hope of exploiting the meager crossings that Walker had made. To do so, he decided to release the 142d Infantry to Walker's control. Walker was not grateful. No success, he insisted, could be claimed until the enemy's main position had been penetrated, which it had not. Keyes, on the other hand, declared that the Germans were "groggy" and believed that another blow by a fresh regiment would turn them out of their position. Walker reluctantly set about making preparations for a third attack on January 23.

During the night of the 22d, however, Keyes underwent a change of heart. He had conferred with Clark and now rescinded his order for the attack by the 142d. He added a dig, "You are not going to do it anyway."

Walker was glad to cancel the attack, because it meant that only two, not three, of his regiments had been shattered. But he was angered by Keyes's remark. It implied a charge of disloyalty and disobedience. "Such a charge is baseless and untrue," he wrote. "I have done everything possible to comply with his orders."[17]

The 36th Division's losses had been heavy: 1,681 men, including 875 missing, out of perhaps 5,000 infantry.[18] On the German side, however, the battle had been viewed as practically inconsequential. Von Senger, for example, wrote,

> At that time neither the 15th Panzer Grenadier Division nor the corps fully realized the extent of the enemy's failure. . . . The German command paid little attention to this offensive for the simple reason that it caused no particular anxiety. The repulse of the attack did not even call for the reserves of the 15 Panzer Grenadier Division, still less from other parts of the front. . . .[19]

The 36th Infantry Division was temporarily broken, and it would once more need rebuilding. The only significant gain in this tragic episode was the phase that went practically unnoticed. The bridgehead taken by McCreery's 10 Corps over the Garigliano would later prove to be worth its weight in gold.

17. Ibid., 313.
18. Majdalany, *Cassino*, 65.
19. Senger, *Neither Fear nor Hope*, 193.

BOOK THREE

LANDINGS AND CONSOLIDATION

The Anzio Landing, 22 January 1944

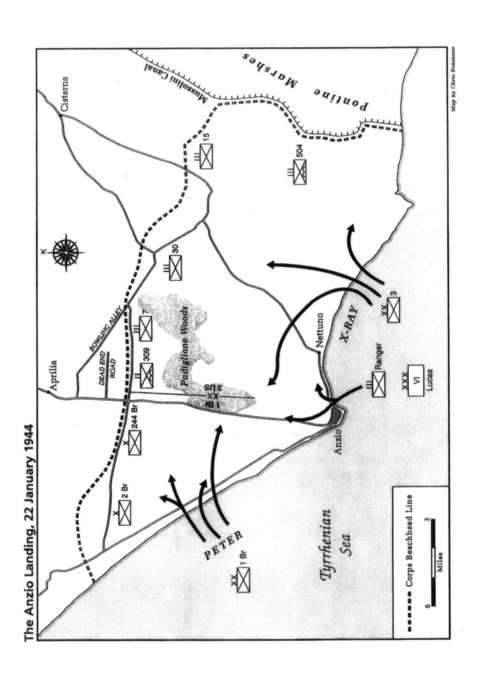

Map by Chris Robinson

CHAPTER 11

ASSAULT

On January 21, 1944, Admiral Wilhelm Canaris, Hitler's doughty little Chief of the Abwehr (intelligence services), dropped into Field Marshal Albert Kesselring's headquarters at Frascati. There he found, perhaps to his surprise, that the "burning question" was the possibility of an Allied landing somewhere behind von Senger's Gustav Line. The intelligence evaluators had noticed that almost all the Allied warships and cruisers had disappeared from the western and southern coasts of Italy, and some reports indicated that 300,000 tons of shipping were being concentrated in the port of Naples. What, he was asked, was the significance of this?

Canaris answered quickly and categorically. "Don't worry," he said. "We're keeping an eye on those ships."[1] The admiral did not go into specifics, but so prestigious was Hitler's "super-spy" that his declaration brought about a moment's relief. It was based at least partially on the admiral's assurances that Kesselring had, at Senger's request, sent the 29th and 90th Panzer Grenadier Divisions to the Garigliano. Canaris's assurances had thus encouraged Kesselring to make a move that would be advantageous to the Allies in the Anzio landing.[2]

The plans of the Allies had been kept remarkably secret, partially because they themselves did not know what they were going to do until the last moment. Some credit, however, must be given to the cover plan they designed to deceive Kesselring into thinking that an amphibious attack on Leghorn rather than Anzio was in the offing. A dummy headquarters

---

1. Heinz Höhne, *Canaris, Hitler's Master Spy,* 538–39. Canaris was later executed by Hitler for collaborating with the Allies. Höhne does not conjecture whether or not he was deliberately being misleading in this instance, quite possibly not.

2. Kesselring, *Memoirs,* 193.

had been set up on Corsica to broadcast thousands of encoded messages to simulate a real headquarters. Fishing vessels were congregated in Corsican harbors, and Allied warships bombarded Civitavecchia and Terracina as well as Leghorn in order to attract attention away from Anzio. To make the picture more confusing, Alexander's headquarters at Caserta had leaked rumors that the Eighth, not the Fifth Army, was about to attack, in this case up the Adriatic coast.

Actually, there is little indication that these deception measures were responsible for the German miscalculation. Peddlers on the streets of Naples were selling postcards of the Anzio-Nettuno area, but their source of information was strictly guesswork.[3] Kesselring did not try seriously to guess Allied intentions; he merely took measures to contain any amphibious landing that might be made. He kept forces to resist landings at Leghorn, Genoa, Ravenna, Istria, and Anzio.[4]

Among the Allied troops bound for Anzio, emotions varied. One of the most optimistic was Major General Lucian Truscott, and the source of his exhilaration would probably be incomprehensible to any but a veteran soldier. As he stood on the deck of the *Biscayne* in the Bay of Naples, he perceived standing beneath the stern of the ship the 3d Infantry Division band. When it struck up "The Dogface Soldier," the division's lilting new marching song, Truscott was stirred deeply.

An emotional man beneath his craggy exterior, Truscott was rapt when he heard the division band play his theme song through in march time. His feelings rose even further when "one hundred and twenty voices roared out the words across the beautiful Bay of Naples."[5]

"It may not have been in the best tradition from a security point of view in this spy-ridden city of Naples," Truscott later wrote, "but it was one of the most inspiring things that ever happened to me. Few who heard it will ever forget it."[6]

---

3. Morison, *Sicily–Salerno–Anzio*, 329.
4. Ibid., 330.
5. "I wouldn't give a bean to be a fancy-pants marine; / I'd rather be a dogface soldier like I am. / I wouldn't trade my old OD's for all the Navy's dungarees / For I'm the walking pride of Uncle Sam. / On all the posters that I read they say the Army builds men / Guess they're tearing me down to build me over again. / I'm just a dogface soldier with a rifle on my shoulder / And I eat a Kraut for breakfast every day. / So feed me ammunition; keep me in the 3d Division. / Your dogface soldier boy's OK."
6. Truscott, *Command Missions*, 296. Truscott was not alone in his feelings. Lieutenant Floyd M. Wells, a replacement bound for the 1st Armored Division, found himself in a bar in Naples where the "Dogface Soldier" was being sung. Told to stand during the rendition, Wells later wrote that he stood, Floyd M. Wells, *From Anzio to the Alps*, 72.

Far less optimistic than Truscott was his immediate superior, Major General John P. Lucas, who was feeling the weight of his responsibilities heavily:

> I struggle to be calm and collected and, fortunately, am associating intimately with naval officers I don't know very well, which takes my mind off things.
>
> I wish the higher command were not so over-optimistic. The Fifth Army is attacking violently towards the Cassino line and has sucked many German troops to the south and the high command seems to think they will stay there. I don't see why. They can still slow us up there and move against me at the same time. I'll know more about this later.[7]

Lucas did not try to hide his pessimism. During the evening before departure, he demonstrated it at a farewell dinner in his command post at Venafro. His principal guest that evening was Major General John A. Crane, the commander of the VI Corps Artillery, a dear friend from the days when the two were lieutenants together in 1911. Aside from the two generals, the only other guests were their aides—a total of five.

First Lieutenant A. Adgate Duer was present with General Crane at the old farmhouse. He had been with General Crane for some time and by now was accustomed to being around the brass, but what he witnessed that evening etched itself deeply in his memory. To his astonishment, the corps commander seemed despondent. In the course of the evening Lucas handed Crane a package. It contained, Lucas said, the personal effects that Crane should send back to his wife in the event that he, Lucas, did not survive the ordeal ahead of him. The package also contained the latest copy of his last will and testament. Before Duer's gaze, Lucas's two aides did the same. The occasion could well be called Lucas's Last Supper.[8]

At nearby Dragoni, Lieutenant Avis Dagit, a nurse in the 56th Evacuation Hospital, was excited as she contemplated what was coming next. She and the rest of the nurses were by this time veterans, having served as hospital staff through the campaigns of Tunisia, Sicily, and southern Italy. Most recently the "56th Evac," as it was familiarly known, had been supporting Lucas's VI Corps in the mountains near Avellino. They had left under mysterious circumstances, and rumors were rife. One theory had it that the 56th Evac would be redeployed to the United States

---

7. Lucas diary, 322–23.
8. Interview of author and A. Adgate Duer, Easton, Maryland, July 30, 2004.

in preparation for going to the Pacific. That prospect, however, was as un-likely as it was unwelcome.

The nurses were sure of one thing, however: the piles of cardboard C ration boxes that they had been using for desks and dressing tables would not be going with them. They therefore decided to enjoy the evening by building a bonfire. It would be a treat for young women who could never get warm in the damp, cold weather. So for a while the nurses luxuriated in the heat. So effective was the bonfire in heating their tent, Lieutenant Dagit recorded, that they had to keep their tent flap open to get a breath of cool air.

Avis Dagit went to sleep wondering where the next move would take them.[9]

The convoy carrying the VI Corps sailed from Naples in the early morn-ing hours of January 21. It followed a zigzag course, partly to enable the ships to pick their way through the minefields laid by the enemy and partly to keep the Germans confused as to the convoy's destination. Both objectives were achieved.

Aboard the *Biscayne,* Lucian Truscott was happy to be included in the main command group. It was not a matter of ego or self-importance; it simply gave him access to Admiral Lowry and General Lucas. He took a moment to enjoy the beautiful calm sea but doubted whether many of his shipmates, especially the commanders, were enjoying the "beauties of a Mediterranean cruise."[10] As was his habit before any dangerous mission, he sat down and penned a letter to his wife. At four minutes past mid-night, he noted that the *Biscayne* had arrived in the "transport area," where the troops would be transferred to landing craft from the ships. Truscott admired that precision; the rehearsal two days earlier had paid off.

At 3:00 A.M., on the morning of January 22, General Mark Clark, at his headquarters, received a message from General Lucas: "PARIS-BORDEAUX-TURIN-TANGIERS-BARI-ALBANY." Clark was relieved, for the message translated into "Weather clear, sea calm, little wind, our presence not discovered. Landings in progress. No reports from landings yet." Two hours later another message came from Lucas: "NO ANGELS YET CUTIE CLAUDETTE." That meant, "No tanks yet, but the 3d Division and 1st Division attacks going well."[11]

---

9. Avis Dagit Schorer, *A Half Acre of Hell,* 116–17.
10. Truscott, *Command Missions,* 307.
11. Clark, *Calculated Risk,* 287–88. Presumably the "angels" in the second message from Lucas referred to friendly tanks.

Landing beaches, Anzio, January 22, 1944. U.S. Army.

The Anzio-Nettuno area was a built-up area, no desolate beach. The famed war correspondent Ernie Pyle, who landed somewhat later, remarked that the two towns were high-class seaside resorts, recently modernized and much bigger and up-to-date than he had supposed. The buildings, lined up in a row about two hundred yards from the water's edge, formed "a solid flank of fine stone buildings four or five stories high," containing apartment houses, business offices, and rich people's villas. These luxurious buildings were now deserted, Pyle noted, for only a very few Italians had returned to town after being evacuated by the Germans. Most of the expensive furniture was wrapped in burlap. No business whatsoever was being transacted.[12]

On the bridge of the *Biscayne*, three and a half miles offshore, John Lucas was astonished by what he saw—or rather what he did not see. Contrary to expectations, all signs pointed to an almost complete absence of German resistance.[13] One landing craft had been hit, but the rest had

12. Pyle, *Brave Men*, 160–61.
13. Lucas diary, Jan. 24, 1944, 324–25.

come through without damage. What Lucas later most remembered, strangely, was a new weapon the navy had developed for giving support to landing forces: rocket ships mounted on LCIs. These rockets, each carrying a payload of about 30 pounds of explosive, could neutralize targets as far as 500 yards inland. Each ship could fire 780 of these rockets in the space of two minutes. But the important thing to all the army officers was that, after the nearly disastrous rehearsal conducted only four days earlier, the navy had landed the army with complete precision.

The main objective for the VI Corps in the first couple of days was a line designated as the "Corps Beachhead Line." For the first phase, however, the objectives were far more modest. On the extreme left, the Second Brigade of Penney's 1st British Infantry Division was to push inland in the direction of Albano, which is about thirty miles from Peter Beach. He was restricted, however, by the beach itself, which was so narrow and limited by shoals that the best he could do was to send the division across the beach in column—that is, one brigade at a time, with the others being held in division reserve to come in later.

In the center, Colonel William O. Darby's three Ranger battalions, reinforced with the 309th Parachute Infantry Battalion, were to seize the towns of Anzio and Nettuno, driving inland about two miles. On the right, Truscott's 3d Division, with the 504th Parachute Infantry Regiment attached, would land with the three regiments abreast at X-Ray Beach. The 3d Division, making the main effort, was to drive inland in the direction of Cisterna.[14]

To the officers and men of the 3d Division, who had been fighting in the cold, wet mountains of the Abruzzi, the landing at Anzio was nothing but a maneuver. The journal kept by the Division Operations Office (G-3) reflects an almost casual account:

> 0145: Rocket Ships fired.
> 0220: 2d wave hit Red Beach. Landed dry.
> 0229: No opposition met by 1st or 2d waves.
> 0245: From 15th Infantry: Landed on Green Beach. Left company advancing rapidly. Right company fair, 4th wave has hit the beach.
> 0300: LCI's are using LCVP's. (Loading onto LCVP's)
> 0330: Message from Liaison Officer, 30th Infantry: "Our leading elements are [meeting no] opposition."

---

14. The 504th Parachute Infantry Regiment had originally been assigned to make a drop north of Anzio, on the Albano Road. General Penney, however, had objected to the drop on the basis that he would have to restrict his fire to ensure the paratroopers' safety.

0335: 15th Infantry reports: Initial operations believed successful. Now regrouping.
0335: 1st Battalion, 7th Infantry Reports: All companies now fairly well together. No opposition. Five boat waves have landed.
0350: 1st Battalion, 7th Infantry, reorganizing on road directly behind Red Beach.
0915: Division command post opened.[15]

The Corps Beachhead Area, about seven miles in depth and fifteen miles in width, defined the limits of Lucas's immediate objectives. On the right, Truscott was to drive out, with the Pontine Marshes to the east protecting his right flank along and across the formidable Mussolini Canal.[16] At the same time, he was to continue his drive northeastward in the direction of Cisterna, which was at a distance of about ten miles. Penney, on the left, was to drive through a series of woods to a line about eight miles north of Peter Beach, in the meantime deploying his 1st and 3d Brigades to form a line abreast of the 2d. The plan seemed reasonable, particularly since German resistance was so light. Lucas does not seem to have even considered pushing the twenty miles up to the Alban Hills.

Colonel William O. Darby, the dynamic thirty-three-year-old commander of Darby's Rangers, was undergoing an experience that he did not like. It was not that the mission of his unit was a tall order—he was used to tall orders—especially at Gela, Sicily, a half year before. What bothered him was the fact that he would perform his mission with only part of his force in the first wave. The shortage of landing craft dictated that he would land with only two of his three battalions, the 1st and the 4th. Other units assigned or attached—the 3d Ranger Battalion, the 309th Parachute Infantry Battalion, and the 83d Chemical Mortar Battalion— would have to await their turn and come in on the second wave. Of special concern was the lack of artillery support.[17]

15. *History of the Third Infantry Division in World War II*, 108–9.
16. Truscott describes the Pontine Marshes thus: "The whole area of reclaimed marshland was passable enough in dry weather. The water line, however, was usually within two feet of the surface. When the rains fell or the pumps stopped working, the area became so marshy that movement off the roads was almost impossible, and fox holes filled with water" (*Command Missions*, 308).
17. Although the Allies did not use chemical weapons (except for white phosphorous and smoke) during the Second World War, the Americans quickly discovered that the 4.2-inch chemical mortar was an admirable infantry support weapon using standard explosives. They substituted for artillery with Darby's Rangers.

Darby had another concern. The beach on which his force was to land was extremely shallow: 1 foot in every 130 feet. This meant, he calculated, "a hundred yard march in water ranging from shoulder high to knee deep." Darby had supreme confidence in his men, but, he observed, "no training in the world can keep men from being hit while thus exposed."[18]

Nevertheless, Darby knew exactly where he wanted to land. During the planning for Shingle, he had selected a stretch of beach in front of the town of Anzio. In its exact center, he later recorded, was a "showy white casino." He wanted to be landed right in front of that casino. "When I get out of that boat, he had told his naval counterpart, "I want to be at the front door of the casino."[19] He planned to use that building as his command post once ashore.

The assault battalions of Darby's Rangers were carried in two LCIs. They departed from their LSTs some time after midnight on January 22 along with the craft carrying the 3d Division. At a certain point in, those carrying the Rangers were to dogleg left, leaving the others, so as to put them on their right beach.

At first all went well. The LCIs carrying Darby's men split off from those carrying the 3d Division. Soon, however, Darby heard the whoosh of rockets on his right,[20] but no rockets were hitting the beach where the Rangers were scheduled to land. Darby was now concerned that the British captain assigned to support him would realize his error and then fire late, thus catching the Rangers in the town without cover. No rockets came, however, and Darby was thankful that the ship's commander had "used his head" and withheld fire on learning that the timing had been thrown off.[21]

The lack of fire, Darby surmised, may have had its advantage: it had contributed to the element of surprise. Whether or not such was the case, Darby's men found resistance very light and scattered when they hit the beach. During the remaining hours of darkness, his men got set for a possible counterattack. The navy had done well in landing Darby at the exact point he had requested. In no time he was set up in the casino and had opened his command post for business. An hour after the 1st and 4th Ranger Battalions had landed, some mortars and engineers troops had landed in LSTs. The Ranger Force was becoming rounded out. Before daylight the 3d Battalion and the other elements of Darby's force had arrived.

18. Darby, *We Led the Way,* 147.
19. Ibid., 147, 149.
20. Those were the rockets that had so impressed General Lucas, aboard the *Biscayne.*
21. Darby, *We Led the Way,* 149.

The mission, or at least the opening phase, was accomplished by noon of the 22d. Though they searched for a pattern of German defense, the Rangers found only scattered detachments. They had knocked out the coastal defense guns in the town and, while killing forty Germans in the process, had made contact with the 3d Division on the right. On the left, the 3d Battalion had met up with the Scots Guards of the British 1st Division. Still, by evening, Darby's patrols had failed to make any substantial contact with German troops.[22]

The void was noticed by everyone along the line right from the beginning of the landing. Captain James F. C. Hyde, Jr., communications officer of the 69th Armored Field Artillery Battalion, was among those most surprised. As an individual officer sent ahead to scout out positions for the self-propelled guns of his battalion, Hyde had landed before dawn with the artillery of the 3d Division. The unopposed landing in a quiet sea had been without incident, and Hyde was amazed at being put on the beach only twenty yards from the muddy road he was to follow on his inland reconnaissance.

Hyde went forward without delay and within forty-five minutes or so he had identified suitable positions for the guns of the 69th. Along the way he ran across no enemy. The only German he saw was a dead one, lying beside the road. Whatever lay in the future, Hyde found the landing amazingly easy.[23]

In the early hours of January 22, Clark joined General Alexander, with some of their staff officers, for a run up to Anzio by PT boat. Clark and Alexander arrived at Anzio in the late morning. Clark headed straight for the *Biscayne* to see Lucas. The reports were good. A large part of the 52,000 men due to land that day were ashore, along with 5,200 vehicles. The Rangers had occupied Anzio, and enemy resistance had been scattered. The landing was off to a good start.

Second Lieutenant Siegmund Seiler, of the 2d Company, 6th Technical Unit, German Army, was expecting trouble that evening of January 21, 1944. He had not been alerted by orders from higher headquarters, but something made him uncomfortable. Seiler was not a combat soldier; actually he could be called a civil engineer in uniform. His technical unit, which consisted of firemen, plumbers, electricians, locksmiths, and welders, had a total strength of some nearly four hundred men, but each

22. Ibid., 147–51 *passim.*
23. James F. C. Hyde, Jr., to author, Feb. 6 and Mar. 30, 2006.

Captain James F. C. Hyde, Jr.
Courtesy Mrs. Enid Griswold
Hyde.

small detachment worked independently. Seiler's job that evening was to blow two channels in the mole at Anzio. His detachment consisted of eighteen men.

At about 9:00 P.M., Seiler heard a loud explosion a couple of miles to the south at Nettuno, and his first reaction was to investigate. He drove the short distance down to Nettuno and reported to the German town commandant. There was no invasion, the commandant assured him; the noise had been caused by the explosion of a German ammunition truck, a sheer accident. Still Seiler remained uncomfortable; the purring sounds out in the waters must have some meaning. But, since the commandant was his senior—and an experienced man—Seiler kept his own counsel.

On the assumption that nothing important was in the offing, Seiler and the Nettuno town commander started back in the early morning of January 22, headed for their headquarters at Frascati. Suddenly, bursts of automatic weapons fire hit the car from the side of the road, one bullet killing the commandant. The Allies were ashore!

In terror, Seiler tried to hide behind the rear seat of their vehicle. Soon an American soldier opened the front door and motioned for him to come out with his hands up, a feat that he managed with difficulty. An American doctor stopped briefly and asked him if he was wounded; he was not.[24] Looking around, Seiler saw that the coast road was crowded with American troops.

Siegmund Seiler, now an American prisoner of war, was being conducted down to the beach for evacuation by sea. His unhappiness at being captured was heightened by the fact that, as a technician, he had never expected to be exposed to this misfortune. In a while, however, his technical expertise made him forget his plight momentarily in his interest to see what was going on. He watched with fascination as an American beach party went about its business.[25] During the time he watched, he never heard a word of command, though everything went like "clockwork." Troops were "running around, unloading, adjusting and correcting here and there; it was like a big market and a medley, without muddle."

Seiler also declared himself impressed by American equipment, especially by the maneuverable jeeps and amphibious vehicles. Bulldozers were operating only a few hours after the landing. "It was an impressive spectacle," he testified, "where every man knew his place and no commands were necessary."

Up to the north, Seiler noticed lights and fire in Anzio. A pathetic German air raid, four waves of four planes each, was apparently having little effect. German fire was almost nonexistent. Seiler had witnessed the beginning of the Anzio landing.[26]

At his headquarters in East Prussia, Adolf Hitler was completely surprised to receive the news of the Anzio landing. Report after report had indicated that a landing in the rear of the Gustav Line was improbable. With this new development, it seemed at first that the effort to hold the Allies south of Rome was futile. General Alfred Jodl, however, stepped in and interpreted the landing to be only an Allied attempt to scatter German forces. The landing, he said, should be eliminated.

24. In *We Led the Way*, William O. Darby says, "On the right, a wheeled personnel carrier was captured just before dawn and its two passengers killed in the fracas" (149). It is intriguing to speculate whether Darby was referring to Seiler's capture.

25. The party, mostly engineers, was doing the job it had performed three times before within fourteen months at North Africa, Sicily, and Salerno.

26. Siegmund Seiler, interview, Jan. 25, 1944. Courtesy of National Archives. Seiler's favorable comments could well have been encouraged to please his captors.

Hitler was hearing what he wanted to hear. "If we succeed in dealing with this business down there, there will be no further landing anywhere," he declared. Immediately he took action. Two motorized divisions earmarked for redeployment to the west, he ordered, were to be retained in Italy. A corps headquarters from Germany was to be moved to Italy. Finally, an infantry division, reinforced by a tank battalion, was to be moved from France into Italy. In Hitler's enthusiasm, it was all that General Walter Warlimont, Hitler's operations officer, could do to stop Hitler from moving two more divisions from the west.[27]

This action on the part of Hitler and his OKW was not what the Allies had hoped for. The German divisions converging on Anzio were supposed to have come from the Gustav Line.

27. Warlimont, *Inside Hitler's Headquarters*, 410–11.

CHAPTER 12

LUCAS CONSOLIDATES THE BRIDGEHEAD

L ate in the morning of January 22, 1944, General John Lucas, satisfied that the American 3d Division was well established ashore, decided to pay a visit to the headquarters of British General W. R. C. Penney, of the British 1st Division, about which he harbored serious doubts. To reach Penney he had to go by water from the *Biscayne* to the HMS *Bulolo,* Admiral Troubridge's flagship, on a circuitous route in order to avoid the minefields the Germans had laid in the harbor. As a result, the trip took an hour and a half.

On arriving at the *Bulolo,* Lucas was surprised at the luxury the Royal Navy enjoyed. "It was very comfortably fixed up," he later wrote, "in contrast to Admiral Lowry and myself on the *Biscayne.*"[1] The remark was probably meant as good-naturedly envious rather than mean-spirited, but Lucas was critical of everything else he saw.

The British, he noted, were "having difficulties in unloading vehicles on the beach." He attributed part of the problem to the fact that Troubridge's men had "mislaid" the pontoons that were used for that purpose. To be fair, however, much of the delay was due to conditions on the beach. The British had never liked Peter Beach, he noted, and he felt that Troubridge and Penney were not "putting out maximum effort to overcome their handicaps." Lucas was never fond of the British, and he gave them no charity. According to Lucas, the Royal Navy did not seem to be as versatile in making expedients as were the members of the American Navy.[2] The fairness of John Lucas's judgments is beside the point; they reflect the beginning of distrust between the corps commander and his principal British subordinate.

1. Lucas diary, 325.
2. Ibid.

Lucas set up VI Corps Headquarters ashore on January 23, at the same time assuming command of the land battle. By the next day he was satisfied that his beachhead was progressing well. The VI Corps had reached the Corps Beachhead Line, making the area occupied by the Americans and British a half moon about eight miles deep and fifteen miles at the base along the coast. This depth of position was considered the minimum to deprive the Germans of observed artillery fire on the port of Anzio. The fact that the VI Corps had taken the port of Anzio without great damage was a matter he considered of greatest importance.

In conducting operations immediately following the landings, Lucas had definite priorities in his mind. After consolidating the Corps Beachhead Line, he would build up his supply reserves and increase his troop strength. Finally, he would move out in the attack. Limited attacks could be conducted in the meantime, but Lucas's attention was definitely focused on securing a solid position. It does not seem to have been a definite decision as such. Lucas was following the priorities he had always assumed were correct.

The flanks of the beachhead were safe. On the left of the British 1st Infantry Division, the flank was protected by the Moletta River, a misnamed, unimpressive little stream. The Moletta had been selected principally because there existed no other obstacle in the vicinity. That weak position caused Lucas and Penney little anxiety, however, because the coast road from that direction was vulnerable to Allied naval gunfire.

The right flank of the bridgehead, as mentioned, was protected by the Mussolini Canal, which emptied into the sea about nine miles east of Nettuno. For the first seven miles inland, it was a single stream. Beyond that point it had two branches, with one branch coming from the northeast and the other from the northwest, thus affording protection to the front. The canal, plus the marsh, afforded such protection to the right flank that Lucas planned eventually to defend it with only Frederick's Devil's Brigade, which he expected to arrive soon. One of the first objectives when the Allies landed on January 22 had been to seize the bridges over the canal, a task that had been achieved handily.

But from the first Lucas seems to have had an uncomfortable feeling that he really should be pushing forward. He therefore instructed the 3d Division to make very limited attacks toward Cisterna, and the British 1st Division was also to move forward, though Lucas was less specific here. "I must keep in motion if my first success is to be of any value," he wrote. But he acted too late. A day after the landing, German reinforcements were already in evidence, and Lucas was concerned that Kesselring's panzers and panzer grenadiers would stop him before he could get very far. "The strain of this thing is a terrible burden," he wrote. "Who the hell wants to be a general?"[3]

Lucas's failure to push ahead more aggressively toward the Alban Hills has become one of the most controversial issues of the war. Kesselring, accustomed as he was to fighting with a paucity of men and supplies— and who always overestimated Allied strength—later wrote that Lucas had missed an opportunity by failing to move forward to seize the Alban Hills the first day. "As I traversed the front," he later wrote, "I had the confident feeling that the Allies had missed a uniquely favorable chance of capturing Rome and of opening the door on the Garigliano. I was certain that time was our ally."[4]

In London, Prime Minister Churchill was also unimpressed by the results of the first few days' action. Possibly desperate to find justification for a flawed plan, he set about to make a scapegoat of an American, specifically Lucas. His account, written later, was typically eloquent:

> But now came disaster, and the ruin of the prime purpose of the enterprise. General Lucas confined himself to occupying his beachhead and having equipment and vehicles brought ashore. General Penney, commanding the British 1st Division, was anxious to push inland. His reserve brigade was however held back with the Corps. . . . The defences of the beachhead were growing, but the opportunity for which great exertions had been made was gone.[5]

And General Alexander, who rarely, if ever, said a word contrary to the opinions of the Prime Minister, stated that ". . . the American John Lucas missed his opportunity by being too slow and cautious. He failed to realize the great advantage that surprise had given him. He allowed time to beat him."[6]

Lucas had no idea at the time that he was being made the butt of such criticism. Alexander, for example, showed nothing but the greatest enthusiasm whenever he visited VI Corps Headquarters. When Alexander and Clark had visited Anzio the morning of the landing, Alexander had bordered on the gleeful. "You have certainly given the folks at home something to think about," he exclaimed.[7] And three days later, though the

3. Ibid., 325–28 *passim.*
4. Kesselring, *Memoirs,* 194.
5. Churchill, *Ring,* 5:481–82.
6. Alexander, *Memoirs,* 126.
7. Lucas diary, 327.

beachhead may not have been expanded as rapidly as Alexander had desired, he was still ebullient in the presence of Lucas. "What a splendid piece of work," he exclaimed. Lucas seemed to consider it necessary to warn Alexander that it "wasn't over yet."[8]

Alexander may have been hiding his real feelings. Two days after their first visit he confided to Clark that he did not believe that the VI Corps was pushing ahead rapidly enough. Clark was not unduly concerned. He knew that Alexander had received a telegram from the Prime Minister complaining about the slowness of the move forward, and he surmised that Alexander was responding.[9]

Lucas's American colleagues, however, stuck by him in this decision. Clark, for example, who usually seemed to think that Lucas needed a great deal of supervision,[10] did not think he could have taken the Alban Hills.[11]

But the most convincing of Lucas's supporters was a man who can hardly be called a shrinking violet, Lucian K. Truscott:

> I suppose that arm chair strategists will always labor under the delusion that there was a "fleeting opportunity" at Anzio, during which some Napoleonic figure would have charged over the Colli Laziali, played havoc with the German line of communications, and galloped into Rome. Any such concept betrays lack of comprehension of the military problems involved. It was necessary to occupy the Corps Beachhead Line to prevent the enemy from interfering with the beaches. Otherwise, enemy artillery and armored detachments, operating against the flanks, could have cut us off from the beach and prevented the unloading of troops, supplies, and equipment. As it was the Corps Beachhead Line was barely distant enough to prevent direct artillery fire upon the beaches.[12]

There the matter stands for a debate which can never be decided. Obviously national loyalty has a great deal to do with a person's perspective.

---

8. Ibid., 335.
9. Later, in private, Alexander described the landing itself as "something of a bluff."
10. Clark set up a Fifth Army forward command post in the Anzio Beachhead, much to Lucas's annoyance.
11. "I have been disappointed by the lack of aggressiveness on the part of VI Corps, although it would have been wrong in my opinion to attack our final objective [the Alban Hills] on this front. [But] reconnaissance in force with tanks should have been more aggressive to capture Cisterna and Campoleone" (Clark, *Calculated Risk*, 296).
12. Truscott, *Command Missions*, 311.

Regardless of his views regarding any lost opportunity on the part of the Allies, Field Marshal Albert Kesselring knew what he had to do. First he had to ring the Anzio beachhead so that the VI Corps could not break out. Second, on Hitler's orders, he had to destroy it. His first chore was, therefore, to reinforce what he had on hand at Anzio.

The few days following the Allied landing were described by Kesselring as "a higgledy-piggledy jumble—units of numerous divisions fighting side by side." He moved two corps headquarters, the 14th Corps from northern Italy and the 76th Panzer Corps from the Adriatic. To command them, he brought the 14th Army, under General Eberhard von Mackensen, to Anzio from its previous location north of Rome. By January 25, three days after the landing, advance guards from eight divisions were in the vicinity, and by the end of the week seventy thousand German troops ringed the bridgehead.[13] German buildup was much faster than was that of the Allies. The vaunted airpower of the Allies had not slowed the Germans, at least not appreciably.

Not all of the adventure of the moment, however, was taking place in the Anzio area. Though the Allies controlled the seas, their lifeline extended a distance of over a hundred miles. Sometimes the trip was dangerous; at other times, as in the case of the 56th Evacuation Hospital, it could be just plain uncomfortable.

On the evening of January 24, the nurses of the 56th Evac were informed that orders had just come in. "We leave at 1900 hours." The nurses, now veterans, automatically ate quick K rations, made trips to the water truck for their rations of a gallon of water each, donned their helmets, and secured their musette bags. Three hours later, cold and hungry, they arrived at Pozzuoli, the port of Naples. Expecting the comforts of a relatively luxurious LST, they jumped off the tailgate of the truck eagerly. Their joy, however, was short-lived. Along the wharf of the crowded harbor they were led to their boat. "Not another LCI!" moaned one of the girls.

"I get sick just thinking of it!" groaned Avis Dagit's friend Danny.

An LCI it was, a British vessel, complete with a welcoming party of a large rat. They were to be packed into close quarters, with bunks three deep and barely room to walk between them. There were no blankets, and

13. The 715th Panzer Grenadiers from France, the 114th Rifles from the Balkans, and three elite infantry regiments from Berlin, the Infantry Demonstration Regiment and the 1027th and 1028th Panzer Grenadier Regiments, Kesselring, *Memoirs*, 194; Morris, *Circles of Hell*, 262. See also Charles G. Starr, ed., *From Salerno to the Alps: A History of the Fifth Army, 1943–1945*, 132–33.

soon over the loudspeaker came the voice of the British captain: "The la-
trine doesn't work down here."

The American commander was quick to reassure him. "Don't worry,"
Colonel Blesse announced proudly. "My girls will manage just fine if
you'll give them a bucket."

With the prospect of a storm facing them, the nurses were immensely
relieved when they were told that they would be transferred to an
American LST. As a sailor tossed a rope to Avis Dagit and she slipped it
around her waist, she mumbled a silent prayer. "Dear God, give me
strength and don't let me fall."[14]

Sometimes the trip from Naples to Anzio was dangerous, and nobody
was exempted, not even the commanding general himself. Dissatisfied
with the progress of Lucas's limited attacks, Clark determined to go to
Anzio to confer with Lucas.[15] On the morning of January 28, he took his
operations officer, his intelligence officer, and his army engineer down to
the mouth of the Volturno to board PT Boat 201.

Clark's trip to Anzio could well have been his last. The seas were rough,
so rough that it was difficult to maneuver the small boat. The prospects
were made even more uncomfortable by word that enemy air raids and
shelling were causing considerable damage at Anzio and that German PT
boats were on the prowl along the coast. Nevertheless, PT 201 made it almost to Anzio without major difficulty.

When Clark's party reached a point about seven miles south of Anzio,
it was still dark. Still they felt no cause for concern when they encountered an American minesweeper, which immediately challenged them.
The commander of the PT boat sent up the routine green and yellow flares
and flashed the designated signal on the blinkers to identify himself. The
minesweeper, however, misread the signal from the PT boat and let loose
with 40 mm and 5-inch shells. The captain of the PT boat was wounded
in both legs and fell to the deck, and a shell caused confusion below. Clark
himself picked up a Very pistol and fired two signal flares, still with no results. Five of the naval officers and sailors had been hit, and one ensign,
despite his leg wounds, got to his feet and swung the boat around.

Clark, though he had no legal authority aboard a navy vessel, took
charge. "Let's run for it," he shouted. He then picked up the ship's captain
so he could direct the movement of the ship. Eventually PT 201 reached a

---

14. Schorer, *Half Acre*, 1321–25 *passim*.
15. Clark, *Calculated Risk*, 291–92. See also Bryant, *Triumph in the West*, 107, for Churchill's
proddings.

British minesweeper, the HMS *Acute,* and unloaded the wounded, a couple of whom were in serious condition. With a new crew and another PT boat they resumed the trip.

By some coincidence, the new PT boat encountered the same minesweeper once again. In Clark's somewhat humorous account of the incident, he says only that "Our new skipper . . . pulled up alongside the AM 120 and through a megaphone delivered an inspiring and profane lecture to the captain of the minesweeper, beginning with, 'You just fired on General Clark.'"[16] The minesweeper captain could not, of course, present an adequate excuse, much as he tried.

Clark's problems were not over. "The [PT boat] incident got the day [of the 28th of January] off to a bad start and it went from there on a downward slant."[17] The PT boat arrived at Anzio just in time for the third air raid of the day, and the Americans had to wait until it was over before they could land. Once ashore, Clark headed for the command post of VI Corps to confer with Lucas. He urged the corps commander to speed up the attack and, to add insult to the situation, arranged for an advance Fifth Army command post to be set up in the grounds of the Prince Borghese palace near the town of Nettuno.

In the early morning hours of January 29, 1944, Major General Ernest N. Harmon, commanding the American 1st Armored Division, was feeling impatient as he looked around Anzio Bay. He wanted to go ashore immediately, but he was advised that such was impossible. There were so many sunken craft in the shallow Anzio Bay, he later noted, that the LST he was riding on would have to wait its turn before landing. Harmon refused to wait. He packed his few possessions in his musette bag and secured a motorboat to take him in to shore.

The refusal to allow obstacles to get in his way was typical of "Old Gravel-voice." It helped to make Harmon one of the truly great combat commanders of the Second World War. A West Pointer from the Class of 1917, he was ruggedness personified. In build he appeared almost square, short and stocky, with a lantern jaw that accurately portrayed his bulldog aggressiveness. His leadership qualities were not of the type advocated in the army training manuals. He did not, for example, pretend to share all the hardships of his troops, though he shared their dangers. Veterans of the 1st Armored Division in Africa loved to tell about Harmon's attitude toward the venerated steel helmet. "You're going to wear that helmet," he an-

16. Clark, *Calculated Risk,* 292–94 *passim.*
17. Ibid., 294.

nounced one day. "It's no goddam good. You'll wear it because I tell you to. I'm going to wear this soft cap. It's more comfortable." His troops loved him for it.[18]

Once ashore, Harmon soon found himself in the three-story building in Nettuno that General Lucas was for the moment occupying as his command post. As he entered the corps commander's office, Harmon noted that Lucas was smoking his "inevitable" corncob pipe, and as Lucas rose to shake hands, they heard the sound of firing in the distance. "Glad to see you," Lucas said. "You're needed here."[19]

As Lucas outlined the situation on the Anzio beachhead, Harmon learned that a portion of his 1st Armored Division was scheduled to participate in an attack the next morning. The corps was going to make a two-pronged attack to seize important points: Cisterna on the northeast and Campoleone directly to the north. The American 3d Infantry Division was to make the Cisterna attack, but Harmon's division was to support the British 1st Division in its attack toward Campoleone. Short as that notice seemed to be, it was feasible. By noon of that day, Harmon noted, the 1st Armored had begun unloading and by evening most of his tanks were bivouacked in an area known as the Padiglione Woods. Harmon described the efficiency of his headquarters commandant with a touch of pride:

> Generals have their troubles, but they don't have to worry about housing. When I reached the Padiglione Woods, my command post was set up. The telephone switchboard was working. I had a "goose-egg" chart which told me where the units were located; and the re-modeled ordnance repair truck I used as an office and bedroom had been magically transported from ship to shore. Some 12,000 men and their machines had been quartered.

In looking around, however, Harmon saw one feature of his command post that he did not like: a British artillery battery was located about twenty-five yards away, and he knew from experience that artillery invites counterbattery fire from the enemy. Harmon had no intention of dying on his first night at Anzio, so he ordered his home moved from the Padiglione Woods to a spot in an open field. Dinner was a warmed-up C Ration. The night was cold. The 1st Armored, or parts thereof, would attack in the morning over unknown terrain.

18. This episode was described to the author during World War II by a member of the 1st Armored Division. Though it cannot be verified by documents, it was the kind of thing the troops believed about Harmon.

19. Ernest N. Harmon, with Milton MacKaye and William Ross MacKaye, *Combat Commander: Autobiography of a Soldier,* 161.

"No one," Harmon noted later, "slept much."[20]

L ucas's VI Corps had done a remarkable job in building up its strength. While executing limited attacks that brought the 3d Division within three miles of Cisterna and the British 1st Division to a point near Campoleone, he had effected an impressive buildup. By January 30, the 45th Infantry Division and a combat command of the 1st Armored Division[21] had been established in the beachhead, along with corps troops, especially artillery. By the end of the month, Lucas had the equivalent of four divisions in the Anzio beachhead.

He was now ready for a serious attack.

20. Ibid., 160–62.
21. The 1st Armored Division had, by this time, been reorganized into three combat commands, each of which included infantry, tanks, and artillery. One combat command (CCA) had remained behind on the Rapido.

Attacks on Cisterna and Campoleone, 29-31 January 1944

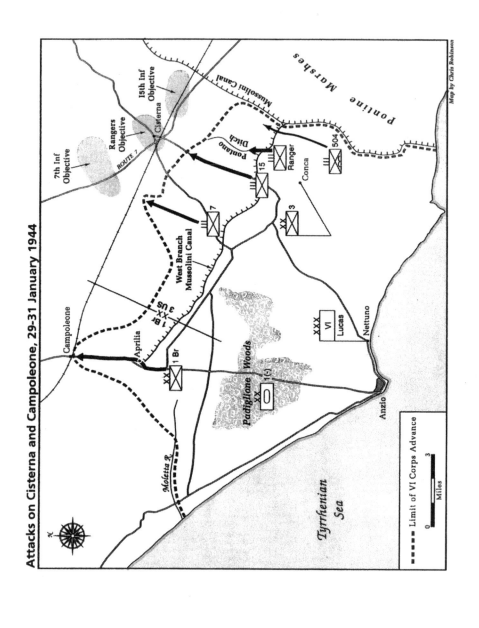

Map by Chris Robinson

CHAPTER 13

CISTERNA AND CAMPOLEONE

The time had come for Lucas to attack. Probably prodded into action by a visit from Alexander, the VI Corps commander finally took the bull by the horns. On Thursday, January 27, he called a council of his commanders to outline his general plan. Those present—Truscott, Penney, and Harmon—listened attentively.

Lucas's plan was logical, if not obvious. He had two divisions with which to make his attack and two major roads leading out of the beachhead. One was the Anzio-Campoleone-Albano Road running to the north in the area of the British 1st Division. The other road ran northeastward between Conca and Cisterna, in the area of the 3d Division. Both were important, but the road to Campoleone was preferable because it led straight to the Alban Hills, the eventual objective. Logically, then, the Campoleone road served as the axis of advance for the British 1st Division, and the road to Cisterna did the same in the zone of the American 3d Division. Lucas gave priority of support to the Albano Road.

Terrain was an important consideration. The Campoleone area was far more favorable for offensive action than that of the reclaimed Pontine Marsh area. It contained the Padiglione Woods, which protected command posts, artillery, and concentrating troops from direct German observation. By contrast, the terrain on the east consisted of flat farmlands that provided little or no concealment. To make matters worse, the ground in the 3d Division sector was cut up by a series of drainage ditches that had been dug to keep the area dry enough to be arable. The land was also dotted by a series of relatively uniform stone houses spaced about eight hundred yards apart, part of the reclamation project of Mussolini's Italian government. These structures were ideal for use as strongpoints for concealed, independent detachments. They were destined to play a significant role in the coming battle.

More specifically, Lucas's plan called for the British 1st Division, supported by Combat Command A of Harmon's 1st Armored Division, to drive up the Albano Road, past the town of Aprilia (The Factory), and on toward Campoleone. On the right, the 3d Infantry Division, with the 6615th Ranger Force[1] and the 504th Parachute Infantry Regiment attached, was to push forward and take Cisterna. The 3d was then to be prepared to push on to Velletri, thereby cutting Route 6.[2] If successful, Lucas would have succeeded in cutting the main supply routes (and routes of retreat) of von Vietinghoff's Tenth German Army.

Lucas's commanders left that meeting feeling confident. Truscott was particularly satisfied. For one thing, he had regained control of the 30th Infantry Regiment, which Lucas had previously held out as part of the corps reserve. The immediate arrival of the 179th Infantry and Harmon's combat command made that possible. Further, intelligence had reported that the 3d Division attack would be opposed only by the Hermann Goering Division, which was spread over a front of some twenty miles. Under those circumstances, Darby's Rangers could easily infiltrate between the strongpoints in the darkness and take Cisterna before the Germans realized what was happening. On the heels of the Rangers would come armor, artillery, and tank destroyers.

Truscott was particularly happy to have the Rangers with him. He and Darby had worked together in London to develop the Ranger Force early in the war, and despite the differences in their ages, they liked and respected each other. When the two conferred after the meeting with Lucas, they agreed that this infiltration mission was exactly what the Rangers had been designed for. As Darby later wrote, "it was down our alley and would have delighted the heart of Major Rogers in pre-Revolutionary days."[3] Darby was just as confident of success as was Truscott.

At that point, a snag occurred. General Lucas, in response to a request from Penney and Harmon, postponed the attack for a day, meaning that the jump-off would occur the evening of January 29–30 rather than that of the 28–29. Ordinarily such a delay would have been of little import, but in this case it enabled Kesselring to move the veteran 26th Panzer Grenadier

1. The three Ranger battalions—the 1st, 3d, and 4th—were now organized under a formal headquarters with Colonel William Darby in command. Darby, *We Led the Way,* 158.
2. Truscott, *Command Missions,* 313. Other accounts say that Valmontone, not Velletri, was to be the ultimate objective. That possibility was so remote, however, as to be academic at that stage.
3. Darby, *We Led the Way,* 160.

Division into the Cisterna sector. Truscott and Darby were now, unbeknownst to them, attacking a force double the strength they had anticipated.

The Truscott-Darby plan called for the closest kind of joint effort. The 3d Division was to attack with two regiments abreast, the 7th Infantry Regiment on the left, bypassing Cisterna on the west; the 15th Infantry to the east of the town. The Rangers were to move forward in a column of battalions down the Pontano. At the end of the ditch they were to dash straight into town. Farther to the west, the 4th Ranger Battalion was to follow the main road, from Conca (where Truscott located his command post), past Femina Morta and Isola Bella and eventually into Cisterna.

Just after midnight of the 29th, Darby's two Ranger battalions crossed the west branch of the Mussolini Canal, the 3d following the 1st. The night was dark and moonless. To their left was the main Conca-Isola Bella-Cisterno road. Darby's trained troops moved in silence, and without incident the leading battalion reached the head of the ditch at a point only eight hundred yards short of Cisterna.

When daylight broke, however, the head of the column suddenly ran into a strong German force led by three assault guns. Moving quickly according to standard procedure, the Rangers deployed and knocked out the three guns in short order. As the light improved, however, they came under heavy fire from German machine guns, mortars, and sniper fire from houses and haystacks all around them. Caught without cover in the open, treeless fields, the advantage of surprise now lost, the Rangers soon realized that they had walked into an ambush. The troops they were facing were veteran elements of the 1st German Parachute Division, brought in within the last twenty-four hours. The sense of security the Rangers had felt in the approach march had been totally unjustified. The enemy had been watching their every move as they had approached up through the Pontano.

The Rangers were now pinned down in the open fields with retreat impossible. Given the choice of fighting or surrendering, they chose to fight. A desperate battle raged throughout the morning against the entrenched Germans on all sides.

Their calls for help were received, but their comrades in the 4th Ranger Battalion and the 3d Division were unable to reach them despite every effort. The 4th Ranger Battalion, which had jumped off with the main attack of the 3d Division at 0200, was stopped by heavy machine gun fire at a point only two hundred yards short of Isola Bella. Casualties were heavy. At about noon enemy tanks attacked the 1st and 3d Ranger Battalions in the pocket below Cisterna. Pinned down, the Rangers had to fight from their positions while the enemy tanks raced back and forth among them, cutting the battalions up into small groups. Finally the Rangers made an effort to withdraw, but it was too late. The Germans had them hemmed in all around, and friendly troops were unable to break through. Of the 767 men in the two Ranger battalions, only 6 escaped; the rest of the survivors were taken prisoner.[4]

Back at Truscott's command post in Conca, Bill Darby, at the end of a radio link, was suffering with his men. At first all had seemed to be going well. At 0415 he had recorded, "No news from 1st and 3d Battalions. Apparently OK. 4th Battalion is getting fire from all houses along the road." A half hour later he recorded that he was still out of contact with the 1st and 3d Battalions. His concern at this time remained with the resistance being encountered by the 4th Ranger Battalion, attacking with the reconnaissance troops of the 3d Division.

It was at 8:35 A.M., four hours after the beginning of the operation, that Darby received the shocking news that the 1st and 3d Battalions had been surrounded. Both battalion commanders were casualties, one killed, the other wounded. It was impossible for the Rangers to adjust artillery fire, and the town of Cisterna, contrary to expectations, was "strongly held." The 504th Parachute Infantry, on the right of the 3d Division, was ordered to take its attached tanks and rescue the beleaguered Ranger battalions as well as a company of American prisoners the Rangers had observed being marched off.

Shortly after noon, the end came, and a distraught Darby, unable to get through, had a last exchange. His old sergeant major informed him that nobody was giving up, that he had given orders to shoot any Americans attempting to do so. In desperation, Darby sent a last order:

> Issue some orders but don't let the boys give up! Who's walking in with their hands up? Don't let them do it! Get the men together and lam for it. We're coming through. Hang on to this radio until the last minute. How many men are still with you? Stick together. . . . Who's with the 1st Battalion? Use your head and do what is best. You're there and I'm here, unfortunately, and I can't help you, but whatever happens, God bless you!

That was the end. At the same time that he sent that message, Darby noted, "They came and got them at the last minute. My old sergeant major stayed with the last ten men. It was apparently too much for them."[5]

4. Starr, *Salerno to the Alps*, 134–35.
5. Taggart, *History of the Third Infantry Division*, 115.

Darby took the loss of his beloved Rangers hard. They were his boys; he had organized them in Northern Ireland and had fought with them from Tunisia to the vicinity of Rome. His anguish was described by one of his men:

> Darby was desperate. His invincible Ranger force was shattered. Two battalions decimated and another battalion, the Fourth, had suffered nearly fifty percent casualties, with three company commanders killed in the last twelve hours. Darby, the iron-willed, resolute commander, fought hard to hold back his tears. But he couldn't. He went inside the farmhouse, asked his staff to leave, and then alone for a few moments, he sobbed out his anguish as enemy shells beat a steady tattoo around the house.

It did not last long. The same witness soon saw Darby come out of the farmhouse, shoulders straight and chin thrust forward defiantly. The war must go on. Darby reported the loss to 3d Division Headquarters and received orders to prepare the remnant of the 4th Ranger Battalion for another attack the next morning.[6]

The failure at Cisterna, unfortunately, involved a great deal more suffering, loss, and frustration than the loss of Darby's two Ranger battalions and the near-destruction of the third, heartbreaking as they were. The casualties sustained by the 3d Division all along the front were staggering.

Of Truscott's three regiments, the 15th had originally been assigned to cross the main road to the right of the Rangers but had later been diverted in a futile effort to rescue them. The 30th Infantry was being held in reserve. The rest of the fighting, therefore, fell on the shoulders of Colonel Harry Sherman's 7th Infantry, a proud unit that had carried the sobriquet of the "Cotton Balers" ever since the Battle of New Orleans under Andrew Jackson. Sherman's objective was a point on Route 7 to the northwest of Cisterna, there to set up a blocking position to protect the town from attack in the direction of Rome.

Conforming his tactics to fit the false information concerning German strength in the Cisterna area, Colonel Sherman moved out in a column of battalions, one following the other. The lead battalion was the 1st, under the command of Lieutenant Colonel Frank Izenour. Izenour, in turn, moved his battalion out in a column of companies. His axis of advance was along the Delle Mole Creek.[7]

6. James Altieri, *The Spearheaders*, 266.
7. John McManus, "Bloody Cisterna," in *World War II*, Jan. 2004, 59.

Izenour's main problem was to find his way. The terrain in his area was so flat that no distinctive features could be discerned as landmarks. The darkness that had provided concealment for the Rangers on their way up the Pontano now worked against the Cotton Balers. Having been provided no time to reconnoiter the area, they had to stumble their way through the darkness, negotiating wire fences that aerial photographs had failed to reveal. At one point, the 1st Battalion encountered a drainage ditch twenty-five feet deep that had appeared as a mere hedgerow on the aerial photographs hastily studied before. Scouting parties failed to find a way around the ditch. It took the battalion a full half hour to negotiate that single obstacle.

At about daylight, after the 1st Battalion had covered a respectable six miles and were a little over halfway to their objective, they ran up against a strong German position, probably a combat outpost of the main line of resistance up ahead on the railroad embankment. Izenour and his men did not know exactly where they were, but they knew they were in a fight. Out in the open, totally exposed, they found themselves nearly surrounded, with German machine guns firing at them from their left rear. Izenour was hit in the shoulder by machine-pistol bullets, and his executive officer was likewise wounded. By about noon, the battalion was down to 250 men, about a third of its original strength. A less experienced unit might have surrendered, but the idea never crossed the Cotton Balers' minds. Instead they dug in.[8]

During the day Colonel Sherman committed the 2d and 3d Battalions of the 7th Infantry on the right of the 1st Battalion. He also reinforced the battalion with tanks and ammunition, providing them with rations to get them through the night. To replace Izenour, he sent Major Frank Sinsel as battalion commander. Sinsel regrouped the 1st Battalion, and its position was now taking the form of a horseshoe. It was now in a position that when the enemy attacked in strength the second morning, the battalion repulsed them handily.

As so often happens in times of crisis, individuals step forward to perform heroic deeds, often with apparent disregard for their own lives. In this instance such a hero was Truman Olson, a baby-faced sergeant in command of a machine gun section from "B" Company, 7th Infantry. On the second night of fighting, Olson's company commander placed his crew, with a single machine gun, out a little ahead of the main line. Olson's heroism is best described in the official citation of his posthumously awarded Congressional Medal of Honor:

8. Ibid., 61.

Although he had been fighting without respite, Sergeant Olson stuck grimly to his post all night, while his gun crew was cut down, one by one, by accurate and overwhelming enemy fire. Weary from over 24 hours of continuous battle and suffering from an arm wound received during the night engagement, Sergeant Olson manned his gun alone, meeting the full force of an all-out enemy assault by approximately 200 men supported by mortar and machine gun fire, which the Germans launched at daybreak on the morning of 31 January. After thirty minutes of fighting, Sergeant Olson was mortally wounded; yet, knowing that only his weapon stood between his company and complete destruction, he refused evacuation. For an hour and a half after receiving his second and fatal wound, he continued to fire his machine gun, killing at least 20 of the enemy, wounding many more, and forcing the assaulting Germans to withdraw. He died before he could be given medical attention.[9]

The 7th Infantry was not to attain relief despite the fact that the 1st Battalion had been fighting for thirty hours. In the early afternoon of January 31, Colonel Sherman, with Truscott's backing, ordered a continuation of the attack toward the enemy's main position along the railroad line. After trying a flanking movement, Major Sinsel decided to make a frontal attack, sending his two hundred men and tank support straight out of the horseshoe. The Americans surged forward, somehow taking the Germans by surprise. Many of the enemy were cut down while trying to flee. Eventually the Americans made it all the way to the railroad embankment. There they dug in.

The 1st Battalion, however, was in for a heartbreak. The 2d and 3d Battalions on its right had not kept up, and Truscott, realistic soldier that he was, decided that the position of the 1st Battalion was too precarious. He pulled the battalion back to put it in line with the rest of the regiment. The survivors of the battalion—only 127 out of its original 800—came back over ground they had fought so hard to take. On the way back they buried the bodies of their fallen comrades.[10]

Heroic as the action was, nobody could deny that the attack to take Cisterna was a failure, for other regiments suffered as did the 7th. The 15th Infantry, for example, was down to a strength of about eighteen men per company. Why had it happened?

As the division contemplated this question, several theories were considered. The enemy was using new tactics. Cisterna was the first time in the Second World War that the 3d Division had attacked an enemy main

9. *History of the Third Infantry Division,* 385–86.
10. McManus, "Bloody Cisterna," 64.

position, as contrasted with a delaying position. But the principal reason was that the tactics did not suit the situation. Expecting light resistance, the division had employed infiltration methods, which simply did not work when attacking a strong position. Though the 3d Division had captured important ground and had inflicted heavier casualties than it had taken, the failure to take an assigned objective always remained a source of grief among the men of the Marne Division.[11]

On the left of VI Corps, the presumed main effort to take Campoleone on the road to the Alban Hills met with the same frustration that had plagued the 3d Division. General Penney's plan was sound enough to succeed against the type of opposition that he expected, but as in the case of the Americans, the intelligence was faulty.

Penney's division was attacking along a single road, employing formations that would be strange to Americans. He sent his main body, the 3d Brigade (the Duke of Wellington's, King's Shropshire Light Infantry Battalion, and the Sherwood Foresters) up the road. But since his various battalions were less amalgamated with their parent headquarters than were the American battalions with their regiments, he broke up the Guards Brigade to protect the flanks. The Scots Guards he placed on one flank and the Irish Guards on the other.

The Germans were ready for them. On the flanks of the road, the Scots and Irish Guards were both stopped cold, and the 3d Brigade was forced to continue on the main road with flanks exposed. That is, if they intended to continue at all.

Harmon's First Armored Division turned out to be no help at all in the initial assault. On the morning of the attack, his Sherman tanks and light tanks, with the 6th Armored Infantry Regiment, left their bivouac areas and made an effort to proceed to the left of the British on the Albano Road. There they found, to Harmon's dismay, that the area over which they were supposed to operate was completely impossible for tanks. Harmon blamed the mistake on intelligence, who had planned the attack based solely on aerial reconnaissance. "What seemed on the aerial photographs to be a series of dimples or minor indentations turned out, when my tankers got there, to be gullies fifty feet deep. When tank commanders attempted to skirt the gullies, they found themselves bogged down in the mud. Off the limited network of hard-surface roads in the beachhead, the January rains had made the area a gluey mess."[12] Harmon thereupon

11. *History of the Third Infantry Division*, 118–19.
12. Harmon, *Combat Commander*, 163.

sought and obtained permission for his tanks to go straight up the Albano Road. With the help of Harmon's tanks, the British drove up to a position just short of the objective. Harmon himself was a witness to the result.

On the day of his farthest advance, Harmon was assigned to relieve a group of British Sherwood Foresters who had "held a position under the most punishing of circumstances." They were located on a bluff that allowed them to look down on the whole German position at Campoleone Station, lying under mortar fire all day. When Harmon's tank could go no farther, he got out and walked. He had never, he later said, "seen so many dead men in one place." He shouted for the commanding officer.

> From a foxhole there arose a mud-covered corporal with a handlebar mustache. He was the highest-ranking officer still alive. He stood stiffly at attention.
> "How's it going?" I asked.
> "Well, sir," the corporal said, "there were a hundred and sixteen of us when we first came up, and there are sixteen of us now. We're ordered to hold out until sundown, and I think, with a little good fortune, we can manage to do so." We got the corporal and his fifteen gallant comrades safely out of there and back to join up with the other British troops.[13]

What Ernie Harmon had witnessed was no isolated case. The corporal encountered the remnants of a company from the Sherwood Foresters' Battalion. Every officer in the battalion at company level and above was a casualty. The battalion was reduced to the strength of 260 men. It was, as it has been called, "finished as a fighting unit."[14]

And Campoleone, like Cisterna, was still in enemy hands.

On the morning of January 30, while Darby's Rangers were going through their last agonies, General Mark Clark arrived at Anzio to inspect his new command post in the Villa Borghese. Everyone who saw him agreed that he was glum and pessimistic. He had not adjusted to the failure at the Rapido a week earlier, and he was now fighting with his forces split, with the enemy enjoying interior lines.[15]

---

13. Ibid., 164–65.
14. Morris, *Circles of Hell*, 263–64.
15. "Interior lines," a military term, means that an enemy concentrated between a split force can move forces from one front to another with impunity. Thus it can be said that Germany, in fighting the Western Allies and the Russians, could switch divisions between fronts with ease, whereas his enemies could not do the same between fronts.

Clark was dissatisfied with the developments at Anzio, and he seemed to be searching for someone to blame. Truscott stood his ground when Clark called the employment of Rangers for the Cisterna mission a misuse. He and Darby, Truscott insisted, had agreed that the Cisterna mission was appropriate. Lucas backed him up. It was a courageous act on the part of Lucas, because he, not Truscott or Darby, was the one losing favor.

After a short stay Clark returned to his main headquarters, apologizing to Lucas before leaving for harassing him so much. Lucas, a generous man, recorded his happiness that Clark had done so, because "I like him very much."[16]

Combat troops and generals, though they belonged to the same army, lived in different worlds.

16. Lucas diary, 353.

CHAPTER 14

THE ARRIVAL OF THE 56TH EVAC

A couple of days before the Cisterna operation began, the ship carrying the twenty-six nurses from the 56th Evacuation Hospital approached the Anzio beachhead. Those on board were the first women to arrive in that area, and they were looking forward to this adventure with keen anticipation.

Once the bulk of the nurses had been transferred from the antiquated LCI to the LST back at Naples, they had found the journey, despite the rough seas, to be nothing noteworthy. As the ship entered the harbor, however, Lieutenant Avis Dagit, whose discerning eye missed nothing, was impressed with the array of ships she saw. "Destroyers, battleships, cargo ships, and landing craft crowded the harbor," she later wrote, and "an umbrella of silver barrage balloons, which interfered with the low-flying aircraft, floated overhead." Lieutenant Dagit concluded that they had come into dangerous waters. "Everyone was anxious to land as we gathered on deck with our gear."[1]

Despite their anxiety to get ashore, the nurses were disappointed; disembarkation was not instant and automatic. Their tensions were increased shortly after the ship dropped anchor, when they experienced their first German air raid. Sirens screamed and the call "man your stations" came over the loudspeaker. Sailors rushed everywhere. The nurses were rushed to the inner cabins for safety, and Dagit was so frightened that her throat tightened up; she actually experienced difficulty in breathing. The fire from the antiaircraft guns caused the ship to shudder. The sky was filled with black smoke and red tracer bullets from guns ashore. The battle went on for forty minutes, and Dagit now realized that the *Luftwaffe* was still

1. Schorer, *Half Acre*, 126.

143

alive. "This was Jerry's way of welcoming us to the beachhead," she noted.[2]

Still the nurses remained confined aboard the ship, most of the time in an uneasy calm. At dawn the next morning came another red alert and Allied planes again met German in dogfights overhead. The raids went on sporadically all day, at the end of which Dagit and her fellow nurses learned that they would have to remain aboard the LST for another night.

By the next morning, the nurses were beginning to feel desperate. They were intensely relieved, then, to hear that their commanding officer had succeeded in making contact with the authorities on shore. When he explained that he had a contingent of nurses aboard, he proudly reported, he was given permission to debark them. It had been thirty-six hours since the LST had entered the Anzio harbor. The date was January 27, 1944.

Once ashore, Avis Dagit observed the surroundings in detail. As the party waited for the combat troops to be moved off the large beach, she noted how flat the beach area was, unlike the mountainous terrain around Naples, where the 56th Evac had previously been. The scene was one of frantic activity. Sailors and soldiers unloaded supplies at a "feverish pace." Soon some men noticed the nurses. Expecting to be welcomed as angels of mercy, they met only warnings: "What the hell are you doing here?" somebody shouted. "This place is hot. Take the first vehicle you can and get out of here." Others said the same thing: "Women don't belong here. Get out as fast as you can."[3]

Eventually a truck arrived, and the nurses scrambled eagerly aboard. Once the tailgate was up, however, a warning siren blared away: air raid. The women piled off the truck and, for want of better cover, snuggled up against what walls remained of the destroyed buildings. The raid over, they mounted up again and continued their journey to their new home.

The new site for the 56th Evacuation Hospital was in a damaged building near the beach, three miles east of Nettuno. The structure had previously been used as a tuberculosis sanitorium, and Dagit noticed that it had recently been hit by a couple of bombs—possibly in the raids the nurses had been witnessing from their spot out in the harbor. Numerous other structures and tents surrounded it. All the tents and the main compound were marked by red crosses mounted on white backgrounds, supposedly to make the area "off-limits" to German bombers. Some of the men assigned to the hospital, however, men who had preceded the nurses,

2. Ibid., 126–27. Ms. Schorer does not make it clear how she could describe the skies in detail when the nurses were huddled in the inner cabins.
3. Ibid., 128.

Lieutenant Avis Dagit (later Schorer) RN, 56th Evacuation
Hospital. Courtesy Mrs. Schorer.

warned them that they had better start digging. Many did, though others
clung to the belief that a hospital would never be bombed. Nurses as well
as men would be fined twenty-five dollars for failing to wear their helmets when out of doors, and that protection would be enough.

Sometime just after landing, the nurses gathered for a group photograph, all twenty-six of them. Together they made an interesting picture.
Outward signs of femininity were missing. The young ladies were clad in
olive drab uniforms with combat boots, sweaters, and GI trousers. By now
experienced, they showed confidence and enthusiasm. As some stood and
some sprawled, they were still very much individuals. Avis Dagit, at the
rear, bore signs of the cheerleader innate in her nature. In the front row,
Lieutenant Grussing looked somewhat shy and uncomfortable. On
Grussing's right was Ellen Ainsworth, kneeling confidently and manag-
ing to look flirtatious despite her garb and the circumstances. Ellen was
the maverick, the flamboyant one, who always led the group and who always seemed to do things a little differently from the others. This was
probably the last time the group ever got together as one.

Shortly after arriving at their new location, the nurses of the 56th Evac received convincing evidence that digging foxholes was advisable. During
the first night, shells burst around their position, causing them to get little
sleep. Strangely, Dagit noted, the girls at first whispered, as if the sound of
a voice would attract the fire. By morning they had discovered two facts. On
looking out they realized that their location was close to the harbor. The

shells hitting the night before had been fired by the "Anzio Express," a large German railroad gun located far to the rear, which came out of a tunnel every night to shell the harbor. Colonel Blesse, always the optimist, had tried to reassure his nurses that there was nothing to be worried about. Their first experiences at Anzio had given them cause for doubt.

The hospital was not assembled all in a day. In fact it was late February, a month after the first nurses had arrived, before the last of the 56th Evac arrived at Anzio. Dagit asked them all about their experiences. Doris ("Danny") Deaver, her best friend, had elected to stay on the LCI back in Naples to take care of the sick. On arrival at Anzio, the skipper of her small ship had considered the seas too rough to land, so that contingent was sent back to Naples. Another friend, Jon Peters, said that his ship had broken in two just a few miles out of Naples. All in all, it had required five ships to move the hospital. Avis Dagit's final words in describing the journey were upbeat: "Now that all the hospital personnel were together again, we were ready to set up the hospital and care for battle casualties."

They did not have long to wait. Hardly had they set up before the first casualties of the Cisterna attack began coming in. Since the 56th Evac was the only hospital yet functioning, the doctors and nurses were overwhelmed.

Lieutenant Avis Dagit was a veteran by this time, but she was unprepared for the suffering she was about to witness:

> Wounded sprawled everywhere in all the ward tents. Seeing so many men with bloody, mangled bodies horrified me. I had barely enough room to walk between the rows of litters in the dimly lit tent. Despite the numbers, it was eerily quiet. No one complained or cried out. The men were in shock from the brutal fighting. I examined each man's wounds and wanted to cry when they thanked me for the kindness. Most quietly lit a cigarette or helped those unable to help themselves. I asked each man if he needed anything. A few with severe wounds asked only to be put to sleep.[4]

There was more to come. Sent up to Pre-op No. 1 to help mix plasma, Davit felt a scream stuck in her throat. "The smell of blood and flesh hit me," she later wrote. "There was litter after litter of wounded men. Stumps of legs were covered with blood-soaked bandages." Some of the men had parts of their faces shot away, while others had abdominal wounds. One episode etched itself into Dagit's mind:

4. Ibid., 137.

I glanced up and saw Captain Madge Teague, an anesthetist, enter the ward. She came to a young, blond soldier [who] lay under the light of a bare bulb. Beads of perspiration stood on his forehead. His face, including his lips, was deathly white. One leg, still in a combat boot, twisted at a crazy angle. Bandages covered a wound on his chest. She crouched down and gently removed the bandage. A five inch square of flesh was gone and his ribs glistened through the gaping wound. Tears streamed down my cheeks, making it difficult to continue mixing the plasma. My fifteen year old brother at home looked much like this young soldier.

"When will I go to surgery?" asked the young soldier weakly. "Will I be all right?"

"We'll get you very soon." She lay her hand tenderly on the soldier's forehead.[5]

Not everyone on the Anzio beachhead was so accepting of authority as the nurses of the 56th Evacuation Hospital. Sergeant Audie Murphy, destined to become America's most-decorated war hero, was already a veteran soldier at the age of nineteen. He had missed the Anzio landing because he had been in the hospital with malaria. Now largely recovered, he was anxious to rejoin the other men of Company "B," 15th Infantry. He had heard vague reports of the Cisterna battle, and he was in no mood to be delayed in getting back to the front.

At 3d Division Headquarters, Murphy ran into another sergeant, who had his own ideas of what Murphy should be doing. Murphy quickly sized him up as a regular army man who "throws his weight around plenty."

"Hey you!" shouted the sergeant.

"Speaking to me?"

"Who'd you think I was talking to? Unload your pack. I've got a detail for you."

"Sorry Mac, I'm going up to my outfit."

"The hell you are. This is an order."

"Oh, go bury your head in the sand."

"I'll report you," he screamed. "You'll get the book."

"Report me. Then come up to the front and get me."

"What's your name?"

"George S. Eisenhower Bradley. Rank: acting private. Serial number one billion two and a half."

---

5. Ibid., 138–39.

Refusing to show the sergeant his papers, Murphy slung his carbine over his shoulder and started up a road marked by a blue diamond, the code signal of the 15th Infantry.

On arrival at the battered farmhouse that housed the command post of Company "B," Murphy was in for a shock. The company was down to thirty-four men. His friends Kerrigan and Swope had been wounded, though not badly. Little Mike Novak was dead. Murphy felt no interest in the fact that he had been promoted to staff sergeant.

That same night, Murphy led a combat patrol behind German lines. In an undramatic way he reported back that the "Krauts" were dug in about four hundred yards to the front, that the ground could carry armor, and that the Germans had only about six tanks in the area, probably for infantry support.

Murphy then collapsed for a few hours' sleep. He found himself quaking. At first he thought it came from the malaria he was supposedly cured of. Then he concluded that it was just the cold and exhaustion.[6]

6. Audie Murphy, *To Hell and Back*, 66–74, *passim.*

BOOK FOUR

THE CRISIS

The German Attacks on the Thumb and Factory, 3-10 February, 1944

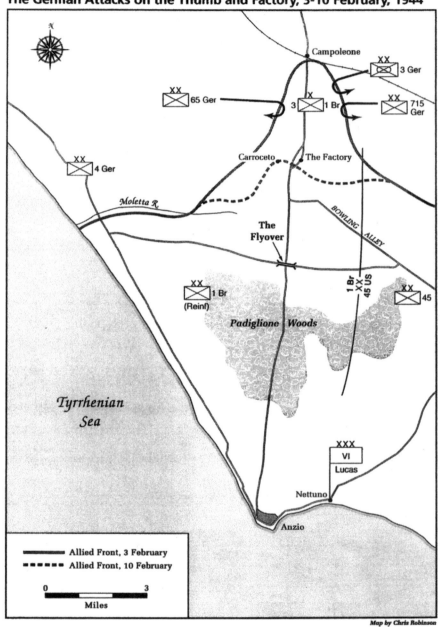

Campoleone

3 Ger

65 Ger

3   1 Br

715 Ger

4 Ger

Carroceto   The Factory

Moletta R.

The Flyover

BOWLING ALLEY

1 Br
(Reinf)

1 Br
45 US

45

Padiglione Woods

VI
Lucas

Tyrrhenian Sea

Nettuno

Anzio

Allied Front, 3 February
Allied Front, 10 February

0   3
Miles

Map by Chris Robinson

CHAPTER 15

THE LOSS OF THE FACTORY

Colonel General Eberhard von Mackensen, whose Fourteenth Army had sustained the attacks on Cisterna and Campoleone, was more elated by his successful defense than the Allies had any reason to believe. The battle had been crucial to the Germans, and the Americans had come closer to success than they realized. The force that Mackensen had built up, while stronger than the Allies had anticipated, was not quite so overwhelming as Allied intelligence had surmised. Their exaggerated estimates of German strength came from what Kesselring had called "a higgledy-piggledy jumble of units of numerous divisions." The many splinters had resulted in numerous identifications of divisions who were only partially represented on the line.[1]

The fifty-four-year-old Mackensen was by all German standards a good choice as the Fourteenth Army commander. A wounded veteran of the First World War, he had served in many responsible positions during peacetime. Like most cavalrymen, he had amalgamated into the panzer force at the beginning of the Second World War, rising in rank and prestige as a tank commander. His First Panzer Army had achieved spectacular successes in the early stages of the Russian campaign, and for his accomplishments, he had been decorated with the Knight Cross with Oak Leaves.[2] However, von Mackensen and Kesselring were no love match. They had an animosity, perhaps because Mackensen was one of those Prussians who refused to accept the Bavarian Kesselring. Mackensen,

---

1. Only a small fraction of the German 1st Parachute Division, for example, had arrived at Cisterna, whereas Truscott believed that the whole division was present.

2. In 1942, at Kharkov, the First Panzer Army had captured 128,000 prisoners, 417 tanks, 827 artillery pieces, and over 1,300 heavy infantry weapons, Web Master, Partner Side, German History, 1919–1945, 2.

however, had adjusted, like a good soldier, enduring the close supervision he received both from Kesselring and even OKW itself.[3]

By February 1, 1944, Mackensen's sizeable force had fulfilled its first mission: it had contained the Allied beachhead. His second, more difficult job, would be to lance the "abscess" that Hitler had pompously referred to in his Order of the Day of January 28.[4] Reinforcements had included the 65th and 362d Infantry Divisions, already part of the Fourteenth Army; the 715th Motorized Infantry Division from the Balkans; and four regiments from Germany, which included the prestigious and crack Infantry Demonstration Regiment, the latter on Hitler's personal orders.[5] Mackensen now had elements of fourteen divisions and two corps headquarters. Logically, he assigned a corps to conduct operations along each of the two main avenues into the beachhead. The 1st Parachute Corps, from Rome, he assigned to the British front at Campoleone, and the 76th Panzer Corps, from the Adriatic, to the Americans at Cisterna.[6]

Despite their personal differences, Kesselring and Mackensen had no difficulty in agreeing on the tactics to be used in destroying the Anzio beachhead. The main effort should be made southward along the Albano-Anzio road to the sea. Wide flanking movements would be impossible. To hit the British along the coast from the direction of Rome would subject the Germans to the devastating power of the Allied naval guns offshore. The other flank, from the east, would entail crossing the Mussolini Canal and the soggy ground, unsuitable for tanks. So the attack would begin by the reduction of the long and vulnerable British salient that reached almost to Campoleone. A continuation of that drive also required taking Aprilia, the Factory, a strongpoint on high ground that controlled all the road network in the region. Only with the Factory in German hands could Mackensen launch his final, all-out drive to Anzio. Kesselring was optimistic.

---

3. "Kesselring did not hold von Mackensen in high regard. Furthermore, von Mackensen had only been in the Anzio area since 25 January, and Kesselring thought him too pessimistic and cautious for an operation he knew would require spirit, imagination and audacity. For his part, von Mackensen viewed Kesselring as an incurable optimist, with no firm idea of the enormity of the task he was assigning to the exhausted troops of the Fourteenth Army. So poorly did the commanders get along that von Mackensen twice submitted requests for transfer; Kesselring twice turned him down flat" (Whitlock, *Rock of Anzio*, 162).

4. Morris, *Circles of Hell*, 284. He mentions, incidentally, that Hitler's order had been picked up by the Allied *Ultra*, and it provided invaluable intelligence as to the German order of battle and plans.

5. Kesselring, *Memoirs*, 194; Starr, *Salerno to the Alps*, 140.

6. Starr, *Salerno to the Alps*, 140.

Aprilia (the Factory), looking south toward Anzio. The Flyover is labeled as "First Overpass." U.S. Army.

... even taking their powerful naval guns and overpowering air superiority into consideration ... we must succeed in throwing the Allies
back into the sea. ... Penned in as they were on the low-lying, un-
healthy coast, it must have been damned unpleasant; our heavy artillery and the Luftwaffe with its numerous flak batteries alone saw to
it that even when "resting," their soldiers had no rest.

As to the timing of his attack, Kesselring was a bit indefinite. "It seemed
to me of paramount importance that we should attack as quickly as possible before the enemy had time to make good their losses. ... On the other
hand, there was the need to acclimatize our unseasoned forces."[7]

February 1, 1944, was a busy day for John Lucas. Despite the failure of
the Cisterna attack and the very limited success of the effort toward

7. Kesselring, *Memoirs,* 195.

Campoleone, he always had attack on his mind. But he was worried about his left flank, so he went to Harmon's command post to meet with him and Penney. He wanted to "see what we can do about the left flank." There they agreed that Penney would "try to advance a little" and that Harmon would help with some tank destroyers.[8] On his return to his own command post, however, Lucas encountered both of his bosses, Alexander and Clark. Clark was about to leave, but Alexander planned to stay overnight. Lucas was not happy about that development. He described Alexander as "not easy to talk to, as he knows very little of tactics as Americans understand it." He added an admission, however. "I don't understand the British very well."[9] That could be an understatement given his distaste for Penney, a feeling that Penney heartily reciprocated. ·

At that meeting, Alexander and Clark agreed that offensive action on the part of the Allies should be suspended, as reports had come in of a heavy German buildup. When he received word of that decision, Lucas was disappointed. "I hate to stop attacking," he confided to his diary. "We must keep [the German] off balance all we can."[10]

Lucas took advantage of the meeting, however, asking for a couple more divisions, which he said he could now support, That request was refused, but Frederick's Special Service Force (Devil's Brigade) was arriving, and Lucas was receiving the 168th Infantry Brigade, part of the British 56th Division. The 168th, having been fighting at Cassino, was tired, but the British 1st Division, badly depleted, could use all the reinforcement it could get.

Before attempting to seize the Factory, Mackensen had to reduce the "Thumb" at Campoleone. The attack to do so began on February 3. The skinny salient was to be reduced by the German 65th Division from the west of the Anzio-Albano Road while elements of the 3d PG Division and the 715th Infantry Division attacked from the east. In the afternoon of the 3d, the Germans bombarded the tip of the salient heavily and infiltrated a company of infantry into the position. At that point British artillery came down heavily, and the Germans withdrew. The British settled down, confident that they had repulsed a major attack.[11]

At midnight, however, German artillery came down heavily on the base of the salient, and infantry attacks soon followed. The two prongs met on

8. Lucas diary, 352–53.
9. Ibid., 353.
10. Ibid., 358.
11. Blumenson, *Gamble*, 109.

the road to Anzio, and the forward portions of the British position were isolated. Rather than give up, however, the British fought fiercely, and the German penetrations were expelled from the salient.[12]

Though the Campoleone salient was once more temporarily in friendly hands, its situation was still precarious. One of Harmon's observers informed Lucas that things were going well, but Lucas was not elated. "The whole situation is confused and uncertain," he wrote. "I am struggling to get a defensive organized that will hold in the face of an all-out effort against me. The confusing part is that the situation has changed so rapidly from offensive to defensive that I can't get my feet under me." But then one of the flashes of optimism that hit Lucas from time to time arose. "There are not enough Huns anywhere to drive us off this beach."[13] Nevertheless, Lucas ordered Penney to withdraw from the Thumb, and Penney did so gladly.

The British defense of the Thumb had been magnificent, and it was fortunate that General Penney had been able to save the bulk of the beleaguered 3d Brigade that occupied it. Nevertheless, the action had been costly. British casualties in that action alone have been estimated at 1,400 killed, wounded, and missing in action.[14]

Lucas's defensive plan visualized two phases. First, he would hold the Factory as long as possible. Though its possession was not completely necessary for the defense of the beachhead, it was very much worth fighting for. But the final line, "Lucas's Last Stand," had to be held. It was nearly identical to the Corps Beachhead Line that the VI Corps had seized back on January 24. The left flank was covered by the Moletta River; the center ran along the east-west road that provided a good defensive position, and on the right were the Mussolini Canal and the Pontine Marshes. If that line were broken, the beachhead could be cut in half, and the Allied ability even to effect an evacuation of VI Corps would be in grave doubt.

During the next three days after the evacuation of the Campoleone Thumb, Mackensen concentrated on regrouping his forces, limiting his actions to small attacks. One such attack, however, caused chagrin on the part of Lucian Truscott and his 3d Division. On orders from VI Corps, he set out to prepare two fallback positions behind the exposed line he was occupying just south of Cisterna. The last position would be part of

12. Ibid., 110.
13. Lucas diary, 360.
14. Starr, *Salerno to the Alps*, 141.

the Corps Beachhead Line—no further retreat from there could even be thought of. But between that last-ditch position and the current line of contact, he was instructed to prepare another, intermediate fallback.

With two regiments on the line, Truscott decided to assign the construction of these positions to each regiment in its own sector. On the night of February 5, during the regrouping after Campoleone, the Germans attacked the 3d Division, laying down a heavy barrage of artillery, mortar, and small-arms fire on the thinly held line of the 2d Battalion, 7th Infantry. The attack carried all the earmarks of an all-out effort. Major John A. Elterich, in a phone conversation with the regimental commander, Colonel Harry Sherman, requested permission to withdraw from his exposed position to the intermediate defense line. Elterich's description of the situation was grim: his strength was much depleted, and he was in danger of being cut off. Sherman reported to Truscott, who granted permission for the withdrawal, even though such a move forced the 30th Infantry, on his left, to withdraw also.

Truscott soon discovered that he had made a mistake. The attack on his front had been only a diversion. Accordingly, he ordered his regimental commanders to attack and regain their original positions. By daylight the main line had been restored, but Truscott resolved from then on never to allow the troops occupying front lines to construct fallback positions behind them. The 3d Division would hold the current front line as the Main Line of Resistance.[15]

Lucas, for his part, was enjoying one of his relatively optimistic periods. Though his spirits always ran high and low, he was confident at this moment, following the retreat from Campoleone, that his corps could "teach the Hun a lesson" if he attacked. The Allies might even give him a "good, stiff crack on the jaw." If he was able to do so, Lucas held the wild hope that he could do enough damage to Kesselring's forces as to "end this Italian campaign now."[16]

Lucas spent much of the day of Sunday, February 6, inspecting his front. First he went to see Frederick's Devil's Brigade, which had now occupied a defensive line along the Mussolini Canal. He then went to confer with General William Eagles, of the 45th Division. Finally he visited the

15. Truscott, *Command Missions,* 316. "Truscott relieved his fighting men of the pick-and-shovel work of setting up those extra defense lines. They were returned to their individual companies, which brought the regiments up to full strength along the front. Only the 7th Infantry, in division reserve, was concerned with construction problems with the help of the division's 10th Engineer Battalion and the VIth Corps' 39th Engineer Regiment" (Fred Sheehan, 100).
16. Lucas diary, 363.

3d Brigade of the 1st Division, where he found the British "all right," highly elated over the appearance of a hundred previously lost men from the Duke of Wellington's Regiment. On the other hand, Lucas was aware that the VI Corps was losing eight hundred men per day. Only three hundred per day were being replaced, so the net loss was five hundred. This, he admitted, gave him "great anxiety."[17]

As the lull of February 4–6 came to a close, the two sides at the Anzio beachhead were approximately equal. According to Lucas's estimate, the VI Corps had a strength of about 100,000, of which about a quarter were service troops.[18] The German forces surrounding the beachhead were about the same.[19]

By now Lucas had, in addition to the original U.S. 3d Infantry Division and the British 1st Infantry Division, the 168th brigade of the 56th Division,[20] the 45th U.S. Infantry Division, a combat command of the U.S. 1st Armored Division, the 504th Parachute Infantry Regiment, and Frederick's Devil's Brigade. The British 1st Division, with elements of the 1st Armored and the 504th Parachute Infantry attached, gritted their teeth and prepared to defend the next critical terrain feature: the Factory and the nearby town of Carroceto.

Penney's 1st Division was in very poor condition. Its units were at about 50 percent strength, and Penney knew that the challenges in the immediate future would be greater than those he had already sustained. To assist him in the defense of the Factory, he had asked Lucas to reinforce him with the two regiments of the American 45th Division that the corps commander had been holding out in reserve. Lucas refused, determined to hold onto his reserve. Furthermore, Lucas regarded the Factory, while important, as nearly incidental to the defense of the Corps Beachhead Line. The critical battle, he held, would be fought at the Flyover, where the beachhead line crossed the Albano-Anzio Road, not up at the Factory.

Lucas and Penney had long been antagonistic, starting from the days when they had been planning the Shingle landings. At that time, Penney had recorded his account of a planning meeting in something less that positive terms:

> We had about fifteen days to get ready, rehearse, and land, and I think it was a remarkable achievement. The planning technique we were

17. Ibid., 364–65.
18. Ibid., 360.
19. Morison, *Sicily–Salerno–Anzio,* 363, sets the figure at 92,000 on February 10.
20. The rest of the 56th, under General Templar, was on the way. It would take three weeks, however, to move the entire division.

subjected to was fantastic. Lucas for various good reasons was not there at the start. We assembled and the G-3 put up on a board a map giving an outline. If it was not acceptable, he pulled it down and put up another. I don't remember any conclusion and certainly no OR-DERS. Truscott, [Darby], myself, and the paratroop commander all had our say and it was a free for all.[21]

But though Penney and Lucas held each other in low regard, the two men, like Kesselring and Mackensen, agreed on tactics for the simple reason that the situation facing them was so obvious. The small rise on which both the Factory and Carroceto stood was an extremely favorable position, worth a strong effort to hold. Each town had its value. Carroceto, five hundred yards to the southwest of the Factory, sat astride the railroad and the Albano-Anzio Road, as well as an amazing network of roads running in all directions, great assets in the boggy countryside. No German force could even consider moving southward against that part of Anzio with those positions left untaken in its rear.

To defend the Factory area, Penney placed three brigades in line. On the left, in the gully area the British called wadi country, sat a low, mile-long ridge called Buonriposo Ridge, a key defensive position. On that he placed the 24 Guards Brigade (1st Bn, Irish Guards; 1st Bn, Scots Guards; and 5th Bn, Grenadier Guards). In the center, facing due north along the Albano Road, he placed the 168th Brigade (10th Bn, Royal Berkshire Regiment; 1st Bn, London Scots; and 1st Bn, London Irish Rifles). On the right he placed the 2d Brigade (6th Bn, Gordon Highlanders; 1st Bn, Loyal Regiment; and 2d Bn, North Staffordshire Regiment).[22] The 3d Brigade, which had borne the brunt of the fighting at Campoleone, was held in division reserve enjoying a well-earned rest.

To give Penney added strength, Lucas assigned one battalion from the American 45th Division, the 3d Battalion of the 157th Infantry, to hold the line of the Moletta River on Penney's extreme left.

On February 6, General Mark Clark made one of his periodic visits to the Anzio beachhead. This time he planned to stay—or at least to leave a Fifth Army presence in the area. Convinced that Lucas had been spending too much time and effort supervising the logistical aspects of the beachhead, Clark established a logistical group from Fifth Army Headquarters to take charge of supply operations. From then on, the ports

21. Penney Papers, quoted in Carlo D'Este, *Fatal Decision: Anzio and the Battle for Rome*, 108.
22. Starr, *Salerno to the Alps*, 142, 472, and 476.

of Anzio and Nettuno would not be under VI Corps, but under the authority of Clark's headquarters. This meant the transfer of the 540th Engineers, who had done such a monumental job in unloading, from Lucas to Clark. At the same time, the 540th was placed in charge of all the other units involved in unloading, such as the 10th Port Battalion.[23]

Lucas made no comment on the move in his diary; he was concerned about the attack on the Factory and Carroceto positions, which he knew was imminent. A precursor of things to come arrived in the form of an attack against the 2d Battalion, 157th Infantry, on the Moletta River. That was only a diversion, however. The main attack would begin the next evening.[24]

During the day of February 7, John Lucas's fears were given added weight by a heavy German bombardment of Anzio and Nettuno. "Anzio Annie" (or the "Anzio Express") was augmented by a group of 170 mm guns located south of the Alban Hills. On the day before, those guns had hit the Nettuno airstrip. Though the incoming fire was not pinpointed, the Nettuno-Anzio area was so congested that any round would hit a remunerative target.[25] As Lucas described it, "The ammunition dump is on fire and making a hell of a racket. I don't know what did that. An enemy shell, probably. . . . It is hard to tell what is enemy fire and what is our own stuff going up in the dump."[26]

One of the buildings hit was Lucas's own command post at Nettuno. An enemy shell that Lucas described as 90 mm went through the roof of his room during the night. Fortunately the shell was a dud. Also fortunately, Lucas had not been present when it hit.[27]

The enemy bombardment had one long-reaching effect for Lucas. In order to get his daily work done, he moved his office into one of the caves that honeycomb the ground below Nettuno. The move seemed to have a salutary effect. But the move gave the casual observer the impression that Lucas was hunkering down, even though he kept his living quarters upstairs in the building. The move was a wise decision from an operational viewpoint but bad public relations.

That night of February 7, at 9:00, Mackensen's serious attack began. Under a heavy artillery preparation on both flanks of Penney's 1st Division, the German 145th Grenadier Regiment began infiltrating up the

23. Blumenson, *Salerno to Cassino*, 395.
24. Starr, *Salerno to the Alps*, 142.
25. Ibid., 142.
26. Lucas diary, 366, dated Feb. 7, 1944.
27. Ibid. It is questionable whether the shell was 90 mm or the more common 88 mm.

gullies through the positions of the 2d Battalion, North Staffordshire Regiment of the 2d Brigade on Buonriposo Ridge. Soon the 5th Grenadier Guards and the 1st Scots Guards of the 24th Guards Brigade were also under attack. By daylight, the Buonriposo Ridge was in German hands. During the next day, the 8th, Penney made a futile attempt at a counterattack with the exhausted 3d Brigade. On the bright side, from the British point of view, three German regiments of Battle Group Graeser made little progress in attacking the 168th Brigade at the Factory from the east.[28]

The next day was not so favorable. In the early morning, four German regiments infiltrated the lines of the London Irish and the 10th Royal Berkshires of the 168th Brigade, and by early afternoon Mackensen's men held both the Factory and the lateral road that ran to the east. A counterattack by the 1st Armored Regiment of the American 1st Armored Division against Buonriposo Ridge failed.[29]

By Wednesday noon, February 10, Mackensen's I Parachute Corps and 76th Panzer Corps held all their preliminary objectives—the Factory, Buonriposo Ridge, and Carroceto. It was not for lack of Allied fire support. Both division and corps artillery, two hundred guns, fired concentrations on enemy positions, succeeding in some cases in breaking up German formations. At the same time, the Allied Air Forces of light, medium, and even heavy bombers attacked targets along the Albano Road in the rear, behind Campoleone and all the way back to Albano. Unfortunately for the Allies, the attacks were short-lived. Before mid-morning a heavy overcast forced air operations to cease. One hundred seventy-four medium and heavy bombers were forced to return to their bases without unloading their bombs.[30]

In London, Prime Minister Winston Churchill was giving vent to his frustrations over the stalemate at Anzio. Unwilling to admit that his idea had been a bad one in the first place, Churchill placed all the blame on John Lucas for failing to take the Alban Hills or at least Cisterna and Campoleone on the day of Shingle. Churchill had his own, characteristically unconventional solution to the problem: he would send Alexander from Caserta to take personal command at Anzio. When he broached the idea to Alan Brooke, the chief of the Imperial General Staff lost his temper. As a customary balance wheel to the Prime Minister, Brooke enjoyed great latitude. "Could you not," he asked, "for once trust his commanders to

---

28. Starr, *Salerno to the Alps,* 142–43.
29. Ibid., 143.
30. Ibid.

organize the Command for themselves without interfering and upsetting all the chain and sequence of Command?" Churchill for once gave in, but he did not for a moment relent in his distrust of General John Lucas.[31]

Mackensen, having taken his immediate objectives, gave Lucas and Penney a short respite, at least enough for Lucas to take action to ease the plight of the British 1st Division. On the 10th of February Lucas released his much-husbanded reserve to take position astride the Anzio-Albano road, thus moving the boundary between Eagles's 45th Division on the right and Penney's 1st Division on the left. Eagles now had responsibility for the main avenue. Penney's men, exhausted and depleted, would have a smaller, less threatened sector.[32]

Both Lucas and Penney refused to give up on the Factory, however. Lucas gave lip service to the idea of retaking it. Late in the morning of February 10, Lucas arrived at the Guards headquarters—for the first time since the fighting began, Penney sneered. Also present, besides Lucas and Penney, were William Eagles, of the 45th Division, Ernest Harmon, of the 1st Armored, and the brigade commanders of the Guards brigades and the 168th.

The informality of the meeting dismayed Penney. After being briefed on the situation, Lucas turned to Eagles and said, "OK, Bill, give 'em the works." Lucas then left.[33]

Eagles gave Mackensen's men something less than "the works." He confined his attack the next day to one regiment, Kammerer's 179th Infantry, who in turn limited the attack to the 1st Battalion. At 0630 on February 11, the battalion, aided by tanks of the 191st Tank Battalion, fought its way into the Factory, only to be driven out.[34]

It was an inadequate effort. A disgusted Lucian Truscott, watching from the sidelines, later wrote,

> General Eagles had used only one battalion, 179th Infantry, and two companies of tanks in these counterattacks. But since the Germans had taken the Factory from a force several times that strength and

---

31. Bryant, *Triumph in the West*, 149.

32. "The first step had been taken on the night of 9–10 February when the 180th Infantry under Colonel [Robert L.] Dulaney took over positions of the 2 Brigade just west of Carano. The next night the 179th Infantry under Colonel [Malcolm R.] Kammerer relieved the 168th Brigade south of the Factory. . . ." (Starr, *Salerno to the Alps*, 144).

33. Wynford Vaughan-Thomas, *Anzio*, 127. Lucas barely mentions the meeting in his diary.

34. Starr, *Salerno to the Alps*, 144.

were obviously holding the area in strength, the contingent was, of course, wholly inadequate. No less than a regiment should have been employed.[35]

Lucas and Penney had seen the picture of the 1st Division front differently. Penney, whose division was being bled unmercifully, lived in constant exasperation with Lucas's tight hold on his corps reserve. Lucas, on the other hand, saw the battle for the Thumb and Factory as only a preliminary. He was saving his strength for what he knew was coming next, Mackensen's all-out drive to cut the Anzio Beachhead in half.

35. Truscott, *Command Missions,* 317.

CHAPTER 16

THE MONASTERY

To the bone-weary, freezing GI or Tommy facing Buonriposo Ridge, the Italian campaign was limited to a circle of perhaps a couple hundred yards' radius. What that lonely soldier did not know, nor did he care, was that the ripple effect of the action he was fighting reached far-off places, to Washington and even more so to London.

In London, Prime Minister Winston Churchill's frustration over the Anzio stalemate was hardly improved by a report he had just received from General Sir Henry Maitland Wilson in Algiers. By the fourteenth day after the landing, Wilson boasted, the Allies had landed some 22,000 vehicles, of which 4,000 were supply trucks coming and going from the beachhead. Of the 18,000 vehicles permanently assigned to the Anzio force, 380 were tanks. Churchill, always annoyed by what he considered the excessive motorization of the Allied armies, penned one of his typical sardonic messages: "We must have a great superiority in chauffeurs. I am shocked that the enemy have more infantry than we."[1] "I had hoped," Churchill later wrote, "that we were hurling a wildcat onto the shore, but all we got was a stranded whale."[2]

Along with most of the British hierarchy, Churchill blamed Lucas for the lack of spectacular success, but Churchill also placed some of the blame on the shoulders of his favorite general, Sir Harold Alexander. Alex, he believed, was too reticent in his dealings with his American subordinates. On the same day he sent his message to Wilson, Churchill also wrote to Alexander:

> I have a feeling that you may have hesitated to assert your authority because you are dealing so largely with Americans. . . . You are however

1. Churchill, *Ring*, 488.
2. Ibid.

Attack of 2d New Zealand Corps, 15-18 February 1944

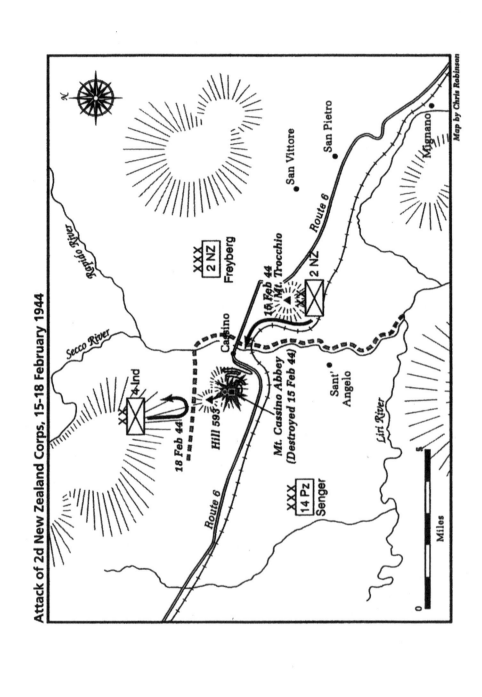

Map by Chris Robinson

quite entitled to give them orders, and I have it from the highest American authorities that it is their wish that their troops receive direct orders. They say their Army has been framed more on the Prussian lines than on the more smooth British lines, . . . Do not hesitate therefore to give orders just as you would to our own men. The Americans are very good to work with, and quite prepared to take the rough with the smooth.[3]

The message, aside from its content, is notable for the fatherly, petulant tone Churchill used in preaching to one of the highest-ranking professionals in the British Army. It illustrates the degree of control that he exerted over his military. Franklin Roosevelt would never have presumed to send a message to George Marshall or even Dwight Eisenhower in that tone.[4]

Though Churchill, in London, railed against the lack of progress at Anzio, the man on the spot in Italy was General Mark W. Clark, as commander of the Fifth Army. Not only did he have two major fronts to worry about (Anzio and Cassino), but Cassino itself broke down into tactical and diplomatic concerns.

The shock of the 36th Division's abortive attempt to cross the Rapido south of Cassino between January 20 and 22 still haunted Clark. Within a couple of days after the end of that fiasco, however, Clark had sent the other division of II Corps, the 34th, to cross the Rapido north of Cassino, as Fred Walker had previously urged. Above Cassino the river was fordable, and the 34th Division attained far better results than had the 36th. Charles Ryder's men secured a bridgehead across the Rapido and clambered up to take at least part of the ridge on which stood the Monastery. Finally, before they were eventually stopped, the 34th had reached a position only about a half mile from the building itself. The losses, however, were staggering, and the men who survived had, through exposure, lack of sleep, and sheer physical strain, become near-zombies.[5] And once they had secured that po-

3. Ibid.
4. "One of Mr. Churchill's idiosyncrasies is known to have been a temperamental allergy to orthodox military men. He became impatient when the generals pointed out the practical aspects of any scheme on which he had set his heart. He had a strong buccaneering streak in him, which tended to favour irregulars—commandos, special forces, and their like—and was quick to assume that more orthodox commanders were unnecessarily making difficulties" (Majdalany, *Cassino*, 75).
5. "I knew from the division emblem they wore on their sleeves that these men had been up in the mountains around Cassino. . . . I thought I had never seen such tired faces. It was more than the stubble of beard that told the story; it was the blank, staring eyes. The men were so tired it was like a living death. They had come from such a depth of weariness that I wondered if they would ever be able to quite make the return to the lives and thoughts they had known" (Matthew Parker, *Monte Cassino: The Hardest-Fought Battle of World War II*, 142).

sition, they were still exposed. As Majdalany puts it, "To reach [the front] they had to make a seven-mile journey obliquely across the flooded valley of the Rapido and then continue up a succession of tortuous goat tracks. Crossing the valley, they were exposed to the glare of Monastery Hill, so that in effect this valley had become a sort of premature no-man's land."[6] And still Monte Cassino remained in German hands.

The American II Corps had now been rendered temporarily ineffective by the losses incurred in the First Battle of Cassino. Its two infantry divisions, the 34th and 36th, were depleted, with the 36th in a state of near rebellion.[7] General Alexander recognized this situation and decided to bring in the 2d New Zealand Corps from the British Eighth Army. The 2d Corps, like so many other formations in the Commonwealth troops, was a mixture of nationalities. It consisted of the 2d New Zealand Division and the 4th Indian Division. Inserting it into Fifth Army was easier said than done.

Part of the problem was the personality of the commander of the corps, Lieutenant General Sir Bernard Freyberg. Freyberg was famous as a hero of the First World War, a recipient of the Victoria Cross, Britain's highest award. His name was a household word throughout the armed forces of the British Commonwealth. His status in Britain had been enhanced by the fact that he had served almost his entire career with the British Army. Had his career been exclusively with the New Zealand Army, he might have been less visible.

Freyberg appears to have suffered from no false modesty about his special status. He knew that he was more than an ordinary corps commander; he held the position of senior New Zealand commander in the theater. Britain had now come to recognize her former colonies as independent countries, so Freyberg, like any senior national commander, enjoyed the privilege of communicating directly with his home government. Alexander treated Freyberg with kid gloves, while the New Zealander seems to have felt no pressing need to reciprocate.

In early February 1944, Alexander summoned Clark and Freyberg to a conference to discuss the future employment of the 2d New Zealand Corps in a renewed offensive against Cassino. The timing of the new attack was set to take the heat off the VI Corps at Anzio, which was known to be facing a German counterattack of major proportions.

When Clark arrived at 15th Army Group Headquarters, he was surprised to discover that Alexander and Freyberg had already been work-

6. Majdalany, *Cassino,* 109–10.
7. Ibid., 108.

ing together without his knowledge. Freyberg, he learned, had already submitted recommendations to Alexander for the employment of his corps. Clark felt, as he later put it, "that 15th Army Group and Freyberg were going to tell me what to do."[8]

Clark protested this way of doing business, and Alexander, always the gentleman, accepted the protest. By the conclusion of the meeting, therefore, the three men had agreed that 2d New Zealand Corps would be placed under Clark's command and be held for the moment as a reserve at the mouth of the Liri Valley. It would be used to exploit a breakthrough in that area, which was expected to be effected by the worn-out Americans in the near future.

On February 4, as the 1st British Division at Anzio was fighting to hold Campoleone, Freyberg arrived for duty at Clark's command post. He did not ask for instructions: he laid out how he intended to move his forces, to include his artillery and other equipment. The commander of II Corps, Geoffrey Keyes, sleep-deprived and never noted for tact, became testy at Freyberg's attitude. Clark did not take sides. He admonished both men to work harmoniously and then departed, leaving "detailed" matters with his staff. In private, he later urged Keyes to recognize the need for diplomacy when dealing with British and Commonwealth officers.[9] It was a policy that he often found difficult to adhere to himself.

Back in his trailer, Clark noted that Fifth Army consisted of five corps, only two of which were American. The others were British, New Zealand, and French.[10] At that, the New Zealand Corps contained an Indian division, and one of his American corps, the VI, was a mixture of British and American.

The 2d New Zealand Corps came into formal being on that same day, February 4, 1944. It was a powerful force. Besides the 25,000-man 2d New Zealand Division and the 4th Indian Division, Clark was attaching Combat Command "B" of the 1st U.S. Armored Division, with some 180 tanks. The corps would also soon receive another division, the 78th British Infantry Division.

Two days later, on February 6, Freyberg's mission was radically changed. Recognizing the bad state of Geoffrey Keyes's two American divisions, Alexander decided that 2d New Zealand Corps could not wait

8. Clark, *Calculated Risk*, 298.

9. Ibid., 299.

10. The British 10 Corps, the 2d New Zealand Corps, and the French Expeditionary Force. Only Keyes's II US Corps was all American; Lucas's VI Corps included the British 1st Division.

for a gateway to be flung open for them; they would have to capture the gate themselves.[11] So it was. The original plan had been unrealistic in any event.

Freyberg's plan of attack, as finally worked out, was generally to follow up on the gains made by the U.S. II Corps. The 4th Indian Division was to relieve the American 34th on the Monte Cassino Ridge and continue the drive down the mountain toward the Monastery. The 2d New Zealand was to attack south of the town of Cassino, across the Rapido, and into the Liri Valley.

Both attacks were important, of course, but the main effort was that of the 2d New Zealand Division. Nobody in his right mind would send the division across the Rapido at Sant' Angelo, where the 36th had broken its back. Instead the attack was to be made farther north, right under the nose of Monte Cassino. Route 6, the main axis of advance, ran through the town of Cassino, but in order to avoid having to clear the built-up area, the 2d New Zealand was to follow the railroad line somewhat to the south of the main road. The troops would form up behind Monte Trocchio and hopefully take the enemy by surprise.

Nobody, not even the cocky New Zealanders and the highly professional men who made up the 4th Indian Division, had any illusions about the difficulty of the task ahead. When Freyberg visited Clark's chief of staff, Major General Alfred M. Gruenther, the American was in a humble mood. "I guess this is where we throw the torch to you. What do you think the chances are?"

"Not more than fifty-fifty," Freyberg answered. Both of his divisions had proud records of success, but neither had ever fought before under these appalling mountain conditions.[12]

On February 9, 1944, as the 2d New Zealand Corps was in the process of relieving the two divisions of II U.S. Corps, Freyberg came to Clark's new headquarters at Presenzano. Clark himself was at Anzio, so he was again represented by his chief of staff, Alfred Gruenther. This was the first time that Freyberg brought up the question of the Monte Cassino Abbey, which in his opinion was being used by the Germans for military purposes and should be destroyed by artillery and air attack. He did not, however, press the matter that day.

Three days later, Freyberg called Gruenther to ensure that he would receive maximum air support for the 4th Indian Division against Monastery

11. Majdalany, *Cassino,* 95.
12. Ibid., 107.

Hill. Gruenther, however, was in no position to reassure him, because the situation at Anzio was so serious that the main air effort was being directed there. Freyberg took that in good part, but when Gruenther asked what targets Freyberg wanted hit, the New Zealander retorted bluntly, "I want the convent attacked."

"The Monastery is not on our list of targets," Gruenther answered. Freyberg insisted that the Abbey had been on the list of targets he had submitted, and battle was joined.

Under normal circumstances, Fifth Army would honor any such request, but the Monastery was no ordinary target. With a large Roman Catholic population in the United States, public attention had been focused on the Benedictine Monastery for weeks. The American public were in suspense over the matter, and the bulk of the American population opposed its destruction. As a result, Clark, with Alexander's reluctant assent, had kept the Monastery off the target list that he submitted daily to the commander of the XII Tactical Air Command (12th TAC).[13]

Freyberg's insistence, however, was enough to sway Alexander, who had always considered the restraint to be "much to our detriment."[14] With the arrival of Freyberg, and the substitution of the 2d New Zealand Corps for the American II Corps at Cassino, he stiffened his position. Finally he instructed General Harding, his chief of staff, to tell Gruenther, who seems to have taken over as the pivotal American officer in the negotiations, that "General Alexander has decided that the Monastery should be bombed if General Freyberg considers it a military necessity."[15]

Gruenther, a meticulous man who during the peacetime years had been a bridge expert in the professional class, refused to give in that easily. He told Harding that General Clark did not think that the building should be bombed, and that if Freyberg had been an American commander, he (Clark) would have denied the request forthwith. Many civilians, he pointed out, had taken refuge in the building. Further, in Clark's opinion, the destruction of the building would "probably enhance its value" as a defensive position.[16]

A decision of such a magnitude as this could never be finally resolved between chiefs of staff, so when Clark flew back to his command post from Anzio on February 13, he called Alexander and went over his objections

13. The army ground force chain of command came together, as it were, at army-TAC level. There a joint operations center passed on army requests to the TAC commander, who hit what targets were possible, given weather and other operational conditions.

14. Alexander *Memoirs*, 119.

15. Clark, *Calculated Risk*, 317.

16. Ibid.

point by point, reiterating what Gruenther had said to Harding and Freyberg.

Alexander was adamant, so the bombing was approved. Clark, because of the structure of the Fifth Army—XII Tactical Air Command organization, had the unpleasant duty of giving the formal request for the bombing of the Monastery.

On that morning, Clark sat in his office studying reports from Anzio, trying to keep his mind off what was going on. Ordinarily the reports of ship damage in the Anzio harbor would have been enough to take his mind off the Monastery, but he found himself checking his watch. When the hour of 9:30 A.M. came near, he heard the hum of the engines and was surprised that a mistaken release had caused several bombs to hit near his command post. Then, in Clark's dramatic terms, "Four groups of stately Flying Fortresses passed directly overhead and later released their bombs on Monastery Hill. . . . I remained at my command post all day and tried to work."[17]

The decision had been made along national lines—British and Commonwealth troops in favor of the bombing; Americans against. To round out the picture, therefore, it is well to cite Alexander's viewpoint as he wrote it:

> When soldiers are fighting for a just cause and are prepared to suffer death and mutilation in the process, bricks and mortar, no matter how venerable, cannot be allowed to weigh against human lives. Every good commander must consider morale and feelings of his fighting men; and, what is equally important, the fighting men must know that their whole existence is in the hands of a man in whom they have complete confidence. Thus the commanding general must make it absolutely clear to his troops that they go into action under the most favourable conditions he has the power to order.
>
> In the context of the Cassino battle, how could a structure which dominated the fighting field be allowed to stand? The monastery had to be destroyed. Withal, everything was done to save the lives of the monks and their treasures; ample warning was given of the bombing.[18]

---

17. Ibid., 319. On 312 he writes, "I say that the bombing of the Abbey, which sat high on the hill southwest of Cassino, was a mistake—and I say it with the full knowledge of the controversy that has raged around this episode. The official position was best summed up, I suppose, by the State Department communication to the Vatican's Undersecretary of State on October 13, 1945, saying that 'there was unquestionable evidence in the possession of Allied commanders in the field that the Abbey of Monte Cassino formed part of the German defensive line.'"

18. Alexander. *Memoirs*, 121.

The bombing did nothing to help the Allied cause. As it turned out, the 4th Indian Division was unprepared to follow up the air bombardment of the Abbey, and it was unable to make a ground attack until February 17, two days after the bombing. When the Indians finally got under way, they were stopped short of the all-important knob called Point 593, once occupied by the American 34th Division. When they attempted to bypass Point 593, they were severely mauled by the German 1st Parachute Division troops, who had taken responsibility for defending the ruins of the Abbey. Indian casualties were estimated at six hundred.[19]

The attack by the 2d New Zealand Division across the railroad bridge south of Cassino also ended in failure. The spearheads succeeded in crossing the Rapido but were soon hit by German counterattacks supported by tanks. Unable to defend against armor, the New Zealanders pulled back to the east bank. The second battle of Cassino was over.

But not the recriminations. Blame has bounced back and forth, largely along national lines. The British and the rest of the Commonwealth blame Clark; the Americans blame Freyberg and Alexander. But all are together on one point: the destruction of the Monastery, in the long run, became a tactical detriment to the Allies. Churchill, in his memoirs, is unusually noncommittal. He justifies the air attack on the Monastery by asserting that "the enemy fortifications were hardly separate from the building itself." He gives Clark credit for attempting to avoid the bombing and is quick to point out that Alexander assumed full responsibility for the decision. He finishes off his gloomy account with a good summary:

> On February 15 therefore, after the monks had been given full warning, over four hundred and fifty tons of bombs were dropped and heavy damage was [inflicted]. The great outer walls and gateway still stood. The results were not good. The Germans had now every excuse for making whatever use they could of the rubble of the ruins, and this gave them even better opportunities for defence than when the building was intact.[20]

19. D'Este, *Fatal Decision,* 261. D'Este places the blame for the delay on Freyberg, who he claims failed "to inform his superiors of the truth for fear the bombing attack would be cancelled."

20. Churchill, *Ring,* 500.

German Attacks, 17-20 February 1944

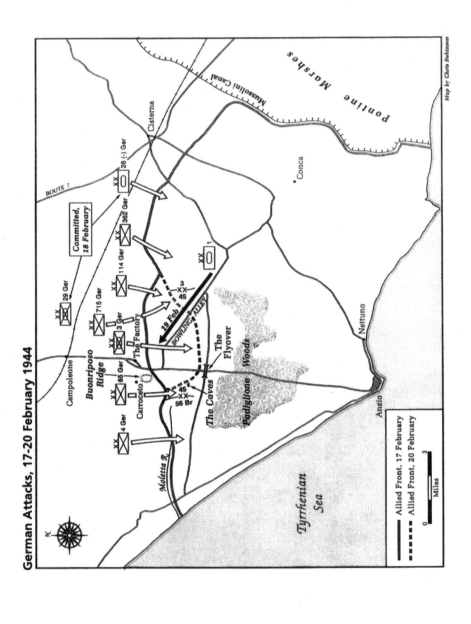

Map by Chris Robinson

CHAPTER 17

THE CRISIS

Today, Sunday, I'd like to drop you a line while I still can. You can't imagine what is going on here. I hope this letter reaches you. It will probably be one of the last. There is no escape. You are either killed or wounded or captured. All the men I came down with here are gone. It's a good thing that I arrived a little later; otherwise I would be gone too. Today or tomorrow I'll be in action too. Beyond that I can't write anything, because I am not supposed to. In my next letter I'll be able to tell you more.

Today there is at least sunshine, although it's pretty cold. And now I wish you all the best till we meet again. The bombs are falling already. It doesn't make any difference any more, for a hero's death is all that is left to me. Goodbye. Willy.

There was to be no next letter. This note was found on the body of a German soldier who had fallen near the Factory. His prediction of his own death had been borne out.

The driving force behind the all-out German attack to eliminate the Anzio beachhead was, as always, Adolf Hitler himself. It was no new phenomenon. Hitler had conceptualized and directed all the military campaigns of the war. After he had orchestrated the strategy for the defeat of the French and British in May and June of 1940, his generals no longer questioned his judgments, at least to his face. It is difficult to conjecture how far Kesselring and von Mackensen would have gone to eliminate the Anzio bridgehead had not Hitler insisted on going all out.

Despite his questionable strategic talents, Hitler was enough of a realist to allow his generals time to bring in the power necessary for an overpowering attack. His plan was to start from the Factory, once it was in

German hands, and drive southward all the way to Anzio, thus splitting the beachhead. While Mackensen was fighting to secure his jump-off line at the Factory and Carroceto, therefore, Hitler was moving heavy tanks, large field artillery pieces, railroad artillery guns, and divisions from France, northern Italy, and the Balkans.

Hitler also dictated the tactics to be employed. The attack was to be executed along a narrow front—only six kilometers wide. It was to be led by the elite Infantry Demonstration Regiment, sent from Berlin to participate as a token of Hitler's personal support. Kesselring had doubts about employing an inexperienced unit to spearhead a major effort, no matter how smart and well drilled it might be. However, he was too intelligent—and his position with Hitler too shaky—for him to protest. He did, however, always assume a share of the blame for the matter in later years.[1]

Hitler placed great store in this operation. When Kesselring's chief of staff, Westphal, went to brief him at Berchtesgaden, he observed that Hitler was full of confidence. "If the enemy could be thrown back into the sea now," Hitler pronounced, "it would be bound to have an effect on the invasion plans in the West." The Allies, Hitler hoped, would be so shaken that they would raise their requisites for a landing in northern Europe to the point that they would be unable to meet them in 1944.[2] Convoluted reasoning, perhaps, but Hitler was grasping for straws.

Evidence of the German preparations for what would obviously be a major attack caused unusual consternation among the members of the Allied command at Anzio. On the day before the expected attack, even Alexander, usually the coolest of commanders, betrayed his own anxiety by an extraordinary outburst at a press briefing. A few days earlier, three newspaper correspondents had hastily left the beachhead, and they had sought to justify their desertion by filing alarming stories predicting a forthcoming Allied disaster. They referred to "another Dunkirk," a term bound to hit the touchy Alexander. When Alexander came to the press conference, he was apparently unaware that the three offenders were not present with the group.

The general, according to Lucas, "launched into a critical discourse on the spreading of false rumors and, by inference at least, accused these men of telling the world we were in momentary danger of being driven off the beach. He was very caustic and rather bitterly sarcastic. It was evident that he was not familiar with the facts and did not realize to whom he was addressing his remarks."

1. Kesselring, *Memoirs,* 196.
2. Westphal, *German Army,* 159.

Lucas tried breaking into Alexander's tirade, but such was almost impossible. At long last he got the idea across to Alex that he was castigating the wrong men; he, Lucas, would vouch for every correspondent present. The guilty reporters were no longer at Anzio. The misunderstanding was finally corrected, but the correspondents were "deeply incensed."[3] Lucas did not take it too seriously that Alexander was nearing the end of his rope with frustration. Nor did he seem to suspect that his own role in the incident may have further jeopardized his own position with Alexander.

Mackensen set his attack for the early morning hours of February 16, 1944. It so happened that the six-kilometer zone of attack coincided almost exactly with the front being held by two Allied divisions, Templar's 56th British Infantry Division on the left (west) and Eagles's American 45th on the right (east). Of the two, the 45th was in better condition. The 56th, newly arrived from 10 Corps on the Garigliano, was tired and understrength. The 45th, due to the greater availability of American infantry replacements, was better rested and nearly up to strength. Only one of its regiments, the 179th, had even been in action at Anzio. It had failed in its halfhearted effort to retake the Factory, but it was far from depleted.

The attack began at 6:30 A.M. with an artillery duel, followed by an attack by German infantry. Nobody was in any doubt that the main effort would be made between the Factory and Anzio, though Truscott's 3d Division, facing Cisterna, had sustained six attacks the day before.

The German columns came along two roads. To the east, the Infantry Demonstration Regiment poured across to hit the American 179th Infantry. The attackers came in waves, through open country, vulnerable to Allied artillery, which fired ten times the number of rounds as did the Germans. Even at that, the front of the 179th began to waver. But then the full effects of the Allied artillery began to take its toll. By mid-afternoon, the morale of Hitler's Infantry Demonstration Regiment had collapsed. Its officers and NCOs were all casualties, and the leaderless men broke, fleeing back a full five hundred yards in confusion.[4]

In the center, along the main, hard-surfaced Albano-Anzio Road, the Germans hit the 157th RCT of the 45th Division without much effect. Farther to the west, the forward companies of the 8th Royal Fusiliers and the 7th Oxfordshire and Buckinghamshire regiments were initially overrun, but the tanks of their parent unit, the 56th Division, restored the line. At the end of the day, despite minor German penetrations of a couple of

3. Lucas diary, 378.
4. Vaughan-Thomas, *Anzio*, 159–60.

miles, Mackensen had failed to achieve a breakthrough. Kesselring now realized that destroying the Allied beachhead would be no pushover.

That night of February 16, General Lucian Truscott, in his command post at Conca, went to bed early, expecting the next day to be a full one. All in all, he was satisfied that so far the fighting had gone well. His 3d Division had repulsed all enemy attacks easily, and reports available to him indicated that German penetrations of 45th Division positions to the west had been small. True, Lucas's VI Corps staff at Nettuno displayed some anxiety, but Truscott did not share it.

Shortly after midnight, Colonel Don Carleton, Truscott's chief of staff, came in with a message. "Boss, I hate to do this," he said, "but you would give me hell if I held this until morning." Carleton was right: in his hand he held a telegram from Fifth Army to Lucas, the critical line of which read, "Major General Truscott relieved from command of Third Infantry Division and assigned as deputy commander of Sixth Corps." Brigadier General John W. O'Daniel, it added, was to assume command of the 3d Division.[5]

Truscott's first reaction was anger, principally because he had not been consulted on this move. It was not that he minded serving as deputy to Lucas, who was a friend, but their methods were different. Further, Truscott felt that Lucas was lacking in some qualities of leadership. For that reason, Truscott could not escape the suspicion that he was being used to "pull someone else's chestnuts from the fire."[6]

Truscott's real disappointment, however, was the prospect of leaving the 3d Infantry Division. He had commanded it for only a year, but what a year that had been! He had whipped the division into a superb fighting unit, partially through his innovation of speed-marching known as the "Truscott Trot." The division had landed in Sicily and had fought its way along the northern shore of that island to reach Messina hours ahead of Montgomery's Eighth Army, much to the delight of his superior, General Patton. Later his men had fought through the mountains of Italy and had made the landing at Anzio flawlessly. And Truscott had a practical misgiving. At 3d Division, he had possessed both command responsibility and authority. At VI Corps he knew he would have neither.

On reflection, however, Truscott realized that he must overcome his first reaction, understandable as it may have been. There was a war going on, and individual preferences were unimportant. Clark's decision, he told himself, had doubtless been made after careful thought. As a soldier, he would carry out his orders loyally.[7]

5. Truscott, *Command Missions*, 319.
6. Ibid., 319–20.
7. Ibid., 320.

One fact gave Truscott comfort: he had great faith in his successor at 3d Division, "Iron Mike" O'Daniel, who had been his assistant division commander. But as Truscott had virtually built the Marne Division himself in the Second World War, his name would always be associated with it.

Truscott did not rush to VI Corps Headquarters the morning of February 17. He held conferences with O'Daniel and his commanders. He then prepared, at about noon, to head for Nettuno. Before he could leave, the corps chief of staff,[8] General Keiser, called asking where he was. Carleton, who took the call, reported a tone of desperation. Keiser, he said, hoped that VI Corps would still be in existence when Truscott arrived. Apparently the situation was more serious than Truscott had surmised.[9]

When Truscott arrived at VI Corps, Lucas did not seem overly concerned with the change in command relationship. He was well aware of the move, of course, because the message from Clark had come through him. In his diary, he mentioned the matter almost casually. "Truscott is relieved of the 3d and is to be my deputy," he noted. "I think this means my relief and that he gets the corps."[10] But he wrote nothing further.

Lucas had, of course, been expecting relief almost from the day he had been assigned to command the Anzio landing. However, General Clark had informed him that he was receiving another deputy, British Major General Evelyn Everleigh, sent to help out in British-American matters. Perhaps the move did not have all that much meaning. Besides Lucas was too tired to worry, and he had a battle on his hands.

On that same Wednesday evening of February 16, General von Mackensen's headquarters realized that their troops had failed to achieve a breakthrough along the road to Anzio. However, they were confident that the American and British forces in their path were exhausted, and the Germans knew that they possessed a superiority in infantry. Against three Allied infantry and one armored division, the German Fourteenth Army had marshaled seven full divisions, three separate infantry regiments, and various independent battalions, including tank.[11] It had been easier for the Germans to build up their strength than it had been for the Allies, because their units came from all over—Italy, France,

---

8. Brigadier General Laurence B. Keiser.

9. Truscott, *Command Missions*, 320.

10. Lucas diary, 385.

11. The divisions were the Hermann Goering Panzer Division, the 26th Panzer, the 29th Panzer-Grenadier (PG), the 114th Jaeger, the 3d PG, and the 65th Infantry Division. The separate regiments included the Infantry Demonstration Unit. The German Operation at Anzio, 41.

Command Post, VI Corps, located in a wine cellar under Nettuno. U.S. Army.

and the Balkans—utilizing numerous available small roads. Allied air-power had been able to restrict German road movements to some extent, but traffic still flowed at night. The inability of the Allied Air Forces to "isolate the battlefield," as advertised, was one of the big disappointments the Allied ground commanders had to bear.[12]

Nevertheless, Mackensen had never expected his attack down the road to Anzio to be easy, despite his advantage in infantry. Obstacles along the path had to be cleared, and he respected the fighting qualities of both British and American troops, so that task would not be easy. Despite Hitler's dictum that the attack should be made on a six-kilometer front, certain terrain features had to be cleared of Allied artillery observers. The

12. Mark Clark, *Calculated Risk*, 286–87, has this to say: "A final factor upon which we counted was the belief of the Air Force that it could 'isolate' the beachhead area. . . . I might as well say right here that this didn't work. . . . [T]hroughout the campaign I saw this iso-lation theory tried out again and again, and repeatedly the enemy moved his forces by rail-road and by highway, with some difficulty to be sure, but with a great deal of effectiveness as far as the progress of the war was concerned."

first of these, on Mackensen's right (west), was the ill-named Buonriposo (Peaceful Rest) Ridge, on which he already had a foothold. A little farther down to the south, also on the west side, stood a series of hills the sides of which were honeycombed with elaborate caves, built probably during the First World War for ammunition storage. The Allies could not be permitted to retain control of that area either.

On the east of the Anzio Road, the biggest threat to Mackensen was a road the Allies called the Diagonal Road, or Bowling Alley, which ran northwestward from the town of Padiglione[13] and led to his rear, ending at Campoleone. He would have to attack or at least hold along that road to protect himself from the east.[14]

The most formidable obstacle that Mackensen would have to overcome, however, was a steep east-west embankment on the top of which ran a road and railroad track. The embankment was called the Lateral Road by the Allies, and Mackensen's advance would either have to assault its sides or drive through an overpass where the Anzio Road ran under it. The British called the overpass the "Flyover." Whether Mackensen knew it or not, the Lateral Road was the Corps Beachhead Line, which General Lucas had specified that the Allies must hold at all costs. No defensive positions lay between the Flyover and Anzio, which was only about six miles to its rear. Because of its absolutely critical importance to the Allies, the Flyover would become the scene of very heavy fighting.

Mackensen's plan could have come out of any military textbook. The bulk of his numerous divisions would be used to make a breakthrough of Allied lines. Once that occurred he would commit his two-division reserve to finish the drive to Anzio.

There was nothing casual about the selection of the units Mackensen held in reserve; they were his best. One was the 29th Panzer Grenadier Division, which he had recently acquired from Vietinghoff's Tenth Army on the Gustav Line. The other was the 26th Panzer Division, one of Senger's favorites, commanded by General Heinrich Freiherr von Luttwitz.[15] They

13. The town of Padiglione and the Padiglione Woods, where supply installations and assembly areas abounded, are six miles distant from each other.

14. It is most important that the east flank of the corps be protected from enemy tank–supported counterattacks. The 1st Battalion, 4th Panzer Regiment, will be prepared for defense against a tank attack from Padiglione, German Operation, 57.

15. Ten months later, von Luttwitz would achieve a sort of dubious fame in Hitler's Ardennes offensive known as the Battle of the Bulge. Luttwitz, having delivered a demand for surrender to the American 101st Airborne at Bastogne, would receive Brigadier General Anthony McAuliffe's famous word of defiance, "Nuts."

were to be supported by the 508th Panzer Battalion, which boasted the new Mark VI Tiger Tanks.[16]

When Mackensen committed these two divisions, it meant that he thought he had the battle won.

L loyd M. Wells, a lieutenant in the 2d Battalion, 6th Armored Infantry, 1st Armored Division, had no idea where in the world he was. He knew only that it was February 17, and that his battalion had been moved out of its assembly area in the Padiglione Woods, and that its members had made their way on foot behind a line of hills that stood on the west side of the Albano-Anzio Road. He did not know that his battalion had been attached to the 45th Division—that was much too high level a matter for a rifle platoon leader to worry about—or that during the previous two days von Mackensen's Fourteenth Army had nearly broken the lines of the 157th Infantry, which stood in its path toward Anzio. Wells was concerned only with his own situation and that of his men.

The tables of organization for an infantry platoon authorized a strength of forty enlisted men,[17] but Wells counted only fourteen. He thought back in his mind. Some of the absences could be accounted for, such as the detachment of a squad of twelve men to occupy a building out to the west. In addition, he knew he had lost several men to enemy shell fire while they were moving up into their position. One of the deaths he remembered well; the sight of it had almost paralyzed him. To the rear of the column, a man had been hit badly. When Wells checked on him, the victim was lying on his back close to death, with a great hole where his belly should have been. "It was almost completely filled with a pool of greenish tinted blood which sloshed from side to side." Some of the man's guts were strewn on the ground. Wells was sorry that he had looked.[18]

The detachment of a squad and the casualties could not, however, make up the difference, in Wells's calculation. Where, he asked Loman, his reliable platoon sergeant, were the rest? Sergeant Loman, an experienced, tough, matter-of-fact man, answered with a touch of resignation. A half-dozen men were missing, he admitted, but he believed that the platoon could do better without "them bastards." The missing men were a group you couldn't trust on guard. Loman thought, however, that the platoon still had enough men to post guard without asking the lieutenant to take

16. German Operation, 57.
17. Three squads of twelve men each, a platoon sergeant, a platoon guide, and two runners.
18. Wells, *Anzio to the Alps*, 57.

Lieutenant Lloyd M. Wells, 6th Armored Infantry, 1st Armored Division. Courtesy Mrs. Lloyd M. Wells.

a turn. Wells, though in command, was a humble man, and he would have agreed to take his turn on guard had his platoon sergeant asked him.

Wells looked around his position. Off to the left, he saw a hill that he estimated to be about five hundred yards away. That hill was supposedly occupied by the British, but nobody in the battalion, to the best of his knowledge, had actually made contact with them. His own platoon had been placed on a bleak hillock, and his left flank was wide open, inviting German infiltration. A few hundred yards to the front stood a ridge that Wells identified as Buonriposo. That ridge, he presumed, was occupied by the enemy.[19] To the right was another unknown hill, believed to be in friendly hands.

Wells's concern was hardly assuaged by a visit from Lieutenant Jarman, his company commander, who had just returned from the hospital. To Wells's many urgent questions, Jarman had no answers. All he could say was, "You know as much as I do."

Wells was getting tired of that answer but recalled that when he had earlier dropped off his detached squad, he had been forced to give the

19. Wells was only partly correct. The Germans surrounded the ridge but it took them days to clear out all of the British garrison.

same response: "You know as much as I do." To Wells that terminology was beginning to wear thin.

Within his own platoon sector, Wells enjoyed complete latitude in setting up his position. In placing his troops, he tried to recall what he had been taught in his officer candidate course at Fort Benning, Georgia. In the tactical exercises at Benning, a defensive line had always been placed on the forward slope of a hill. Wells soon discovered, however, that during daylight hours that practice was costly. Enemy gunners to his front had him and his men under constant observation. The result was heavy artillery fire. Fortunately, Wells also remembered something else from the instructors at Fort Benning: "Always learn from the enemy." So, aware of German tactical doctrine, Wells placed his main defenses on the reverse slope of the hill during the daytime, leaving only a screen on the crest. At night, he moved his men into their proper positions on the forward slope. He was glad he did.

Still Wells was disturbed by the sounds of German infantry infiltrating to the left of his position during the hours of darkness. And the incoming artillery was nearly unbearable:

> They pounded us without let up until after dark. I cursed myself for not having dug [my foxhole] deeper. Several rounds came so close they threw up great clouds of dust and rained down rocks on my unprotected back. I was so terrified I barely felt the pain. I remember urinating in an empty C ration can and waiting for a lull before daring to raise my hand and pour it over the side. . . . There was no infantry attack coming in under the barrage. . . . Apparently the [enemy] were simply trying to neutralize us while they went for the big stakes. If that was their purpose, I have to count their efforts a success. They neutralized the hell out of me.[20]

At one point, Wells decided to see for himself what unit was on that hill off to his right. Leaving Sergeant Loman in charge of the platoon, he made his way down the gentle slope in front of his position and entered one of the deep ditches the British called wadis, after similar formations in North Africa. There he passed by the bodies of at least a dozen Germans, apparently the victims of American artillery fire. Crossing a wadi, Wells made his way up the slope of the hill, shielded from any observation from Buonriposo Ridge. When he was challenged by an American sentry, he knew that he was in safe hands. He soon learned that he was in an area called the Caves, being occupied by remnants of the 2d

---

20. Wells, *Anzio to the Alps*, 65.

Battalion, 157th Infantry, 45th Division. This battalion had been in the direct path of Mackensen's spearheads on the night of the 16th, and the survivors had fallen back into this area, south of the Buonriposo.

Wells was immediately ushered into one of the caves, where he met the company commander, a young captain. The captain was on the phone with his battalion commander but interrupted the conversation to greet Wells. "How did you get here?" he asked. When Wells told him, he observed that the path Wells had followed had been beset by snipers.

The captain seemed very much in control of things. He wore the stubble of a red beard, and his eyes were red-rimmed. He looked tired, Wells noted, but in good spirits. The 2d Battalion, 157th Infantry, he said, had been cut off by the Germans from the rear, and he was unable to evacuate his casualties, a few of whom were lying quietly in the back of the captain's cave. Wells had many questions: Where was the rest of the 157th? Did he expect reinforcements? What were his orders? Where were the British, who were supposed to be on Wells's left? The captain had answers to none of these, though Wells was relieved that he did not say, "You know as much as I do."[21]

There was nothing much else to say. The captain proudly pointed out the stacks of German bodies that lay around his position, for which Wells expressed his admiration. Then they shook hands and wished each other luck. Wells was uneasy on his trip back, being now aware of the presence of snipers, but he encountered nothing.

His problem now was simply survival, for both himself and the few remaining men of his platoon.

General Lucian Truscott did not allow the title of "deputy" to deter him from exercising authority when he arrived at VI Corps. After all, he had reconciled himself to assuming this dubious position by seeing it as an opportunity to improve the procedures—and provide some leadership—at that higher echelon.

When Truscott first met with Lucas, Keiser, and the corps staff in the basement command post in Nettuno, he was struck by the defeatism of the group. On the other hand he came to realize that the situation on the Albano-Anzio Road was more serious than he had previously realized. That day, despite the formidable air support provided by the air force's Flying Fortresses, medium, and fighter bombers, the enemy had pushed the front of the 45th Division all the way back to the Corps Beachhead Line. A couple of German tanks had actually gone under the Flyover before they

---

21. Ibid., 64.

were knocked out by antitank guns. The situation was bad, but Truscott tried to convince the group that "nothing ever looked as bad on the ground as it did on a map at Headquarters." To escape the aura of "pall-like gloom,"[22] Truscott decided to see for himself. He left for the front in the mid-afternoon.

His first destination was Harmon's CP in the Padiglione Woods. He then went to visit Eagles, at the 45th Division. Both men realized the seriousness of the situation, but Truscott found neither of them to be unduly worried. Eagles had lost contact with all his frontline battalions, but he expected communications to be reestablished soon, at which time they would find the situation to be not so bad as thought. He planned a counterattack by a battalion of the 157th Infantry for the following morning, to come to the aid of the hard-pressed 179th. Truscott arranged for Harmon to support the attack with tanks. He then headed back to his trailer, which was now located near the beach. He noted wryly that this was where he had spent the first night at Anzio. A conference called by Lucas that evening concluded nothing.[23]

At the end of the day, John Lucas wrote a gloomy estimate of the situation in his diary. Typically describing his position as a "not particularly happy one," he was not much worried about the 3d Division, which he described as in good shape for the moment. The 45th was largely committed at the Flyover with just a little held in hand as a reserve to use "as a last resort." The British 1st Division he described as "so weakened from continuous battle that it was incapable of offensive action." He seemed to derive little comfort from the fact that Harmon's 1st Armored Division (two regiments of armor, one regiment of armored infantry and one reconnaissance battalion) were in good shape and "itching for a fight." The 56th British Division would require a week for rest and reorganization as it had been in action with 10 Corps.

In other words, Lucas concluded, the Germans outnumbered him about three to one in infantry. He had the advantage in medium and light artillery, and an estimated advantage of as much as about a hundred more tanks and control of the air.

Based on these facts, which did not appear too unfavorable, Lucas decided to attack. He did so for a strange reason. "The only recourse of the weaker of the two opponents," he concluded, "is to attack." The alternative was to stand still and be cut to pieces. "The German pressure," he concluded, "must be relieved."[24]

22. Truscott, *Command Missions*, 321.
23. Ibid., 322.
24. Lucas diary, 386–88.

Major General Ernest N. Harmon, commanding the U.S.
1st Armored Division. U.S. Army, Eisenhower Library.

The morning of February 18 still found the Americans and British at their last-ditch line. The brunt of the fighting had been borne by the 45th Infantry Division, and during the course of three days its accomplishments—and losses—had been such as to form the basis of its claim to the title of "Rock of Anzio."

When General Eagles had assumed responsibility for the Albano-Anzio Road from Penney's British 1st Division, he had placed all three of his regiments on line. On the right he had placed Colonel Robert Dulaney's 180th Infantry Regiment about three miles north of the town of Padiglione. In the center, just south of the Factory, he had deployed Colonel Malcolm Kammerer's 179th Infantry. On the left, between Buonriposo Ridge and the Albano-Anzio Road, he had placed Colonel John Church's 157th Infantry. Just behind Buonriposo Ridge he had placed the 2d Battalion, 6th Armored Infantry, attached to him from the 1st Armored Division.

The 45th would be in the path of three German divisions, the 715th Infantry Division on the east, the 3d Panzer Grenadier Division in the center along the Anzio Road, and the 65th Infantry Division on the west, in the wadi country, facing Buonriposo Ridge.

On the first day of the attack, it will be recalled, the German offensive had made some but not much progress. In fact the most memorable aspect of the German activity on that day was the failure of the Demonstration Regiment.

The German advances on February 17, the day that Truscott arrived at VI Corps Headquarters, had been more substantial than those of the 16th. By noon of that day, the German 3d PG Division had driven the 45th Division a couple of miles back to a line called the Dead End Road. At that point the Germans also split the 157th Infantry, driving between the 3d Battalion on the Anzio Road and the 2d Battalion to the west. The 2d Battalion dropped back to the hill mass on which its command post was already located, the area referred to as the Caves (which Lieutenant Wells visited at about this time).

The area of the Caves restricted Mackensen's room for maneuver, and if he were to continue all the way to Anzio, he would have to reduce that position. However, he had his orders as to the width of his front, and he was currently concentrating on breaking through at the Flyover. He would have to attend to the 2d Battalion, 157th Infantry, later.

The German drive continued on February 18, and for a while it appeared as if the Flyover, the critical point in the line, might be lost. For a while a single American company, "I" Company, 157th Infantry, stood alone in the path of the German drive to Anzio. General Eagles soon discovered this emergency and reinforced "I" Company with "K" and "L" Companies. This reconstructed 3d Battalion held—but barely. By now most of Eagles's battalions were down to about two hundred men, the strength of a company. Each battalion was given missions, however, as if it was at full strength. As the pugnacious Ernest Harmon saw it, "Not only our line troops but many of our officers were despondent, and, as I could readily see, at the point of cracking up."

Fortunately, Harmon was correct in another observation: If the Allies were near exhaustion, the "Germans must be tuckered too."[25] They certainly were. Even before that last attack of the 18th, the German Fourteenth Army was exhausted. Its units had been reduced to tatters, and morale was now at a dangerously low point. It had, in fact, been a

25. Harmon, *Combat Commander*, 170.

difficult decision for Mackensen to even make that attack. But perhaps he was afraid not to take the gamble.[26]

At noon of that day, February 18, General Lucas called a conference at his corps command post, a conference at which Clark and Truscott were present. At that time, Harmon, as he later wrote, proposed that his 1st Armored, which Lucas had described as "itching for a fight," should counterattack against the German east flank northwestwardly along the Diagonal Road, or Bowling Alley, toward Campoleone, in the German rear. Truscott agreed with Harmon, but Lucas opposed the attack. He should, he felt, keep his corps reserve intact for a worsening situation.[27] Over Lucas's head, however, Clark approved the attack. The 6th Armored Infantry (minus Wells's 2d Battalion) with the 3d Division's 30th Infantry and a tank battalion attached, would attack on February 19th up the Bowling Alley. At the same time, a British brigade from Templar's 56th Division, just unloading in Anzio Harbor, was to attack directly up the Albano Road from the Flyover. It soon became apparent that the British brigade could not be ready in time, but the attack by Harmon was to go ahead anyway.

That evening Lucian Truscott made an assessment of the situation facing VI Corps. He found it puzzling that with all the firepower of the Allies, including that of tanks, artillery, and airpower, there should have been any fear of their destruction from recent attacks. It occurred to him that the Allied divisions (other than the 3d) were not using their overwhelming artillery superiority efficiently. To confirm his suspicions, he checked over the ammunition expenditure reports of the heavy fighting on the 17th and discovered that a single battalion of 3d Division artillery had fired more rounds than the entire division artillery of the 45th Division, which had borne the brunt of the fighting.

Over dinner that evening Truscott discussed the problem with Colonel Carleton, who was still chief of staff of the 3d Division. The answer seemed to be that the 45th Division had lacked any system to cope with the very real problem of how to continue fire even when out of contact with frontline units. Artillery forward observers and commanders could become casualties, and wire and radio communications could be disrupted. In 3d Division, he noted, the artillery had worked out a system of laying down prearranged final protective lines based on previous registration of various

26. Whitlock, *Rock of Anzio,* 217.
27. Truscott, *Command Missions,* 323. Lucas's diary, obviously highly edited for the benefit of future historians, is always suspect, even more than most military memoirs, which generally place the writer at the center of the action.

targets. That was all well and good, but how to remedy the problem that evening?

Truscott hit upon a bizarre scheme. He instructed Carleton to contact the operations officer of 3d Division Artillery, Major Walter T. "Dutch" Kerwin, with instructions to report to corps headquarters prepared for an all-night mission. When Kerwin received the word, he was astonished but he naturally obeyed. By 10:00 P.M., according to instructions, he reported to Truscott at Nettuno.

A diplomatic problem presented itself through nobody's fault. The newly arrived corps artillery commander, Brigadier General Carl A. Baehr, was an experienced officer, dating back to the First World War, but he was unfamiliar with both the terrain of Anzio and with Truscott's methods. So Truscott did the unconventional. He put a major in charge of a task force of two, the other member of which was a brigadier general.

The incident was fresh in Trucott's memory years later. Most of the offices in the dark caverns were empty except for a few sleeping men and clerks on duty. The dim, flickering lights "gave a ghostly aspect to surroundings already eerie." He explained the problem to Baehr and Kerwin and then turned to Baehr: "General, I am confident that if we had two or three days I could handle this through normal artillery channels, but it has to be done tonight." He then asked Kerwin if he understood what Truscott meant when he said he wanted all the fires of the corps organized and coordinated as they were at 3d Division. Kerwin said he did.

"If you had the authority," Truscott went on, "could you ensure that these fires are so organized tonight—before daylight tomorrow?" Again Kerwin said he could. "Well, Major, you have that authority. You are to go to Corps Artillery and to each division. You are to examine their plans. You are to issue any orders necessary to insure that these artillery fires are organized and coordinated as I want them to be."

Truscott then turned to General Baehr. "General, your sole duty tonight is to accompany this young officer. If anyone questions his authority or any order he may issue, you are to say, 'That is the Corps Commander's order.' Do you understand?" General Baehr said he did.[28]

They made an odd couple. Thirty years of service separated the two officers, Baehr from the Class of 1909 at West Point, Kerwin from the Class of 1939. In a long and distinguished career that culminated with the position of vice chief of staff of the army, Kerwin later recalled that he had never before felt the pressure that he felt that evening.[29] But they worked together well.

28. Ibid., 325–26.
29. Interview, author with General Walter T. Kerwin, Alexandria, Virginia, Apr. 2, 2002.

At daybreak, Truscott received a phone call. It was General Baehr. At first Truscott was irritated, because he had ordered Kerwin, not Baehr, to report to him. But what Baehr said placated him. "I told Major Kerwin that I would report to you. I wanted to tell you that I have had the best lesson in artillery that I have had in thirty-five years service." Truscott felt better.

While Truscott was organizing the artillery fires on the VI Corps front, Ernest Harmon was trying to grab a couple of hours' sleep. At 2:00 A.M. the phone rang, with General Lucas at the other end. The Germans had begun a tremendous offensive at the Flyover, Lucas said, and it might be best to cancel the offensive planned for the next morning. Harmon disagreed and was able finally to secure permission to go ahead with it.[30]

Two hours later Harmon received another message, this one even more disturbing. His chief of staff informed him that a battalion of the 45th Division, for reasons unknown, was located forward of the "no-fire line." The normal artillery preparation for Harmon's attack would therefore kill some American troops. The question was, should Harmon call off the artillery? Harmon agonized. He was convinced that saving the beachhead depended on his attack, so, as he put it, "The brutal, naked choice seemed to be between the loss of some hundreds of men and the loss of many thousands." He decided to fire.[31]

The attack began at 6:30 A.M. on February 19, and by 3:30 P.M. the Germans on Harmon's front were disorganized. An hour later, Harmon's men were on their objective at the eastern end of Dead End Road. Apparently the artillery barrage that Harmon had ordered caught a full German division moving down the Bowling Alley to attack him. The German division, Harmon later claimed, had been destroyed and the Americans had taken 1,700 prisoners. Every effort had gone into the attack, including the fire of four hundred guns. Naval gunfire had played a prominent role as had two hundred medium bombers. A soldier who had been taken prisoner and had escaped reported seeing enemy dead "stacked up like cordwood." Harmon was also relieved to learn that the unit he had been told was a battalion of the 45th Division had actually been only a platoon, and not located in the spot where it had been reported.[32]

---

30. Harmon, *Combat Commander*, 170. Harmon does not specify that he actually talked with Lucas, though it would seem unlikely that such an important call would be delegated to a staff officer.

31. Ibid., 171.

32. Ibid.; Truscott, *Command Missions*, 326.

In the mid-afternoon, Truscott met with Harmon to assess the situation. The two men agreed that the attack had broken the back of Mackensen's offensive, but Harmon had lost whatever tanks could be committed in the restricted road network, and his infantry was sitting in an exposed position. Truscott therefore recommended to Lucas, who agreed, that Harmon's men be withdrawn to a position just west of Padiglione while the defenses were being reorganized.[33] Harmon, never one to hide his successes under a basket, later boasted,

> By the evening, we knew we had won our battle. What a difference a will can make! There was to be desperate fighting for another fortnight, but the frontal rush down the Albano Road was never seriously renewed after the Bowling Alley counterattack. We no longer needed to worry about being driven into the sea.[34]

33. Truscott, *Command Missions*, 326.
34. Harmon, *Combat Commander*, 172.

CHAPTER 18

TRUSCOTT TAKES COMMAND

It was easy enough for Harmon and Truscott, in writing their memoirs, to look back and say that the Anzio beachhead was no longer in danger after Harmon's attack on the Bowling Alley on February 19, 1944. But what they thought at the time of action, rather than at the time of writing, is difficult to ascertain. The same applies to the German side; at what point did von Mackensen and Kesselring really know that their attempt to push the Allies into the sea had failed?

German records say little. However, a single fact stands out. Mackensen's reserve, consisting of the 29th Panzer Grenadier Division and the 26th Panzer Division,[1] had been committed as of February 18, and even against those powerful units, the Allied lines had held firm.[2] Whatever Mackensen and Kesselring realized, however, they felt that they could not inform Hitler until they had made another effort a week later. That meant that they had to keep their troops fighting and dying. Dealing with Hitler meant a great deal of compromising with reality.

From the 19th on, Mackensen ceased trying to break through at the Flyover and turned his attention to widening his penetration to give him more space for maneuver. Extended operations toward Anzio could never be sustained with Allied Forces entrenched in positions squeezing both of his flanks.[3] But where to attack to widen the corridor? On the east, the

---

1. Kesselring, *Memoirs*, 196; also German Operation, 61.
2. German Operation, 57.
3. Truscott has this tidbit regarding the meeting of February 18: "General Clark placed his fingers on the shoulder of the salient on the map which lay before us. Then in a somewhat pontifical manner rather reminiscent of an instructor at a service school, he remarked, 'You should hold these shoulders firmly, and then counterattack against the flanks of the salient'" (*Command Missions*, 323).

Americans were obviously strong, with both the 3d Infantry Division and the 1st Armored covering that flank. So Mackensen's big hope lay to the west, where the exhausted British and a few Americans promised to be a softer target. He had already taken Buonriposo Ridge, so the next objective should be the area of the Caves to its south. It fell to a single American battalion, the 2d Battalion of the 157th Infantry, to play the role of Leonidas at Thermopylae. At all costs it had to buy time for the rest of the army to reorganize.[4]

When Mackensen's attack was launched back on February 16, the 157th Infantry had been deployed on a narrow front across the Anzio Road, in his direct path. The German 3d PG Division, it will be recalled, managed to drive a wedge between the 3d Battalion on the east and the 2d Battalion on the west. The 2d Battalion fell back along its line of communications into the area of the Caves, and had been relatively safe until the 19th, when Mackensen gave up trying to take the Flyover.

It was a strange area, as described by a participant to the historian Flint Whitlock:

> There were some six caves in all. . . . These particular caves were very large, about a normal city block long and a half a block wide and about fifteen feet high. Each cave contained maybe fifteen ten-by-twelve rooms. The cave I was in sheltered me and five other members of my company, as well as at least fifty Italian women of assorted ages, some with babies. They were all refugees from nearby Aprilia [Factory], trying to survive the bombing and shelling of both sides and so they were actually living in these caves.[5]

Since the caves were several hundred yards apart, communication between the companies was difficult, and some were unaware at first of the location of the others. When Lloyd Wells of the 6th Armored Infantry Regiment visited one company, it will be recalled, the company commander was at sea as to the situation, though he was in telephone contact with the battalion commander, Lieutenant Colonel Laurence C. Brown.[6]

Even after the situation was clarified, the position remained precarious, because the various units were not in mutual supporting positions;

4. Starr, *Salerno to the Alps,* 142. Leonidas, King of Sparta, held the vital pass of Thermopylae, in northern Greece, in 480 B.C. against the Persians under Xerxes. Leonidas and his 300 Spartans were all killed, but the time they bought allowed the main Greek Army to organize. Leonidas has been credited with saving Greece from Persian conquest.

5. Kaufman, Henry. *Vertrauensman: Man of Confidence,* 21, cited in Whitlock, *Rock of Anzio,* 211.

6. See chapter 18, 286–87, above.

the Germans were able to pick them off one by one. A German tank rolled up to the entrance of one of the caves and began firing a flamethrower. Desperately, the men responded with unlikely weapons, hand grenades and armor-piercing machine guns. The tank withdrew.

Two days later the men in the same cave were less lucky; the Germans used tear gas. Since most of the Americans had long since discarded their gas masks, the tear gas was effective. Six men surrendered, and the Germans freed three German prisoners who had been taken a few days earlier. One witness claimed that when the Italian women and their coughing children came out of the cave, hyped-up German soldiers turned machine guns on them, calling them collaborators. Their officers quickly put an end to that atrocity, so the witness said.[7]

And so it went throughout five days of siege. The battalion front, originally two thousand yards in length, was reduced to an area six hundred yards across.[8] But still the Americans held out.

On February 21, in order to give the British responsibility for a continuous front on the west, General Gerald Templar, now commanding both the 1st and 56th British Divisions,[9] sent the 2/7 Queens[10] forward to relieve Brown's 2d battalion. The move was a mistake, even in the eyes of those who were about to be relieved. Mackensen had stepped up the pressure on the western shoulder of his bulge, and the 2/7 Queens was caught in heavy fire, losing all heavy weapons and cut off from its supply train. Still the Tommies came on. Lloyd Wells, near whose area they passed, was astonished by what he saw:

We first saw the Queens in the fitful light of the flares as an almost ghostly manifestation in a column of twos coming up the road from our rear, at route step with rifles slung. . . .

Before they could reach us, a single German plane coming from the rear of their column swooped low and shoveled out antipersonnel bombs which flashed and exploded pop, pop, pop, pop down the middle of their road like a long string of firecrackers. . . . The plane was gone in a split second and the sound of firecrackers was replaced by the cries and moans of the wounded. . . .

It took some time to get things sorted out, the wounded started back and the able-bodied reorganized. The remaining British officers

7. Whitlock, *Rock of Anzio*, 240–41.
8. Starr, *Salerno to the Alps*, 162.
9. General Penney had been wounded.
10. 7th Battalion, The Queen's Royal Regiment (West Surrey). The 2 designates that this was the second such unit to be so named. Sheehan, *Anzio*, 147.

moved with cool efficiency to get the job done. They left a very few men on our hill. I have no difficulty crediting reports which conclude that the 2/7 was itself in need of relief when it got there.[11]

The 2/7 Queens, or what was left of it, reached the Caves without their equipment. The next day, Templar made an effort to send supplies and weapons to the two battalions, but the task force was beaten back. In the meantime, however, the howitzers of the 158th Field Artillery Battalion, 45th Division, wrought havoc on the attacking Germans. Mackensen's dwindling attack was broken up.

The British and American battalions fought side by side until the evening of February 22, at which time a message came through ordering Brown's 2d Battalion to turn all heavy weapons over to the British and fight their way back to friendly lines. Leaving their wounded behind with the British, Brown's battalion began its perilous journey shortly after midnight. They trudged their way in the rain in a column of companies. About halfway back to the Allied line, the battalion was ambushed by Germans firing machine guns. The 158th Artillery laid down smoke to hamper enemy observation, but the resulting miasma served only to make reorganization more difficult. The leading companies of the battalion, under Brown's direct control, stayed together as a unit; the following companies disintegrated into small groups.

Only 225 officers and men of the 2d Battalion, 157th Infantry, made it back, out of an original strength of about 1,000. Of the 225, 90 were walking wounded.[12]

Truscott, at VI Corps, was lavish in his praise. "In the annals of American wars, there are few deeds more gallant than the defense by this gallant battalion, and no unit has ever received a more richly merited Presidential citation."[13]

While the 2d Battalion of the 157th Infantry was enduring its ordeal, a personal tragedy of another sort was being played out in Nettuno. On the evening of February 22, as Brown's men were leaving the Caves, General Clark called Truscott to his quarters in the cellar of the Villa Borghese and informed him that Lucas was being relieved of the command of VI Corps. Truscott was to replace him.

Truscott protested, as he had before. He harbored no desire to replace Lucas, he said, and he feared that a change in command so soon after the

11. Wells, *Anzio to the Alps,* 69.
12. Sheehan, *Anzio,* 147–48.
13. Truscott, *Command Missions,* 327.

corps had finished its recent ordeal might be bad for morale. It could be taken as a criticism of their conduct in the recent crisis. Truscott admitted that he had hated to leave the 3d Division, but he now believed that the current arrangement was a wise one. He was willing to continue as deputy to Lucas, and he felt sure that Lucas was willing for him to do so.

Clark brushed off these arguments. The discussion was only a repetition of one they had had three days earlier, when Clark had come to Anzio to confer on Harmon's counterattack. Further, he added, the decision had already been made. He would do everything possible to avoid hurting Lucas, Clark said. He would appoint him Deputy Fifth Army Commander, at least for the time being. He had already sent for Lucas and would break the news to him. There being nothing further to do, Truscott returned to the command post and informed the staff.[14]

Lucas returned to the command post a little later, deeply hurt but bearing no rancor toward Truscott or even Clark. He blamed the British, especially Churchill, for his removal. He left Anzio the next day, telling himself that he had won "something of a victory" and consoling himself that he had commanded the finest troops in the world in their moment of danger.[15]

Lucas was only half correct in blaming British influence for his removal. Certainly his friction with Penney, who had Alexander's ear, had exerted some influence, and he was right that Churchill, fretting over the lack of quick, decisive results, was using all his influence to make Lucas a scapegoat. Furthermore, Alexander lacked direct authority to relieve an American general, and that fact placed him in an extremely awkward position.[16] But that was only part of the story.

Had Lucas's removal been based solely on his failure to push on to the Alban Hills on January 22–23, the American command, from Truscott and Clark all the way up to General Marshall, would have stuck by him. But Lucas was actually removed for his negative attitude, manifested by his reluctance to commit his reserve when doing so could be decisive. Lucas had always expected to be relieved of command, so his fate could almost

14. Ibid., 327–28.

15. Lucas diary, 395.

16. Alexander, perhaps incorrectly, claims credit for Clark's decision to remove Lucas in this way: ". . . some time was to elapse before Mark Clark could be persuaded to relinquish the services of General Lucas—in fact precisely one month. His appointment was entirely an American affair, and it would have been quite inappropriate for me to have intervened. However, at the last I brought myself to remark to Mark Clark, 'You know, the position is serious. We may be pushed back into the sea. That would be very bad for both of us—and you would certainly be relieved of your command.' This gentle injunction, I am glad to say, impelled action" (Alexander, Memoirs, 126).

be seen as a self-fulfilling prophecy. A corps of 100,000 men in a precarious situation needed positive, not negative, leadership. Even Truscott admitted that much.

Perhaps the view of the troops was best expressed by Lieutenant Lloyd Wells, who upon learning the news, reacted strongly:

> There were two items of good news that day. The best was that General Truscott had assumed command of Sixth Corps, replacing General Lucas. I never thought a change in command at that high level would mean anything to the men in the line. Generals were all alike. . . . but somehow this change was different. I shared the views of everyone around me. It was about time.[17]

By February 22, Mackensen and Kesselring knew that their hopes of destroying the Anzio beachhead were slim, but they felt obligated to make one last major effort. Accordingly, they planned another attack, the main effort of which was to be conducted against the 3d Infantry Division on the east.

The Americans had received warnings of this German attack and had made preparations for it. The members of the 3d Division did not, however, expect it to come in the strength that it did. On February 27, for example, the 3d Division intelligence report contained this confident statement:

> It can be logically assumed that the *Hermann Goering Panzer Division,* the chief elements of which have been out of the line resting for some days past, will spearhead this effort. The offensive capabilities of troops now in contact in the 3d Infantry Division sector are not believed great enough to lend much assistance to this effort.

The estimate was in error. In fact, as the 3d Division history admits, the attack that finally came on February 29 contained elements of six German divisions: the 362d Grenadier, the 26th Panzer, the 715th Infantry, the Hermann Goering, the 29th Panzer Grenadier, and the 114th Jaeger Divisions.[18] Mackensen's best, their objective was to drive the 3d Division back to the west branch of the Mussolini Canal. Despite its strength, however, the German attack failed completely. The 362d Grenadier, the 26th Panzer Division, and the Hermann Goering Panzer Parachute Division lost 361 prisoners and many dead and wounded while hardly denting the

---

17. Wells, *Anzio to the Alps,* 72. The other piece of good news was the pulverizing of the Monte Cassino Abbey.

18. Taggart, *History of the Third Infantry Division,* 131.

3d Division's defenses. A continuation on the next day was even less effective, the American effort augmented by air raids of 351 heavy bombers, a concentration even greater than that of February 17. By March 4, 1944, Kesselring and Mackensen admitted failure.[19]

The time had now come for Adolf Hitler to be informed of the failure to push the Allies into the sea. Kesselring prudently avoided taking on that unpleasant task himself. Instead he sent his chief of staff, Siegfried Westphal. He knew that if anyone could present the grim facts in such a way as to make them halfway palatable to Hitler, it would be this highly respected staff officer.[20]

Westphal, well aware of the challenge that lay before him, left Kesselring's headquarters a couple of days after the last futile attack had ground to a halt in the 3d U.S. Infantry Division sector. He flew to Hitler's luxurious headquarters at Berchtesgaden, arriving on March 6. Instantly, he was aware that his worst fears regarding Hitler's frame of mind had been realized.

Colonel General Alfred Jodl, chief of the operations staff, was reluctant to allow Westphal into Hitler's office. It was better, Jodl said, for him to speak to Hitler himself.[21] Perhaps the idea was good, at least from Westphal's viewpoint, in that Hitler had taken out at least part of his wrath on Jodl before he was admitted to his presence. Nevertheless, as Westphal was ushered into Hitler's office, he was greeted by an outburst and a demand to see the man who had been "slandering his troops."[22]

For over three hours Westphal went over the reasons why the attack to throw the Allies into the sea had failed. After five years of war, he explained, the troops had become exhausted to a frightening degree. The losses were not only in personnel; they were in equipment also. It was now impossible, with the current state of men and materiel, to really coordinate the fire of the various weapons.

Hitler interrupted Westphal's presentation frequently, but he listened. At the end, Hitler melted a bit. Showing great emotion, he admitted that he realized how great was the war-weariness that afflicted both the German populace and the *Wehrmacht*. He himself would like to bring

19. Starr, *Salerno to the Alps*, 163–64.
20. Westphal's professionalism allowed him to serve various temperamental commanders, starting with Erwin Rommel as far back as 1942 in the North African Desert. He had been described, it will be recalled, as "one of the best horses in the stable" by von Senger during the previous summer.
21. Westphal, *German Army*, 160.
22. Ibid.

about a speedy solution to the war, he said, but to do so he needed a victory. With Germany's dwindling strength, it was impossible to achieve a decisive victory on the Russian front. That was why he had so much counted on success in what he called the "Nettuno assault."

Westphal left Hitler's room with a feeling that he had "met with understanding." Field Marshal Wilhelm Keitel was impressed. Westphal had been lucky, he said. "If we old fools had said even half as much, the Führer would have had us hanged."

Nevertheless, despite Westphal's persuasiveness, Hitler decided to conduct his own investigation. He ordered twenty officers of all arms and ranks to be brought from the Italian front so he could question them about conditions in that theater. For the two days following his conference with Westphal, Hitler kept him waiting while he personally conferred with these officers, coming to the same conclusion.[23] Westphal was then permitted to return to Kesselring's headquarters.

The Anzio situation was unusual, in a way, because the stalemate caused frustration on both sides. Churchill, however, made an effort to paint his frustration in the best possible light. On February 22 he spoke before the House of Commons. After emphasizing the intensity of the fighting and the heavy German losses, he took some time to praise Alexander:

> General Alexander has probably seen more fighting against the Germans than any living British commander, unless it be General Freyberg, who is also in the fray. Alexander says the bitterness and fierceness of the fighting now going on both in the bridgehead and on the Cassino front surpasses all his previous experience. He even uses in one message to me the one word "terrific.". . . [The Allied] leaders are confident and the troops are in the highest spirit of offensive vigor.[24]

Churchill did not mention the Allied losses, including the fact that the American 3d Division was 2,400 men understrength, that the 168th Brigade of the British 56th Division stood at half-strength and the two other brigades, the British 167th and the 169th, had been reduced to one-third authorized strength.[25]

---

23. Ibid., 161.
24. *New York Times*, Feb. 23, 1944, cited in Sheehan, *Anzio*, 150.
25. Sheehan, *Anzio*, 150.

Lucian Truscott had made all the proper noises when discussing the possibility of his replacing Lucas. He was doubtless sincere, because he was a man who did not carry a burning desire for personal advancement. However, he had been in his position as deputy to Lucas for about a week when he took over, and it is inconceivable to think that he was not planning in his own mind what he would do when the inevitable occurred.

General Clark left Anzio on the morning of February 23, the day that Lucas left. Before going, however, he dropped in for a conference with Truscott. There he told of the impending attack at Cassino, to be made by Freyberg's New Zealand Corps, with II Corps out of the line for refitting. Clark had high hopes for success. He also conferred with Major General Evelyn Everleigh, who had been serving temporarily as Lucas's deputy for coordinating British affairs. Truscott was eager to keep Eveleigh in that capacity, and the British officer stayed on for a month, much to everyone's satisfaction. Clark, incidentally, noting Truscott's experience with the British Commandos earlier in the war, had every confidence that he could heal the rift with General Penney and General Templar. Truscott, as he later recalled, was not quite so optimistic.[26]

Finally Clark gave Truscott his immediate instructions. He was to reestablish the former position held by VI Corps before the German counterattack. Later he was to be prepared to attack toward Velletri and Albano in conjunction with the main thrust up the Liri Valley, which Clark seemed to think would come relatively soon.

Truscott's first decision as official corps commander involved the British. As soon as Clark had left, Templar came in to discuss the situation of his 56th Division, especially the desperate plight of the 2/7 Queens, which had been in the Caves for two nights. Templar wanted permission to withdraw it. Truscott agreed, noting ruefully that his first decision, to withdraw a unit, was not a particularly good omen.

The overall front was a broader matter than that of the 2/7 Queens, however. At this time it was obvious that the U.S. 3d Division was in far better condition than either the 45th or the 56th British Division. Truscott therefore transferred a whopping half of the 45th sector to the 3d on the east. At the same time he committed part of the reserve that Lucas had been holding out. He now placed one battalion of the 30th Infantry, 3d Division, to take over part of the sector being held by the 180th Infantry of the 45th Division. He also released the 3d Brigade of the 1st Division to take over a sector just to the east of the Flyover.

26. Truscott, *Command Missions*, 331–32.

Another high priority item was that of the VI Corps staff. In Truscott's eyes, it had not been disciplined and utilized to anything like its full potential, even though he considered many of its members to be competent officers. As is usual with a commander stepping up to a higher level of command, Truscott reached down to the 3d Division and transferred some of its members to VI Corps. First of all, he moved Colonel Don Carleton, his old chief of staff, to the corresponding position at corps. He also took the 3d Division operations officer (G-3) and the executive officer of 3d Division Artillery. "Otherwise," he wrote later, "I made no change in the Corps staff."[27] Perhaps he had not; he had replaced only the most important officers.

One item that Truscott had noticed, and that he could fix in a moment, was that of the VI Corps command post. Lucas, who seemed to feel an undue concern for safety, had moved his living quarters into the underground wine cellars of Nettuno along with the staff. To counter what Truscott considered the wrong image to the subordinate units, he moved his own office into a building above ground, including his general staff. He found a duplex house a couple of blocks away, with two apartments, one above the other. He took one of these apartments and placed Colonel Carleton in the other. But there was no reason to expose the bulk of his staff, so he left the staff departments in their caves underneath the town.[28]

One problem, a knotty one, could not be solved by Truscott on his own authority, because it involved General Clark and Fifth Army Headquarters. Earlier in the month, in an effort to get Lucas more active on the VI Corps front, Clark had established the rear boundary of the corps along a line somewhat to the north of the port area. That meant that Fifth Army troops now were responsible for the port area, the unloading of vessels, and the administration of the rear area. If Truscott had a weakness as a commander, it was of a passion to control everything he dealt with. The presence of Fifth Army troops, to whom he could issue no orders, rankled him. He also accused these rear-echelon people of excessive pessimism and lack of discipline.

Truscott had clashed with Clark over the matter soon after Truscott had taken command. He wished authority to control the port, as Lucas had at the beginning. Clark, who customarily gave Truscott everything possible, was adamant, considering it a matter of personal pride that no corps commander should give orders to Fifth Army troops.

27. Ibid., 333.
28. Ibid.

Truscott went on with his arguments. It would be one thing, he said, if Fifth Army troops at the port were commanded by a high-ranking officer, capable of making decisions on his own authority. As it was, the lieutenant colonel in charge was forced to refer back to Fifth Army for instructions on all matters of importance.

For a while, the two strong personalities stood at an impasse. As one expedient, Truscott suggested that he himself be designated as Clark's deputy in addition to his position as corps commander. Clark refused. Finally, however, Clark agreed to assign a senior officer to command his advance command post. His instructions were that he would "command these units under [Truscott's] control." Colonel L. K. Ladue soon arrived to fill that position, and he became, in reality, Truscott's staff officer. He and his successor attended all staff meetings and worked in close harmony with Truscott's staff as if they had actually been assigned to him.[29]

Those were busy days for Lucian Truscott, but the Anzio beachhead was now an established entity. Anglo-American forces had repulsed the best that Hitler had to offer. The beachhead was now under the command of the best major general the American Army could provide, and it was there to stay.

29. Ibid., 339–40.

CHAPTER 19

STALEMATE

The hardships, suffering, and death at Anzio were not confined to the frontline troops. The rear areas, except when the Germans were launching a major attack, were often considered to be more dangerous than the front. Among those installations vulnerable to bombardment from German air and artillery was the 56th Evacuation Hospital, located only a couple of miles from Nettuno. Almost immediately after the hospital had been set up, the authorities had discovered that the red crosses on the tops of the tents and buildings would never ensure safety; accordingly, all tents were dug into the ground so that only the tops could be seen from the outside.

To insure the maximum possible safety of the nurses, the hospital commander of the 56th Evac built an air raid shelter strong enough to afford reasonable protection from anything short of a direct hit. Nearly all the off-duty nurses automatically headed for the shelter when the hospital was under shell fire or aerial bombardment—which was often. One notable exception to this practice was Lieutenant Ellen Ainsworth, who was always, it seemed, disposed to do things a little differently from her colleagues. She refused to use the air raid shelter, for reasons of her own. When Avis Dagit mentioned the shelter at breakfast one morning, Ellen answered insouciantly, "I'm not going to use it. Everyone would be killed if a bomb hit that shelter. I'll take my chances elsewhere."

Ellen's luck ran out in mid-February, when the hospital had been ashore only a couple of weeks. During the height of von Mackensen's ground offensive at the Factory, the *Luftwaffe* unexplainably hit the 56th Evac with the heaviest raid that Avis Dagit ever experienced, before or after. When the alert sounded, Nurse Dagit joined the other nurses in heading for the shelter, reaching it just as the first German planes were dropping flares to guide the wave after wave of planes that followed. Antipersonnel bombs crashed around the hospital area. Inside the shelter the nurses were terrified but unharmed.

Once the raid was over, the natural relief that everyone felt soon turned to shock. A soldier appeared at the shelter shouting frantically for a doctor; Ellen Ainsworth had been hit. Two other soldiers quickly found a litter and carried the bleeding nurse to the pre-op ward. None of her colleagues would know of her condition until morning. Avis Dagit spent a nearly sleepless night. "When, O God, is this madness going to stop?" she prayed.

The next morning at breakfast, Dagit learned more about Ellen's condition. A piece of shrapnel had pierced her chest, causing a sucking wound. But the doctors and nurses held high hopes for her recovery. While being carried to the operating room, it was rumored, Ellen had taken her own blood pressure, reporting it as 130/80. Typical Ellen! Without difficulty, Avis arranged to be assigned as Ellen's nurse during the day.

When Avis's shift began, she examined Ellen's wound and noted that it appeared small. And her spirits were good, despite the nasogastric tube in her nostrils and the intravenous fluids dripping into her arm. Sensing Avis's natural concern, Ellen assured her: "Don't worry, Avis. I'm tougher than anything Jerry can throw at me." Avis felt better, even though she knew that Ellen's internal injuries were severe, with stomach contents spread throughout her lungs and abdomen. Ellen asked if anyone else had been hurt in the raid. On being assured that they had not, she whispered, "Oh thank God," and closed her eyes.

Despite her courage, however, Ellen Ainsworth lost ground every day. She lived in a state of lethargy, which was broken only when German shells hit nearby. It was difficult for Avis to tell if Ellen's drowsiness was due to heavy sedation, but there was no denying that her abdomen was swelling. Finally came an unexpected shock. When Avis and her fellow nurses started to attach some lucky charms to Ellen's dogtags, the doctor shook his head. "She might as well throw this away," he said. "She won't need it."

Four days after she had received her wound, Ellen Ainsworth's life was obviously nearing its end. Her breathing was becoming increasingly shallow and her skin was pale. In the mid-morning she tried to reach up and remove her oxygen mask. When Avis protested, Ellen rolled her eyes and took her last breath.[1]

L ife was hard and humdrum in the 56th Evac, but there was occasionally a little time for a social visit. Captain Jim Hyde, of the 69th FA

1. Schorer, *Half Acre*, 147–50 *passim*.

Battalion, on learning that the hospital was on the beachhead, determined to look up a nurse he had formed a friendship with back at Fort Chaffee months before. During a lull, he took a jeep, found the hospital, and made a date. A few nights later he drove up through the blackness to take up where he had left off.

His nurse greeted him warmly, obviously quite glad to see him. She was clad in GI trousers and combat boots, the overall effect only slightly softened by a pink sweater. They sat for a while in her tent, lit by a single lightbulb, and chatted. But the time passed quickly. Before they had a chance to finish catching up with what had happened since Chaffee, the sentry outside shouted, "Visiting hours is over!"

As Jim Hyde drove back to his unit, he was not sure whether he resented more the interruption in his social activities or the triumphant tone in the sentry's voice.[2]

By March 1, 1944, it had become clear to both sides that neither the Allies nor the Germans possessed the capacity to break the other's lines at Anzio. The Fifth Army's main preoccupation therefore turned back, at least for the moment, to the Cassino front.

Nevertheless, the calm at Anzio was only relative. Under constant bombardment from the air and from German artillery, the port was required to sustain about 100,000 men, which involved bringing in supplies, replacements, ammunition, food, and equipment. Doing so under bad weather conditions constituted a major task for both the British and American navies.

The task was made more difficult by the fact that the largest cargo ships being used by the Allies could not use the Anzio port. The main available bases in the Mediterranean were Bizerte, Algiers, Oran, and Casablanca, but cargo shipped to Anzio had to be transshipped at the closest bases, Palermo and Naples, from which smaller ships bore the burden. Each day, six LSTs made the trip from these ports to Anzio. There they followed the quick on-and-off loading procedure that had been officially disapproved at Marrakech early in January. Each week another fifteen LCTs (Landing Craft, Tank) arrived at Anzio, and every ten days a Liberty Ship arrived.[3]

Losses were heavy. During the latter part of February alone, Allied naval forces at Anzio lost three ships to German submarines and one to enemy aircraft.[4] The psychological impact on the men was severe, cooped

2. Hyde to author, Mar. 30, 2006.
3. Tomblin, *With Utmost Spirit*, 353.
4. Ibid., 355–56.

up and helpless as they were in ships vulnerable to fire they could not return. As one sailor later told a war correspondent,

> The air attacks were so frequent that the red flag denoting the presence of enemy aircraft [was] seldom taken off the halyards. There is no warning of the shells that come screaming over the beach.
>
> The nights are worse than the daytime since the explosion of shells can be seen more clearly. . . . After watching a Liberty ship hit by bombs and set afire, it tears your heart to see those ships hit at night. You realize men are in the icy water but you are afraid to light lights. Some ships do take chances to look for survivors.

Admiral Lowry was well aware of the strain his men were enduring. "Most of our Navy casualties," he later wrote, "were the result of 'nerves' or battle fatigue which took some unusual and quick turns and developed after the strain was over."[5] The Allied high command, therefore, strained every effort to knock out both the German Air Force and the heavy artillery.

The troops and sailors tended to lump all enemy guns under the nickname of "Anzio Annie" or "the Anzio Express." However, the incoming artillery shells were of all calibers.[6] And even "Anzio Annie" and the "Anzio Express," the names the troops used interchangeably, were two guns, not just one. One, which the Germans called "Leopold," was located southeast of Rome near the Ciampino Airfield. The other, which they called "Robert," was situated several miles to the south of Ciampino at Frattocchio Station.[7]

Both were railroad guns, the descendants of the long-range gun the Germans had used in the First World War to shell Paris, only modified to make them more practical.[8] The main limitation of this type of weapon was its extreme complexity. It took a skilled gun crew six to ten hours to set it up and put it in operation. To eliminate the chance of its being spotted by Allied

---

5. Ibid., 355.

6. "Wait'll old Annie opens up" [said Kerrigan to Thompson]."

"That's the big gun?" says Jacoby.

"Well," Kerrigan replies, "you wouldn't call it an air rifle. Rumor says the barrel's not more than a quarter of a mile long. The Krauts use old railroad cars for shells, and a pile driver for a ramrod. Ever hear it?"

"No."

"You will" (Murphy, *To Hell and Back*, 90).

7. D'Este, Carlo, *Fatal Decision*, 454.

8. The 75-mile range of the Paris Gun was cut in half, but the shells of the new weapons, being of 280 mm caliber, were far more deadly. They were towed by Diesel electric locomotives, and the entire unit consisted of four cars. The total shipping weight of each unit, gun and cars, was a whopping 416 tons.

aircraft, therefore, a gun had to be fired only at night or in heavy weather. So most of the shells that hit troops in the rear areas of the beachhead during the daytime were neither Anzio Annie nor the Anzio Express but guns of another caliber.[9] As the army ordnance history described it,

> Every time a shell from a long-range gun hit the Anzio beachhead, the troops blamed it on Anzio Annie, but the Germans had a formidable array of heavy artillery in addition to the railroad guns: 220 mm howitzers, 210 mm howitzers, and 170 mm guns. The 170's on surrounding hills, possessing a range of about 30,000 yards, did more damage than the railroad guns. . . . The railroad guns were freaks; but the Germans had in the 170 mm, a gun that outranged the best gun the Allies had, the 155 mm Long Tom, with a maximum range of 25,500 yards. It was at Anzio that the clamor for heavier artillery began.[10]

The Allies made every effort to knock out the railroad guns, which General Clark described as "one of the most disturbing factors about life on the beachhead." He consulted with General Urban Niblo, his ordnance officer, and with General Aaron Bradshaw, the Fifth Army antiaircraft officer. Together they devised elaborate schemes, none of which worked. The guns were damaged but never knocked out.[11] They were silenced only after the Allies captured them following the breakout from the beachhead later in the spring.

On March 15, 1944, the 2d New Zealand Corps, facing the German Gustav Line, launched another attack on the town of Cassino in an operation that came to be known as the Third Battle of Cassino. Some among the Allied ranks would have preferred a day other than the Ides of March, but the date had not been chosen as a calculation. It had resulted from delays of nearly two weeks due to abominable weather that precluded the use of heavy bombers in what was designed to be the heaviest close air support of ground troops by air force support in history. Every day, on twenty-four-hour alert, the New Zealanders and Indians had picked up radio signals hoping to get word that "Bradman batting tomorrow,"[12] but every day up to the middle of March the message had

9. D'Este, *Fatal Decision*, 454–56.
10. Lida Mayo, *The Ordnance Department: On Beachhead and Battlefront* (Washington, D.C.: 1968), 200–201, cited in d'Este, *Fatal Decision*, 455–46.
11. Clark, *Calculated Risk*, 323–24.
12. Sir Donald Bradman, a famed cricket star of Australia, was known to all New Zealanders. Fred Majdalany, however, viewed the use of his name sniffingly, because the troops involved were New Zealanders, not Australians.

been negative. During that time of waiting, the 6th Brigade of the 2d New Zealand Division had lost 263 men, and the Indian Division had lost about an equal number.[13]

The amount of tonnage in bombs and artillery shells to be placed on the small town of Cassino, by now a ruin only about a mile square, was astounding. Admittedly, some of the tonnage was to be used on German positions on Monte Cassino, but the lion's share was reserved for the town itself.

The Germans were confined to fixed positions and could not maneuver. General Freyberg, therefore, could attack Cassino from any direction he wished; the enemy was powerless to interfere. For this attack, he planned to employ his two divisions abreast, the 2d New Zealand on the right and the 4th Indian on the left. The attack was to be made on a remarkably narrow frontage; the roads followed by the two divisions were only a hundred yards apart.

The 2d New Zealand was supposed to make the initial breakthrough. It was to hit Cassino from the north, send some of the 6th Brigade partway up Monte Cassino to take Castle Hill and continue on south to meet Highway 6, on the all-important western bank of Rapido. The 4th Indian was to follow the 2d New Zealand, relieve its units on the side of the mountain, and continue up across the hairpin turns of the road to attack the Monte Cassino Abbey itself. The British 78th Division, fresh from the less active Adriatic front, was to follow the other two divisions as corps reserve.

On the afternoon of March 14, the magic message came through: "Bradman batting tomorrow." All was placed in readiness.

General Mark Clark, like many others, was not overly optimistic about the prospects for the attack, the chances for success being about even, he calculated. And even the aggressive Freyberg, in reporting to Alexander, quoted the words of General Thomas Wolfe just before he assaulted Quebec in 1758, "I am faced with a choice of difficulties."[14] Still, the attack had to go on.

After receiving word of the attack, Clark lost no time in heading for Freyberg's headquarters near San Pietro. Arriving early on the morning of the 15th, he found that Alexander was also present, along with General Ira Eaker, commanding the Allied Air Forces in the Mediterranean. All the top commanders were thus together, both ground and air force.[15] From

13. Majdalany, *Cassino*, 168.
14. Ibid., 165.
15. General Ira Eaker, former commander of United States Air Forces in London, had been sent to the Mediterranean on the arrival of Air Chief Marshal Sir Arthur Tedder, deputy to General Eisenhower for Overlord and Eisenhower's chief airman.

Freyberg's main headquarters the party drove forward to an old stone house at Cervaro, on top of Monte Porchio. There they could see Cassino, only three miles off. Ironically, all those high-ranking officers could do nothing to affect the battle they were about to witness below.

At 8:30 A.M., the first wave of Allied bombers appeared over Cassino, and the B-17 Flying Fortresses dropped their loads with great accuracy, causing the heart of Cassino, as Clark later described it, to "go up in sharp, stabbing flames of orange, followed by a great eruption of smoke and debris." Wave after wave came over, each dropping its lethal packages. All in all, the Fortresses dropped 1,320 tons of bombs on Cassino in attacks that went on until noontime. Unfortunately, some bombs hit short of their targets. One bomb hit a New Zealand artillery battery, killing several men.[16]

After the last of the bombers had passed, Allied artillery began a series of barrages. In the space of two hours, Allied guns of all calibers fired a total of 200,000 rounds. Under the cover of the artillery, the 6th New Zealand Brigade, with the 19th New Zealand Armoured Regiment in support, moved into town.

They were too late. Even the stupendous bombardment had failed to wipe out the German defenders, nor did it destroy their morale. Certainly the effects on such German troops as were caught in exposed positions had been devastating; two companies of paratroopers were reportedly wiped out in one location. The bulk of the German defenders, however, had previously taken refuge in steel-and-concrete pillboxes and even caves. When the New Zealanders arrived, the Germans were ready for them.[17]

The fighting went slowly, impeded by heavy rains that same evening of March 15. It took three days for the New Zealanders to take two-thirds of the town, but they kept on pressing. At a certain point, according to plan, the 1st Battalion of the 9th Gurkha Regiment, of the 4th Indian Division, passed through the New Zealanders and made their way up the hill toward the Monastery. They were stopped after taking Hangman's Hill, three hundred yards short of their objective. German counterattacks effectively cut them off. The Allies resorted to supply by air, but most of the tonnage fell into enemy hands. The situation, Clark later recorded ruefully, was "not encouraging."[18]

By March 20, five days after the attack began, General Alexander held a conference at Caserta to decide what to do next in the light of the slow progress at Cassino. At that time, he disclosed his decision to shift the

16. Clark, *Calculated Risk,* 330.
17. Ibid., 330–31.
18. Ibid., 331.

boundary between the Fifth Army on the left and the British Eighth Arm. on the right. The Eighth Army was to be given responsibility for the Liri Valley, while the Fifth would be concentrated on the Tyrrhenian coast, along Route 7. As to Cassino, the issue remained in doubt.

The next morning, a pessimistic Clark drove up to Freyberg's head-quarters. There he found Freyberg grim but optimistic. Further progress of only a few hundred yards, on both the town and Monastery Hill, Freyberg insisted, would mean success. Reluctantly Clark acceded.[19] The attack was resumed two days later, on March 22, and once more the New Zealanders and Indians failed to break through. Clark later summarized the Third Battle of Cassino in frank terms: "From March 15 to 23, the New Zealand Corps suffered 1,594 casualties. It had killed many Germans, but in terms of progress we were still looking at the battered ridges of Monte Cassino, and it still barred our road to Rome."[20]

Back at Anzio, the 2d Battalion, 6th Armored Infantry Regiment, was headed once more from its reserve position in the Padiglione Woods to the front lines. Its members knew nothing of the Third Battle of Cassino, which was going on many miles away; all they knew was that they were leaving a comfortable rest area and heading back into the face of danger.

To Lieutenant Lloyd Wells, of Company "B," however, the conditions of the battalion's employment were greatly improved over those they had undergone during the harrowing weeks of February, just south of Buonriposo Ridge. The situation was now quieted down to defensive war-fare and, more important, the battalion knew where it was going and what it was supposed to do. The front line was continuous, which meant that the battalion's rear would be safe—no more German infiltration to sur-round the battalion.

This time the officers of the battalion were afforded an opportunity to look over the ground during daylight. On the morning before they were scheduled to relieve a battalion from the 45th Division, Wells and the other platoon leaders of "B" Company took a jeep up the Albano Road and then turned right to reconnoiter their future position, which was just east of the Flyover. A short distance behind the lines they dismounted and went on foot most of the way up. In the last few yards they crawled on their bellies.

The position appeared strong. The ground in front of the battalion looked "deceptively flat" except for the outline of the Alban Hills in the far

---

19. Clark quotes himself as saying to Freyberg, "I think you and the Boche are both groggy" (*Calculated Risk*, 332).

20. Ibid., 333.

distance. The area was nearly devoid of trees, but even that early in the spring splotches of green were appearing in various spots. Wells would bet ten to one that the isolated stone farmhouses scattered through the area were occupied by Germans. Off to the left front they could see the Factory—or what was left of it.

Wells and the others were allowed only a brief moment to study the ground. Their presence was almost immediately picked up by a German observer, and soon a shell from an 88 mm gun hit near them. A second round confirmed that the shot had been nothing random. In a moment, the Americans were trying to sneak back to their partially concealed jeep, chased by the explosions of incoming rounds at their heels. There was no doubt about it, Wells thought; they were a very specific target.[21]

That night the company hiked up the Albano Road in darkness—no talking, no smoking—and were guided into their position. Here they found a situation far different from that of their previous experience. In place of individual foxholes, the platoon would occupy a continuous trench that much resembled those the doughboys had carved out of the earth during the First World War. It was possible, Wells observed, for a man to walk almost the entire length of the platoon position without the need to bend over. Spaced along the trench were dugouts providing over-head cover from rain (not enemy shells), each of which housed three or four men. At least, Wells observed, the proximity of comrades spared the men the terrible loneliness that came with individual foxholes.[22]

The company position being established by the previously prepared trench line, Wells had no responsibility for deploying his squads. At the outset, Wells's platoon was placed in the "support line," a position be-tween and slightly behind the two frontline platoons. Being in company reserve, though it sounded good, did not mean that his platoon was ac-tually safer than the other platoons. All three were subject to direct German observation. There were advantages and disadvantages to both situations. The frontline platoons supplied the men for the combat patrols and were in greater danger from aggressive German probes at night. The support platoon, on the other hand, was charged with the onerous task of hauling up supplies—food, ammunition, and the heavy barbed wire being used to improve the position. The presence of the barbed wire meant that, for the moment at least, the high command had no intention of continu-ing the attack northward. All in all, Wells thought, most men held up pretty well.

21. Wells, *Anzio to the Alps*, 76–77.
22. Ibid., 82.

As always, Wells relied heavily on his platoon sergeant, Sergeant Loman. A professional soldier to the core, Loman was a great admirer of the German soldier. He was favorably impressed with the way the Germans made themselves comfortable without exposing themselves to unnecessary danger. Wells quoted him with a touch of amusement:

> Take a wet night [Loman once said]. Old *Tedeschi*'ll build hisself up a big farh to get warm and dry out. You come in on 'im, he'll grab 'is gun and shoot your ass off. Then he'll go back to his fahr. We jest set around shiverin' and frostin' our balls.[23]

By and large, despite the exposure of the company position and the danger in conducting night reconnaissance patrols, the casualties among Wells's men were relatively light. "One day in the trenches," he later wrote, "was pretty much like all the others. Once again the calendar lost significance. . . . We couldn't even keep an accurate account of how many days we had been in the line." Eventually, however, the 2d Battalion was relieved by the Irish Guards. When the men of the 2d Battalion dropped their packs back in the Padiglione Woods, April had arrived and with it the first touches of spring. Wells's outfit then returned to something approaching garrison duty in the now-familiar reserve area.

If there was anything approaching levity at the Anzio operation, it was to be found in the unconventional approach to war exhibited by the First Special Service Force (FSSF), commanded by Brigadier General Robert Frederick. Though trained especially for mountain warfare, the so-called Devil's Brigade[24] quickly adapted to fighting in the flat country of the Pontine Marshes. There they kept the enemy off balance.

The brigade took charge of the right flank of the Anzio bridgehead in early February, relieving the 39th Engineer Combat Regiment,[25] which had succeeded the 504th Parachute Infantry in the area. The sector ran along the Mussolini Canal from the Tyrrhenian Coast northward to the point where the western branch of the canal joined the eastern, a distance of some eight miles. The men of the brigade took pride in the fact that they had been entrusted to defend about a quarter of the entire beachhead perimeter, which came to only about thirty-two miles. With a total

23. Ibid., 83. "*Tedeschi*" was the name the 1st Armored used in referring to the German enemy, much like "Joe Chink" referred to the enemy in the later Korean war.
24. The nickname apparently derived from the Germans' referring to the men of the brigade as "black devils," owing to their habit of blacking their faces when on night patrols.
25. The 39th Engineers had a strength between double and triple that of the FSSF.

strength of 1,165 officers and men available for duty, that meant that each man, if the brigade were stretched out in a single line, would be covering about twelve yards.[26]

Even the Devil's Brigade needed artillery support, and that task fell to the 69th Armored Field Artillery Battalion, of which Captain Jim Hyde was the communications officer. Hyde had his work cut out for him in running wire among a motley collection of tanks, tank destroyers, and howitzers. The equipment he had on hand was designed for eighteen guns; Hyde used it to connect fifty. He found the role of Frederick's men somewhat ironic. "Here was a super elite force," he wrote later, "trained for mountain warfare . . . deployed on the flattest of terrain in a fixed defensive position."

The fire direction center of the 69th was located about a mile behind the Mussolini Canal in one of the stone houses distributed through the area. "Occupants were not evicted," Hyde recalls, "but were forced to cram themselves in the remaining rooms. I still have a vivid picture of a toothless grandmother busy cooking a meal on the stove, a few feet away, as fire direction center personnel worked on an enormous kitchen table to concentrate the fire of our eighteen guns on an all-out German attack several miles away."[27]

The Devil's Brigade was a tough, elite unit, no doubt about that. But no sensible corps commander would assign it such a frontage if the area of the Pontine Marshes had been a logical place for either the Allies or the Germans to make a major attack. But it was not. A glance at the map should suffice to convince anyone to write it off as an area for a major attack—both sides recognized as much. The sector, therefore, was a "quiet" one, resembling the St. Mihiel sector of the First World War before the American offensive was launched there in September of 1918. Such an area offered the men of the brigade an opportunity to put its audacious side forward—which they did.

When the brigade assumed responsibility for its new sector, it was quickly obvious to everyone, from Frederick on down, that merely holding the line of the canal would never do. Certainly the waterway itself was a formidable obstacle, with steep banks and swift current, but if the enemy were allowed to occupy the entire east bank, he could shoot across the narrow canal into the already restricted area of the Anzio beachhead. So the brigade, making use of the five bridges that provided crossings in

26. Robert D. Burhans, *The First Special Service Force: A History of the North Americans, 1942–1944*, 166.
27. Hyde to author, Mar. 30, 2006.

that eight miles, initiated a program of patrolling so aggressive that the Germans prudently withdrew from the banks and established their main battle position along a line between one and two miles back. A space of no-man's-land developed between the two antagonists.

The main target for the brigade's patrolling was the small town of Littoria, which stood about three miles east of the canal. It served as an outpost for both sides, with neither the Americans nor the Germans occupying it permanently. In general, the Germans occupied it during the daytime and the Forcemen during the nighttime hours. It was the scene of many a battle between patrols. Throughout the area were a series of smaller towns, some of them of only a few houses. One of them became famous because the Forcemen actually occupied it permanently, attracting the attention of the American press.

The Italian name of the town was Sabortino, and it was located across the canal, in the southern part of no-man's-land, almost at the coast. When a platoon entered it, found it empty, and decided to set up housekeeping there, its members quickly named it Gusville, after their lieutenant, Graham "Gus" Heilman, a colorful character admirably cut out for the swashbuckling role he was playing. The Italian name of the town was far too complicated for the men of the Devil's Brigade.

Gus Heilman, a big strapping man, was already something of a legend, even among this group of Canadian-American roughnecks. He was not an enthusiastic soldier; he had, in fact, done everything legally possible to avoid service in the army. His reasoning made sense, at least to him. As of 1941, Gus was a varsity football player at the University of Virginia, and to defray some of his expenses, he had established a bar in nearby Charlottesville, which he had named the Cavalier Bar and which had turned a tidy profit. The Cavalier, with its reasonable prices, was popular in town, but the local draft board rejected Heilman's argument that closing it down would be detrimental to civilian morale. Losing that fight, he retained ownership of the Cavalier for some time after being called into service, but eventually he gave up and sold it at a loss. He was accepted in officers' candidate school at Fort Benning but was obviously failing when a recruiter from the FSSB came to his rescue. It was not so much dread of service in the military that made Gus Heilman a reluctant soldier; it was the anguish of having to sell the Cavalier bar.[28]

Here in Gusville, Lieutenant Heilman lost little time in setting up another bar. He stocked it with wines and other liquors that his platoon had

28. Adelman and Walton, *Devil's Brigade*, 75–78 *passim*.

stolen from the Germans. He also appointed town officials and even established a small newspaper. His novel community soon caught the attention of a reporter from the *Stars and Stripes*, the army newspaper:

> On the surface, this fantastic community appears to be just a collection of huts and tents and a few buildings; the home of cows, chickens, horses, and a few pigs. But it is also the home of sudden death—for Gusville is the base used by our reckless Anzio Commandos whose motto is, "Killing is our Business."
>
> And these night raiders are not lacking in civic enterprise. They issue their own newspaper, the *Gusville Herald-Tribune*, so that the troops in town can follow the war outside the beachhead, and they have given picturesque names to their town's two streets—for example, "Tank Street," so named because a Nazi tank has a habit of moving forward at frequent intervals and pumping lead down their thoroughfare. . . . Gusville's existence as a community will be short-lived, but she needs no chamber of commerce. Her reputation is being assured by the deeds of her citizens.[29]

Gusville provided only a fraction of the lore that surrounded the deeds of the Devil's Brigade at Anzio. Tales of their exploits circulated around the Allied troops and provided a touch of humor. At the same time, the Forcemen caused consternation among their German adversaries, consternation not really justified by the facts. For the strength of the Germans facing the brigade was very little more than that of the brigade itself—possibly a little less.[30] But the Germans, puzzled because captured Forcemen refused to talk, estimated the brigade's strength as that of a division.[31] As a result, Mackensen kept a couple of units in reserve behind the Pontine Marshes, units that might have been employed elsewhere.[32]

The members of the 56th Evacuation Hospital, having received more than their share of air strikes and artillery fire, were showing signs of real fatigue. Various incidents, some of them small, were getting on their nerves.

29. Ibid., 164. The *Stars and Stripes* article failed to mention the name of the other street of the town, "Prostitute Avenue," because a man walking down it would find himself "without visible means of support."

30. Burhans, *First Special Service Force*, 170, places the strength of the Hermann Goering troops on the brigades' front at 1,250 men.

31. Ibid., 185.

32. Ibid., 170.

One such incident involved a pickup baseball game in late March, organized as a lark with the arrival of milder weather. No sooner had the two teams gathered in the flat area near the hospital than the mellifluous voice of Axis Sally, a German propagandist, came on with her radio broadcast: "Hello fellas of the 56th Evac. I hope you're enjoying your ball game and your camp." Almost immediately the artillery shells started coming in.[33] There was no doubt that the enemy was able to watch every detail of the hospital's daily life.

Another incident at about that time could have had more dire consequences. The hospital was notified that General Clark intended to pay a personal visit. That visit, of course, meant a great deal of sprucing up; the general must never see the hospital in its normal state. But upon his arrival on March 29, he was greeted by a red alert and an air raid. Then again came Axis Sally's broadcast. To everyone's chagrin, she "gave a report of the day's activities and accurately named those involved." That night, the *Luftwaffe* launched one of its heaviest air raids on the 56th Evac.[34]

A week later, on April 6, Axis Sally brought welcome news to the 56th Evac: "Happy days are here again for the 56th Evac," she said. "You'll soon be leaving the beachhead, and I'm dedicating my program to you as a parting gift."

A dumbfounded Lieutenant Dagit was perplexed. Could it be true? Confirmation soon came. The hospital would be leaving the following Sunday, Easter. It was admitting no more patients as of that very evening.

When relieved by the 38th Evacuation Hospital on schedule, Avis Dagit envied the high spirits and fresh look of its members. Conscious of the fact that she herself had lost twenty pounds during her two and a half months at Anzio, she still felt regret at having to leave some of the patients behind. As the truck carrying the nurses passed the cemetery, Avis Dagit gave a short prayer for the friends, including Ellen Ainsworth, whom she had left behind.[35]

As the month of April passed, it was becoming obvious to everyone that their period of relative quiet was about to come to an end. Lloyd Wells, the great observer, recorded the atmosphere:

> By the middle of April a constant cascade of men and materiel added to the noise level and threatened to inundate the already congested

33. Schorer, *Half Acre*, 165.
34. Ibid., 163.
35. Ibid., 168–70, *passim*.

beachhead. New divisions, parts of divisions and assorted other units flowed in to prepare for the breakout. The remainder of our division which had been kept on the southern front until late in the game rejoined us at this time.[36]

It did not require an observer of Wells's stature to realize that the end of the stalemate was near.

36. Wells, *Anzio to the Alps*, 90. One combat command of the 1st Armored Division, it will be recalled, had been held behind to fight at Cassino.

BOOK FIVE

BREAKOUT
AND THE CAPTURE
OF ROME

CHAPTER 20

PLANNING DIADEM

During the month of April 1944, as the men and women of the Italian campaign were enjoying a relative lull in the heavy fighting, two of their commanders, one American and one German, were ordered home for consultations. Mark Clark and Frido von Senger, opponents on the Rapido, left Italy at about the middle of the month. Both were scheduled to pay calls on their respective heads of government. Clark was to visit Roosevelt, and Senger was to visit Hitler.

Clark's trip to Washington was upbeat all the way. He was traveling first class, under specific orders from General Marshall, who was anxious to receive a firsthand report on the situation in Italy. Marshall was particularly interested in Clark's assessment of the chances that the Allies in Italy might take Rome before the launching of Overlord, the cross-Channel attack, in early June.[1] Despite the somewhat disappointing results of the fighting in Italy so far, Clark was returning as a conquering hero.

Clark's experience in the United States demonstrated dramatically the extent to which the American military could call on the civilian sector for all its needs in time of war. Since General Marshall desired that Clark's visit be kept secret, Clark's movements were highly restricted. His plane landed secretly in Washington at 3:00 A.M., April 16, and on hand waiting was a representative of Marshall accompanied by Clark's wife, Maurine. The newly reunited couple had no chance to visit, however, because they were taken directly to the chief of staff's home, Quarters Number One, at Fort Myer.

---

1. Clark, *Calculated Risk,* 336. Although the exact date of Operation Overlord could not be decided until the last minute, it was no secret in Allied circles that it would come in early June. All planning, especially the allocation of landing craft, hinged on the date of the Normandy invasion.

After a couple of days the two Clarks, joined by Clark's mother, were flown to the Greenbrier Hotel at White Sulphur Springs, West Virginia, which the army had taken over as a hospital but also as a rest area.[2]

During their stay at the Greenbrier, Clark was flown to South Carolina for a brief call on President Franklin Roosevelt. Though that visit was short, Clark left feeling ebullient. He was amazed, he later wrote, at the grasp the President demonstrated on the details of the Italian campaign.[3] Back in Washington, Clark was guest of honor at a small dinner at a restaurant the army had hired for the evening. Marshall reluctantly allowed Clark and his wife to stay at the Kennedy-Warren Apartment on Connecticut Avenue, but they were required to come and go through the service entrance, where a security agent was temporarily acting as the elevator operator. Clark returned to Italy without more than a few people learning that he had been home in the United States. Before he boarded his plane, Mrs. Marshall gave him a couple of packages for her two sons, both of whom were serving in Italy.[4]

Frido von Senger's experience was very different from that of Clark. Apparently under little pressure to reach Hitler's headquarters at Berchtesgaden, he left Cassino by car on April 17. He drove up the boot of Italy and crossed the Alps, stopping at spots of aesthetic interest along the way.

The official purpose of Senger's visit to Berchtesgaden was to afford Hitler a chance to decorate him with Oak Leaves of the Knight's Cross, a high award. He surmised, however, that the reason for his visit was something else. His decoration, he observed, had been given out so freely that it no longer was coveted. Its presentation could never justify his leaving the front.[5]

At the decoration ceremony, Senger was struck by the obvious physical degeneration of Hitler himself. Part of the poor impression was attributable to Hitler's uniform, which consisted of a military blouse with a yellow tie, white collar, and black trousers—hardly a becoming outfit, Senger thought. But it was Hitler himself, not his getup, that was most discouraging:

2. It was known at that time as Ashford General Hospital.
3. Clark, *Calculated Risk,* 336.
4. Ibid., 336–37. The reason for all this secrecy is not clear. General Dwight Eisenhower went through much the same routine in December and January of 1944, but that was understandable, given the fact that the Germans were expecting an invasion of northwest Europe any day. One receives the impression that General Marshall somewhat enjoyed the exercise.
5. Senger, *Neither Fear nor Hope,* 241.

His unprepossessing frame and short neck made him appear even less dignified than usual. His complexion was flabby, colorless, and sickly. His large blue eyes, which evidently fascinated many people, were watery, possibly due to his constant use of stimulating drugs. His handshake was soft, his left arm hung limp and trembling by his side. Yet a striking feature, contrasting with his notorious screaming during his speeches or fits of rage, was the quiet and modulated voice that almost inspired compassion since it barely concealed his despondency and weakness.[6]

There was another side to Hitler's demeanor, however, that surprised Senger even more than his pathetic appearance: his change in attitude when describing the situation confronting Germany.

More noteworthy than this outward impression of Hitler were the words he spoke to this small circle of fortuitously assembled frontline soldiers when he sat down with them at a round table. He described the disastrous situation on the Eastern front, where one defeat succeeded another. He informed us that the Battle of the Atlantic had entered a critical phase for the Germans because of the enemy's use of radar. He barely mentioned our successes on the Italian front. . . . He made no secret of his anxiety over the impending invasion in the West and the prospect of a second front that would use up his forces. The only consolation that he gave these fighting men was a muttered sentence to the effect that all difficulties must be surmounted by "faith."

Senger had some doubts as to whether his personal impression of Hitler was fair, in view of his dislike of the man for other reasons. His concern was later eased, however, when he conferred confidentially with a respected fellow officer. "The government and the Army," his friend said, "are finished—defeated over and over again in the field, damned by history, heading for downfall—and they know it."[7]

The meeting with Hitler at an end, Senger was subjected to a short indoctrination course at Sondhofen, which may have been the real purpose of his being called from the front. Speakers included Keitel and Himmler, and their message was uniformly optimistic—and unconvincing. Senger believed that many officers in the audience shared his own strong misgivings,

6. Ibid., 341. One is tempted to question whether Senger, writing after the war, had his dates misplaced. Hitler's limp left arm was universally noticed after July 20, 1944, when the revolt of the generals had resulted in damage from a bomb meant to kill him. This incident occurred three months before that assassination attempt.

7. Ibid., 241–42.

but none dared to speak their minds. All of them feared incurring the suspicion of being an "unreliable general."

Senger was undergoing a feeling of helplessness himself. What was to be done? Even if Hitler were gotten rid of, the rest of his gang would still be in power. And did anyone believe that the Allies would negotiate a peace after the declaration issued by Roosevelt and Churchill of the "Unconditional Surrender" doctrine at Casablanca a year earlier? Some German generals clung to the hope that the Allies would treat them as instruments of Hitler's demise, if Hitler were removed, but Senger predicted that they would instead be blamed for Hitler's rise to power in the first place. Senger looked back with regret to the days of 1918, when the German people took matters into their own hands and brought the First World War to a close. Today, he mused, the average German was "not disposed to act on his own initiative."

Senger arrived back at the Italian front on May 17, after a month away.[8]

The Allied 15th Army Group had tried three times to break the German Gustav Line at Cassino—once in January, once in February, and once in March, 1944. Each effort had failed at heavy cost, and General Alexander had no intention of undergoing any more such humiliations. Operation Diadem, as the forthcoming attack was code-named, would be conducted with the three-to-one advantage the Allies considered necessary for an assault on a fortified position. It would be planned meticulously. "Alexander's masterpiece," Fred Majdalany calls it, "an operation in C major with full orchestra." He goes further, declaring that it represented "the vindication of Churchill's Mediterranean strategy: the justification for the long winter agony: the triumphal salute of the Mediterranean veterans to those new armies poised to strike across the English Channel. . . ."[9]

Majdalany, himself a veteran of the Cassino battle, may be excused for waxing a bit dramatic in describing the campaign, but the vindication belonged more to the valor of the soldiers of several countries. Logic and strategy aside, the spirits of the Allied troops both at Cassino and Anzio were high at the prospect of fighting with overwhelming force in a period when good weather, vital to air support, could be expected to prevail.

To assist this massive attack, the 15th Army Group instituted an elaborate cover plan, designed to convince Kesselring that the Allies were intending to launch another amphibious landing, this one north of Rome at Civitavecchia. If Kesselring could be thus persuaded, the Allies hoped,

8. Ibid., 242–43.
9. Majdalany, *Cassino*, 221.

the field marshal might be induced to keep enough divisions in the vicinity of Rome to make the breakthrough on the Gustav Line easier.

The deception plans were elaborate. The U.S. 36th Division, still being held in reserve, was sent to the Salerno-Naples area to carry out training in amphibious operations; fictitious assembly areas and embarkation areas were marked out extensively in full view of German agents. Since the Canadian corps had not yet been identified on the Gustav Line, the roads in the area also carried the Canadian Maple Leaf. Radio traffic in the Naples area was raised to the volume commensurate with that to be expected of a corps and a division headquarters. The navy conducted fictitious exercises, and the Mediterranean air forces carried out repeated reconnaissance missions over the beaches near Civitavecchia. All troop movements at Cassino were limited to the hours of darkness. Artillery fire was to continue in its usual patterns to look completely normal.[10] The problems of secrecy in troop movements were facilitated by the fact that many of the forces to be employed were already in place. They had been moved as a result of Alexander's redeployments back in March.

Diadem was visualized as a one-two punch, the first punch being against the Gustav Line. Since the force at Anzio was not deemed to be strong enough to break out on its own, the initial rupture of the German lines would have to occur on the Rapido, where the Allies enjoyed a preponderance of twenty nearly full-strength divisions over eight vastly understrength German.[11]

For the outset of the attack, Alexander's main effort was to be made by Oliver Leese's Eighth Army up the Liri Valley, which was still considered to be the most desirable avenue along which to approach Rome. Alexander, however, sensed Clark's fears that giving Leese the Liri Valley would mean that Eighth Army would take Rome. He sought to allay Clark's concern by assuring him that his beloved Fifth Army would be given the honor of taking the city.

Leese had stacked up a great amount of power around the Cassino area. On a ten-mile front he planned to employ two whole corps, the British 13 Corps on the left, facing the valley, and the Polish Corps on the right, flanking Monte Cassino from the north.[12]

10. As it turned out, the deception plan was only partially successful. Kesselring, *Memoirs*, 199, claims that he did not substantially change his plans based on current intelligence reports, though he kept some force in the vicinity of Rome.

11. *West Point Atlas*, Map 104.

12. Clark reportedly had serious doubts that Leese was aggressive enough to accomplish his task.

The seventy miles between the right flank of the Polish Corps and the Adriatic Sea would be held thinly. To cover that distance, Leese employed only two British Corps of two divisions each. On the left was McCreery's 10 Corps, which had finally been transferred from Clark to Leese, and on the right was General Sir Charles Keightly's 5 Corps.[13] Leese's plan suffered from one glaring weakness: his advance up the Liri Valley depended on Clark to clear the rugged heights that dominated his left flank, a hill mass called the Esperia.

The Esperia, the mountain mass between the Liri Valley and the Appian Way along the coast, was a formidable piece of ground, filling the space between Route 6 on the north and Route 7 on the south. From the viewpoint of the Fifth Army, Clark observed that that hill mass made the narrow plain along Route 7 "like a little gutter at the edge of a steep roof."[14] There was therefore little question as to how Clark's attack would begin: he would attack and clear the Esperia mountain complex before attempting to move up the Appian Way.

In sheer numbers, Clark's Fifth Army was a powerful formation, boasting a total of thirteen divisions. They were, however, a variegated lot: seven American, four French, and two British divisions. Of these, both of the British and four of the American divisions were at Anzio, leaving only three American divisions and four French divisions on the Gustav Line.[15]

Fortunately for Clark, the task of his troops on the Gustav Line would be greatly facilitated by the bridgehead that the British 10 Corps had seized over the southern portion of the Garigliano back on January 18. That foothold meant that some of Clark's divisions, but not all, would be spared the need to make an assault crossing of the river. By utilizing the bridgehead in the southern portion of the line, he could launch an attack northward into the Esperia complex with a couple of divisions from one corps. But the terrain was rugged, so rugged that the Germans had neglected its defense. The Hitler (or Senger) Line, designed to back up the Gustav Line a few miles west, was concentrated on the Liri Valley; it was incomplete in the hills to the south.

13. *West Point Atlas*, Map 104.
14. Clark, *Calculated Risk*, 338.
15. At Anzio were the British 1st and 56th Infantry Divisions, the 3d, 34th, and 45th U.S. Infantry Divisions and the 1st U.S. Armored Division. On the Garigliano were the 85th and 88th U.S. Divisions. The French divisions were the 3d Algerian, the 2d Moroccan, the 4th Mountain, and the 1st Motorized. The 36th, at least for the outset, remained in reserve, Clark, *Calculated Risk*, 337–38.

For the difficult mission of assaulting the Esperia, Clark chose the elite French Expeditionary Corps (FEC).[16] The II U.S. Corps, in the meantime, would push up the Appian Way, along the coastline.

The commander of the FEC, General Alphonse Juin, was delighted to receive the toughest mission on the Rapido front: it would afford the French Colonial troops an opportunity to at least partially avenge France's humiliation at the hands of Hitler's panzers in the summer of 1940. The reporter Eric Sevareid described these French Colonial troops vividly:

> These men had a cold, implacable hatred of the enemy that was almost frightening; they were driven by such a fierce desire to show the world and regain their pride that one knew at once they could be stopped only by death and that in victory they would show no mercy. . . . They did not love Americans; they did not love the British; they were callous and cruel toward the Italians. Yet it was good to be among them now; it was a reassuring vindication of faith in these people. I went so far as to predict on the radio that they would make a sensational fight, and this time I was not wrong.[17]

Juin set about making his plans with alacrity. It was not difficult for him to realize that the dominating height in the mountain complex was the 940-meter Monte Majo, in the center, whose height made it tower over the hills around it. He would concentrate three of his four divisions to taking Majo at the outset. Since speed was essential, Juin decided to attack with all four of his divisions abreast. The 1st Motorized Division on the right would cross the Garigliano and head in a northward direction, passing in front of Monte Majo and pushing forward to the heights of the Liri Valley before turning westward. In the center, the 2d Moroccan Division would drive northwestward directly toward Majo. The 3d Algerian Division would bypass Monte Majo to the south and swing northward behind the mountain. On the extreme left of the French Corps, the 4th Mountain Division would operate alone, taking Castelforte and then driving westward to seize Monte Revole.

The U.S. II Corps, on the left of the French, consisted of two newly arrived American divisions, the 85th and the 88th Infantry Divisions. Clark

---

16. The French Expeditionary Corps, under General Alphonse Juin, were superb troops, especially for fighting in the mountains. They were all Moroccans or Algerians, native troops with French officers. Their location was always a source of concern to German General Frido von Senger und Etterlin, but he was unaware at this time of their exact location.

17. Eric Sevareid, *Not So Wild a Dream,* 378–79.

General Alphonse Pierre Juin, commanding the French Expeditionary Corps.

took a special interest in those two units because they were the first AUS (Army of the United States) divisions[18] to go into combat. All the troops heretofore employed in the Mediterranean had been Regular or National Guard. Clark himself had been much involved in the organization of these AUS divisions a couple of years earlier when he was on the War Department staff.

Clark's plans for the attack on the Gustav Line—so far as he could make them—were now complete. He could now turn to the area of his primary interest, the prospective breakout at Anzio.

At his headquarters in Nettuno, General Lucian Truscott had been planning for the breakout for a long time, expecting the event to take place far sooner than it did. When Clark informed him of the delay on a visit in late March, Truscott was disappointed but made use of the extra time to make thorough plans for the eventual employment of VI Corps.

---

18. The AUS divisions corresponded to the National Army divisions of the First World War. In both instances, it took nearly two years into the war before they were fit for battle.

Truscott's studies produced four possible alternate plans, two of which could be potentially decisive. One, code-named Turtle, envisaged breaking out of the bridgehead northward on the much-contested route toward Rome by way of Albano and Campoleone. The other, code-named Buffalo, involved an attack to Cisterna and Cori, eventually to Valmontone, thus cutting Route 6. The other two plans consisted only of small attacks on the flanks to deprive the enemy of observation over the beachhead and the port of Anzio.[19] For each of these alternatives, Truscott's staff worked out complete plans.

On May 5, less than a week before the scheduled launching of Diadem, Alexander visited Truscott, and in his "charming way," as the American put it, "let me know very quietly and firmly that there was only one direction in which the attack should be launched, and that was from Cisterna to cut Highway 6 in the vicinity of Valmontone. . . ." Alexander would reserve the decision as to timing to himself.[20] Alexander seemed fixated on the idea that Buffalo and only Buffalo would be decisive; it would trap the German Tenth Army at Cassino and result in its annihilation.

The conference made Truscott uncomfortable, not so much with Alexander's instructions per se, but from the fact that his immediate boss was Clark, not Alexander. He was conscious that Clark's orders had been different from those now being issued by Alexander, and Clark had not been present at that meeting. Immediately on Alexander's departure, therefore, Truscott reported the incident to his American chief, adding a new twist, that Alexander was planning to send the American 34th Division to Anzio also.

On receiving that word, Clark was understandably disturbed. Not only was he unwilling to confine himself to a single plan for the Anzio breakout; he also feared that Alexander was trying to micromanage Fifth Army. A telephone call to Alexander reassured him that the misunderstanding had been a great mistake. Alexander insisted that he understood Clark's feeling and had not intended to interfere.[21]

Alexander's assurances, however, were only cosmetic. His official written order, published the same day as his visit to Truscott, specified that the Fifth Army would "Launch an attack from Anzio Bridgehead on the general axis CORI—VALMONTONE to cut Highway 6 in the VALMONTONE area, and there prevent the supply and withdrawal of the

19. Grasshopper and Crawfish were the plans for limited attacks on the flanks, Truscott, *Command Missions*, 366.
20. Ibid., 368.
21. Clark, *Calculated Risk*, 340–42.

troops of the German Tenth Army opposing the advance of Eighth and Fifth Armies."[22]

Clark, for his part, refused to be hog-tied in his plans. He directed Truscott to continue planning for an alternate attack toward Rome by way of Campoleone (Turtle). Truscott was quite conscious that Clark was obsessed by the fear of seeing the British Eighth Army reach Rome before Fifth Army.[23]

The seeds of future disagreements had been planted.

Not all the planning for the breakout involved high-level maneuvers of troops. Everyone, generals and sergeants, was interested in finding devices to minimize casualties when the attack began. A few days before the scheduled jump-off, Clark visited Anzio to see demonstrations of some of these devices.

One device consisted of a means of retrieving tanks that had been mired into minefields. Some expert in tracked vehicles had devised a crane to be welded on the front of a tank, equipped with a hook that could be attached by cable to the stalled vehicle. The process of such tank rescue proved, in Clark's words, to be "smooth and fast."[24]

Another device, one that soon became common in the army, was the "snake," a long, thick piece of metal tubing loaded with high explosives. In appearance it resembled a huge boa constrictor, with a ball-shaped runner out in front to enable it to be pushed by a tank into a minefield. When the snake was exploded, it blew a pathway through the minefield wide enough for another tank, likewise pushing a snake, to follow. When one snake had blasted a pathway a certain distance, the next would take its place and continue blasting the pathway.[25]

The most intriguing scheme that Clark observed, however, was that of the tank-infantry sled team, an innovation to be used by the 3d Division in the coming breakout. Each team would consist of a single Sherman tank towing two columns of low-slung sleds. Each individual sled would carry one man, and its metal sides would afford its rider protection from shell fragments and spent small arms, at least from the sides. Conveniently, since the infantry squad in the Second World War had twelve men, one team consisted of a single tank and a single infantry squad. Since a tank

---

22. Operation Order No. 1, Allied Armies in Italy, dated May 5, 1944. NARA. "Allied Armies in Italy" was the new designation of the former Fifteenth Army Group. Hence the Number 1.

23. Truscott, *Command Missions*, 369.

24. Clark, *Calculated Risk*, 342.

25. Ibid., 343.

platoon had five tanks, a regimental sled team consisted of five of these tank-infantry combinations, involving sixty infantrymen in all. Ideally, such teams should move rapidly with minimum exposure to enemy fire. It was an intriguing idea, and the demonstration for Clark was witnessed with approval also by both Truscott and O'Daniel.

Though the generals thought the sled teams were a great idea, their enthusiasm was not shared by the men who were going to participate. According to Sergeant John Shirley, a nineteen-year-old replacement, "There were few volunteers."[26] In order to attain the necessary sixty doughboys, therefore, each regimental commander was forced to order each of his nine rifle company commanders to provide one sergeant and several men. No company commander was going to send his most reliable and experienced men, and Shirley attributed his own selection to the fact that he had just arrived and was therefore untested in battle. The men ate and slept with their own parent companies but during the training phase for Buffalo they trained with their sled team a couple of hours a day.

Shirley accepted his lot philosophically, but one circumstance, as the day drew near for the attack, took him aback. Floods of mail from home—forty letters—had been en route at the same time that he had been making his way to the front. They all arrived on the same day. Shirley was feeling a bit apprehensive that day, because Axis Sally had announced over the radio that the organization of the battle sled teams had been discovered and promised that they would be annihilated. Shirley wondered if he would survive long enough to read all of his forty letters.[27]

All was in place. Eric Sevareid described the ominous forthcoming events with a touch of literary license:

> Beyond the Allied fronts the earth trembled in the night under the travel of silent convoys. Whole armies switched positions unnoticed by the enemy; the Americans on the central front moved down to the Tyrrhenian Sea; the French faced impossible peaks to our right; the British and the Poles looked at Cassino and the Liri Valley. Each prong of the steel rake was imbedded in position; very soon the signal would be given, and the rake would move northward up the length of the peninsula, furrowing the earth, heaping the mangled houses and bodies together as it moved. It was May. Everywhere the fields were delicately tinted with flowers.[28]

26. John Shirley, *I Remember,* 3.
27. Ibid., 4.
28. Sevareid, *Not So Wild a Dream,* 386.

Breakout at Cassino, 11 May 1944

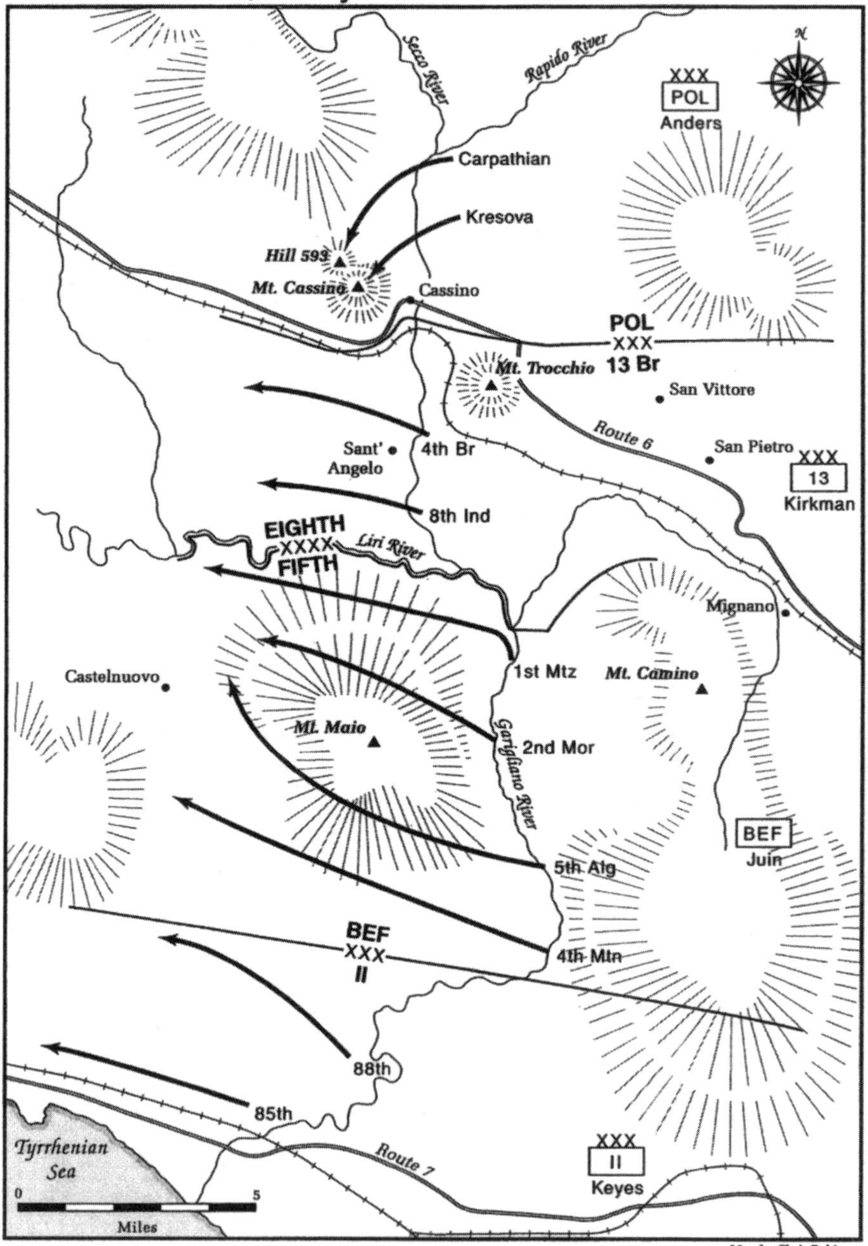

Map by Chris Robinson

CHAPTER 21

BREAKOUT AT CASSINO

G eneral Alexander's elaborate deception plan may have confused German intelligence, but it failed to induce Kesselring to redeploy his divisions to any great degree, or so he later claimed.[1] On the other hand, the Allied measures to maintain an atmosphere of "normalcy" on the Cassino and Anzio fronts were highly effective. Lulled by that "normalcy," Kesselring permitted several of his generals to be absent from the front during the early days of May besides von Senger, who was still in Germany. Heinrich von Vietinghoff was in Germany also, and Kesselring's chief of staff, Siegfried Westphal, was home recuperating from some vague malady, probably fatigue.

At 11:00 P.M. on May 11, 1944, the Allied front along the Gustav Line burst into flame. A barrage of two thousand guns fired simultaneously in what has been called the "biggest artillery barrage since El Alamein."[2] With plenty of time to register in, the thousand artillery pieces supporting Fifth Army put on a performance that General Clark called "perhaps the most effective artillery bombardment of the campaign," destroying a great number of enemy artillery batteries and vital communications centers. The artillery supporting Fifth Army, according to Clark, fired nearly 174,000 rounds during the first twenty-four hours of the attack, and at dawn of the 12th of May the Allied Air Forces came in with approximately 1,500 sorties.[3]

Nevertheless, despite the overwhelming artillery and air bombardment, the German defenders along the Gustav Line were not obliterated

1. "The first days of the battle . . . confirmed our guess at the points of the enemy's main effort" (Kesselring, *Memoirs,* 200).
2. Morris, *Circles of Hell,* 320.
3. Clark, *Calculated Risk,* 346.

or even neutralized. As a result, Allied progress was painfully slow, so slow that the first three days of Diadem have been called "ominously reminiscent of previous failed operations."[4]

The first Allied setback—and the most dramatic—was the disaster that befell the 2d Polish Corps in its effort to take the Monte Cassino Abbey from the north and northwest. The Polish Corps, like the French Expeditionary Corps, was a unit fired with an unusual motivation to kill Germans. Its commander, General Wladyslaw Anders, was a zealot, and his subordinates almost matched him. It was composed largely of survivors from that mass of Polish men, women, and children—a million in all—that Stalin had sent to labor in Siberia after the Germans and Russians had overrun Poland in September of 1939. In captivity, the Polish hostages had been brutally ill-treated, some of them spending time in the notorious Lubianka Prison in Moscow. Their plight was somewhat eased when Hitler's invasion of the Soviet Union in June 1941, made Poland at least theoretically an ally. Using that argument, Churchill had secured the release of many and some had managed to make their way to the west by way of Iran.[5] Eventually a number of able-bodied male survivors were formed into the 2d Polish Corps, which was later assigned to the British Eighth Army.

As a result of their harrowing ordeal in Russia, Anders's men hated their Slavic cousins as much, if not more, than they hated the Germans. But Cassino was far from Russia, so for the moment Anders's preoccupation was to put his corps in a position where it could prove itself to the world. He therefore eagerly seized on General Leese's suggestion that the 2d Corps take the assignment of assaulting the Monte Cassino Abbey. That despite the fact that the Americans, Indians, and New Zealanders had previously failed to do so.

Anders and his Poles had taken on a gargantuan task. The Abbey and part of the town of Cassino were being held by the elite German 1st Parachute Division, whose members were nearly as fanatical and proud as the Poles themselves. Their commander, Lieutenant General Richard Heidrich, was one of the toughest and most competent division commanders in the German Army. The German position had been organized in every possible detail, with interlocking machine gun fire between positions and every spot on the landscape registered for the mass of artillery and mortars it had in support. The Germans enjoyed perfect observation

4. D'Este, *Fatal Decision*, 347.
5. Churchill had encountered General Anders when visiting Moscow in August of 1942.

General Sir Oliver Leese, commanding the British Eighth Army, and General Wladyslaw Anders, commanding the 2d Polish Corps. U.S. Army, Eisenhower Library.

of every foot of ground the Poles would have to cross. Anders was aware of all this, but it did not dampen his enthusiasm.[6]

Anders's corps was relatively small, with a strength totaling only about forty thousand men, comprising two divisions, the Carpathian and the Kresowas, organized into two brigades each. A certain amount of mutual jealousy had grown up between the two division commanders, and they vied with each other for the most difficult and visible missions, each demanding the honor of leading the corps attack. To placate them, Anders compromised: the two divisions would attack abreast, each with one

6. A member of Anders's staff wrote: "The enemy positions had not been adequately reconnoitered. In particular their defence works (bunkers and shelters) could not be located. In addition, some of them were built on reverse slopes, putting ground reconnaissance out of the question. There were no orthodox defence works on the position, such as old-type trenches and barbed wire—nothing, in fact, which could give any clue in the system of fortifications" (John Ellis, *Cassino: The Hollow Victory,* 322).

brigade leading and the other following. Each division was assigned an objective north of the Abbey. The Carpathian, on the left, aimed for Hill 593, and the Kresowa, on the right, was designated to take the Phantom Ridge.[7] The ultimate objective of the Kresowa Division was the Piedmont, farther on, the hinge of the Hitler Line.[8] Once those objectives were in Allied hands, Anders and Leese expected the Abbey to fall of its own weight.

When the Allied artillery fires lifted late that night of May 11th, the two Polish divisions, according to Majdalany,

> began to pick their way through the boulders and thickets, across the gullies, and above the ravines which unpredictably cut across these mountains: through thorn and gorse: through the corpses that still littered the entire area: and soon the ubiquitous machine-guns, that had been there so long they seemed almost to have grown into the rock, began to mow them down as they had mowed down the Americans, the Indians, and the British.[9]

Nevertheless, the Poles did not wilt under that heavy fire. For the rest of that night they pushed on, fighting hand to hand in human waves toward their objectives. For a while both divisions made progress, and before dawn both were on their preliminary objectives, despite heavy casualties.

With the arrival of daylight, however, the two divisions were in untenable positions. Incoming fire was so heavy that the frontline troops lost communications with their rear headquarters. German snipers were picking off the leaders, especially officers of rank. Reinforcement and resupply were impossible. Finally, in the early afternoon of May 12, General Anders sadly sent an order for both divisions to withdraw.

Anders was understandably shattered over the loss of four thousand men with not a foot of gain, but the depth of his emotion was lost on the British commander, Sir Oliver Leese. Leese was a genial, optimistic man who could not comprehend—nor totally approve of—the depth of Anders's passion. When the army commander came by Anders's command post to offer a word of consolation, Anders murmured in French,

7. Anders, *Army in Exile*, 175.

8. The Hitler, or Senger, Line began on the northeast near Cassino, and slanted rearward so that its southwest anchor was at Aquino. According to D'Este, *Fatal Decision*, 347, the name had been changed to the Senger Line in January of 1944, but was still referred to by most people as the Hitler Line. It seems logical that the change in name was due to the fact that it consisted of mobile pill-boxes, not sufficiently grand for it to be referred to in dispatches as the Hitler Line. As mentioned in the previous chapter, the line was strong in the Liri Valley but weak in the Esperia.

9. Majdalany, *Cassino*, 247.

their only common language, *"Ah, mon general, tout est perdu, tout est perdu."*

Leese burst out profanely and somewhat impatiently, *"Ah, mon general. Nothing is fucking perdu."* He then explained what the Poles had accomplished. Their attack had drawn German troops away from the critical battle to the south, where the 13 British Corps had made a small penetration into the Liri Valley. Their sacrifice had not been in vain.

Anders's spirits rose, and without hesitation he offered to try again. The commander of the Carpathian Division, who was present, agreed. Leese assured them both that their chance would come. For the moment, however, Anders and his Poles should await orders.[10]

South of the Poles, at the Liri Valley, the British 13 Corps, as the main effort for Diadem, was a powerful formation. It consisted of four divisions, the British 4th and 78th Infantry Divisions, the 6th Armoured Division, and the 8th Indian Division. For the assault across the Rapido, Lieutenant General Sir Sidney Kirkman, commander of the corps, chose the 4th British and the 8th Indian Divisions.

As with most organizations in the British Army, the various formations differed in many respects. One important difference lay in the amount of experience a unit might have. The 4th Division, which would attack on the right, had seen difficult service in North Africa, so difficult that four of its original infantry battalions had been destroyed, later replaced by units from Gibraltar and other quiet sectors where they had not seen previous action. Also in common with most other British units, the 4th Division was understrength. For the crossing of the Rapido, therefore, each assaulting company consisted of only ninety officers and men.[11]

The 8th Indian Division, on the left, was a more established, confident formation. Its commander, Dudley Russell, had been with the unit ever since January of 1943, and he had developed such a rapport with his troops that he had come to be known to them as "Pasha." He was described as being "beefy of build, with a square bristling moustache, and a touch of flamboyance." The officers of the division, according to one authority, were "tied to their troops by bonds of mutual devotion that could never be fully comprehensible to an outsider."[12]

10. Morris, *Circles,* 323. The source of this exchange is a letter from General Leese to the author, Nov. 1968.

11. Blaxland, *Alexander's Generals,* 85.

12. Ibid., 81.

The position from which the two divisions were to launch their attack was the same as that from which Fred Walker's 36th Division had met with tragedy nearly four months previously. The evidence was still there:

> The ghosts of Texans haunted the banks of the Rapido. They emerged from the many easily recognisable [*sic*] items of American equipment that were strewn among the shell holes in dishevelled abandon, from countless rounds of eroded ammunition, from pieces of torn uniform, and from the odd bodily remnant that had escaped detection by burial parties. Everyone knew that the Texans had met disaster. Their agony still lingered, sensed where it could not be smelt.[13]

Such an eerie scene could be expected to have a depressing effect on the men of the 13 Corps. Perhaps it did to some extent. They knew, however, that the situation in May was far different from that of the previous January. For one thing, the ground over which the assaulting parties would have to carry their boats, though soft for tanks in places, was no longer a swamp. Further, the weather in May would be clear, allowing for maximum air support. And the Germans, who had been fighting steadily over the months without sufficient replacements, would be a less formidable foe. Finally, the Allied attack would be conducted in overwhelming force. The crossing would be difficult, to be sure, but the prospects for success were good.

The 4th would cross the Rapido just to the south of Cassino. General Ward would employ two brigades abreast, each brigade going in column, with one battalion leading the other. Since each battalion sent only two companies forward, each brigade was being led by about 180 men. Rigid techniques had been set down for the troops crossing the Rapido. Each canvas boat was designed to carry eighteen men, of whom three were specialists in the actual handling of the boats themselves. The other fifteen—the fighters—were to be delivered to the other side. That arrangement seemed to make sense, but once the assaulting troops lowered the boats into the river, they found the current to be much stronger than they had expected. As a result, when the Tommies reached the other side of the narrow river and clambered up the side of the steep bank—which most of them succeeded in doing—the three boating specialists lacked the sheer strength to buck the current. As a result, they were consigned to be swept down the river, if not sunk. Few boats were to be used twice in that day's assault.[14]

13. Ibid., 79.
14. Ibid., 85–86.

Despite that difficulty, the 10th Brigade of the 4th Division quickly established a foothold on the opposite bank of the Rapido. Though unable to move freely because of the heavy German resistance, they were assisted to some extent by the heavy fog that protected most of them from direct, aimed fire.[15] Unfortunately, the division's procedures for artillery support of infantry lacked flexibility. The attack had been planned with a rigid timetable, which called for the artillery barrage to move forward at an interval of a hundred yards every six minutes. As the men were delayed, fighting on the banks, their artillery support, according to plan, was creeping inexorably toward the planned objective, two thousand yards ahead.[16]

On the left of the 10th Brigade, Brigadier C. N. Shoosmith's 28th Brigade ran into serious trouble. Their mishaps were due to some extent to incompetence, but mostly they resulted from plain bad luck. Shoosmith had assigned his Somerset battalion to launching duties, which included fixing cables on the opposite side, while his battalion of the 2d King's Regiment was to make the assault. The 2d King's however, were delayed by a minefield and for a while lost their bearings, arriving at the river over a half hour late. Like the 10th Brigade on their right, therefore, the 28th Brigade lost the services of their artillery. Their barrage, according to Gregory Blaxland, had "rolled onwards with impervious disregard for the unpunctual."[17]

Shoosmith's troubles did not end there. Two battalion commanders went off on reconnaissance together, and both disappeared. A single artillery shell killed two majors from different battalions, together with several of the staff. By 10:00 A.M., it was estimated that the 28th brigade had only 250 men in position on the west bank of the Rapido.[18] The historian John Ellis puts it bluntly—and rather unkindly—saying that the contribution of the brigade had "failed badly."[19]

The task of the 8th Indian Division, south of the 4th British, was even more difficult, because its sector included the redoubtable ruin Sant' Angelo, a major strong point that had wrought such havoc on the 36th Division in January. The terrain around the town was especially choppy, and the river's banks formed "veritable escarpments."[20]

15. Opinions have varied, and have never been completely agreed, as to the main source of the fog. Some have attributed the source to German smoke shells, others to the mists rising from the river. Perhaps it was a combination of both.

16. Blaxland, *Alexander's Generals*, 86.

17. Ibid., 87.

18. Ibid., 88.

19. Ellis, *Hollow Victory*, 300.

20. Blaxland, *Alexander's Generals*, 88.

To help the Indians to cope with these difficulties, General Kirkman had given Pasha Russell twenty additional assault boats to enable his brigades to cross the Rapido with two battalions abreast, in contrast to the one battalion per brigade in the 4th Division. Apparently by chance, a group of Sherman tanks from the Canadian Armoured Brigade appeared on the scene and was pressed into service.

Russell placed the 17th Brigade on the right, north of Sant' Angelo, and the 19th Brigade on the left, south of the ruined town. The crossing was at first encouraging, with the support of the Canadian tanks. Once the brigades were across, however, the Germans laid down a heavy and effective smoke barrage. The 17th Brigade began to wander in confusion while the division's artillery, as with the brigades in the 4th Division, continued to proceed on its steady course toward the corps objective two thousand yards away. Eventually, the 17th ran up against a strongly defended terrain feature called the Platform, and there was forced to dig in and wait.

The 13 Corps had crossed the Rapido but had been unable to penetrate beyond a distance of five hundred yards. But if everyone else was discouraged, the corps commander, Lieutenant-General Sidney Kirkman, put the matter in perspective. Recalling the fate of the American 36th Division over the same terrain, he remarked, "But we are across!"[21]

Engineers are always important, but they are the stars of the show in a river crossing. Infantry can assault a river line, but it cannot go far inland without the support of armor and artillery, and that means bridges. Therefore, no matter how shallow the bridgehead, Kirkman's engineers, even at great cost, could not wait in their efforts to install bridges to get the tanks across. Seven bridges had been planned for this operation, three in the zone of the 4th Division and four in the zone of the 8th Indian, codenamed alphabetically from north to south.[22] From the outset, the bridges in General Ward's 4th Division sector came under heaviest fire, and even though Blackwater Bridge had a little work done during the first night, by morning all bridge construction in his zone had come to a standstill.[23]

In the zone of the 8th Indian, things went better. Work was held up but never abandoned. By mid-morning of the 12th of May, two of Russell's

21. Ibid., 88–89.

22. Starting at the north, the bridges in the sector of the 4th Division were Amazon, Blackwater, and Congo. In the sector of the 8th Indian, they were Cardiff, London, Oxford, and Plymouth, Ellis, *Hollow Victory,* 301.

23. Ibid.

four bridges were in operation, and during that day the best part of four Canadian armored squadrons had driven across. That success spurred Ward and Kirkman into renewed efforts to get a bridge in the sector of the 4th "at all costs," and by the morning of the 13th a bridge was in place. Of the two engineer units involved, nearly half of their men—eighty-three out of two hundred—were casualties.[24]

With the bridges in place and the armor crossing, the 13 Corps began to move. The Indians took Sant' Angelo on the 13th, and the Germans defending the Platform further on seemed impressed enough to surrender, an unusual occurrence for the German Army. To the north, the 4th Division received a new brigade—the 12th—and together they pushed on, although "there was no such thing as an easy attack in any part of the Liri Valley."[25]

Thirteen Corps had crossed the Rapido. Reinforced by the British 78th Division, which Kirkman sent into the sector of the 28th Brigade of the 4th Division, the corps went on to take its objective two thousand yards from the river. But decisive exploitation of the initial successes would be impossible until the hill mass dominating the Liri Valley from the south should be taken. That area, the Esperia, was the sector of the French.

The French Expeditionary Corps, which consisted of troops recruited from North Africa—Goumiers and Berber irregulars among them— proved to be the key to the success of Diadem. Those groups were very much at home in mountain terrain. Others, more conventional, were also tough Algerians. The officers of the four divisions were Frenchmen, at home with their troops and highly competent.

The commander of the FEC, General Alphonse Juin, was a remarkable man, though easy to underestimate. He was small in stature, and that fact was unfortunately emphasized when he was photographed beside the towering Clark. Most noticeable was his left-handed salute, the result of his losing the use of his right arm in a North African action back in 1912. The British seemed prone to sniff at Juin's military knowledge and his sharp brain, overlooking the fact that he had graduated first in his class at the French Military Academy, St. Cyr (a classmate was Charles de Gaulle). Born and raised in North Africa, he understood his troops thoroughly.

Not everyone underestimated the FEC, however. General Frido von Senger was always concerned about the location and future plans of Juin and his troops. Senger had a respect for these North Africans. Further, he

24. Ibid., 302.
25. Ibid., 303.

believed, as did Mark Clark, that the key to the Gustav Line position was not Cassino but the mountainous area south of the Liri Valley. The prospect Senger dreaded most was that the FEC might attack in that area.[26]

When Diadem was launched late in the evening of May 11, the French were the first to crack the Gustav Line. The 1st Motorized Division, according to plan, crossed the Garigliano in the north, while the 2d Moroccan Division, on their left, headed straight for Monte Majo. By the end of the second day of the attack, Monte Majo was in Moroccan hands, and the Gustav Line had been penetrated.

As General Clark wrote later,

> The next forty-eight hours on the French front were decisive. The knife-wielding Goumiers swarmed over the hills, particularly at night, and General Juin's entire force showed an aggressiveness hour after hour that the Germans could not withstand. Cerasola, San Giorgio, Mt. D'Oro, Ansonia, and Esperia were seized in one of the most brilliant and daring advances of the war in Italy, and by May 16 the French Expeditionary Corps had thrust some ten miles on their left flank to Mount Revole, with the remainder of their front slanting back somewhat to keep contact with the British Eighth Army.

Clark added, "For this performance, which was to be a key to the success of the entire drive on Rome, I shall always be a grateful admirer of General Juin and his magnificent FEC."[27]

The French feat in clearing the heights above the Liri Valley allowed the British 13 Corps to drive some three miles into the Gustav Line, and by May 16, Alexander felt free to report his confidence that such had been accomplished.[28] Kesselring, his adversary, had come to much the same conclusion. The German plan, anticipating events such as those facing them, had been for the units north of the Liri Valley—the LI Corps—to retreat from the Gustav Line by way of the Abruzzi Mountains. The XIV Panzer Corps would use the valley. On that date Kesselring, in a conversation with von Vietinghoff, declared that the time had come to with-

26. "I was therefore particularly anxious about this sector . . . because of the nature of [the opponents]—Moroccan and Algerian troops under General Juin. These were native mountain people, led by superbly trained French staff officers, equipped with modern American weapons and accoutrements. The formidable opponent naturally aggravated the already critical situation of 5 Mountain Division." Senger, *Neither Fear nor Hope,* 189.

27. Clark, *Calculated Risk,* 348.

28. Alexander to Sir Alan Brooke, CIGS, May 16, 1944, cited in D'Este, *Fatal Decision,* 349.

draw into the Hitler Line, the first fallback position after the Gustav Line.[29] Both men agreed that it was now necessary to give up the Monte Cassino Abbey and the town.

The next day was one the Allies had been awaiting for a long time. General Leese gave General Anders the order to resume his attacks on the Monte Cassino Abbey and Cassino. The Poles jumped off with great élan, only to find that the Abbey had been evacuated by Senger the evening before. The members of the German 1st Parachute Division would have preferred to stay and die in the Abbey in which they had developed a proprietary interest. Senger, however, had pulled them out against their will. That event made taking the Abbey, after all these heartbreaking months, something of an anticlimax.

The Allies were now engaged, not in attacking a position, but in pursuing a beaten enemy. The impregnable German position on the Rapido, the killing ground of Monte Cassino, had been broken.

29. Paraphrased conversation, D'Este, *Fatal Decision*, 349.

Plan for Breakout from Anzio, 23 May 1944

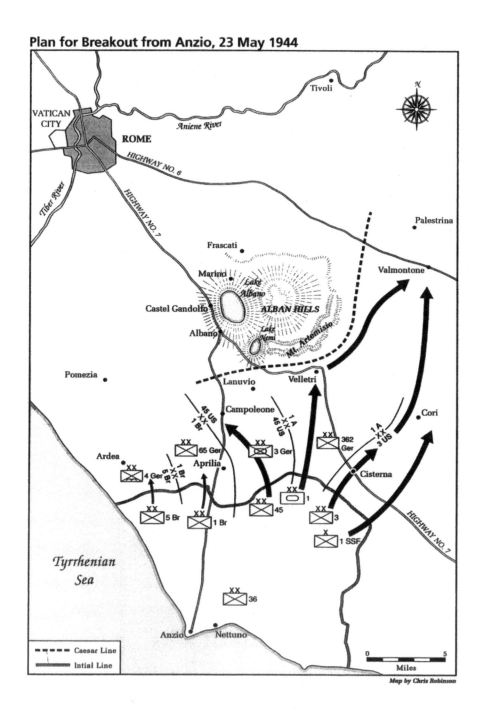

CHAPTER 22

ROME IS THE PRIZE!

We [the Fifth Army] not only wanted the honor of capturing Rome, but we felt that we more than deserved it; that it would to a certain extent make up for the buffeting and the frustration we had undergone. . . . My own feeling was that nothing was going to stop us on our push toward the Italian capital. Not only did we intend to become the first army in fifteen centuries to seize Rome from the south, but we intended to see that the people back home knew that it was the Fifth Army that did the job.

Mark W. Clark

By early May 1944, when Diadem was launched, Clark and Alexander had developed different views as to the relative importance of the Gustav Line and the Anzio Beachhead. The two men had never seen eye to eye on much, but in this case they had, oddly, switched positions.

When Shingle had been launched back in late January, Clark had seen the amphibious landing as secondary to operations on the Gustav Line. It was at Cassino, he believed, that the decision would be made. Alexander, on the other hand, had seen Shingle as the master stroke. Now Clark focused on Shingle while Alexander emphasized the breakout on the Gustav Line.

The changes in attitude should not be surprising. In late January, the VI Corps, at Anzio, had consisted of only two divisions, the British 1st and the American 3d. By May, however, VI Corps had grown to a force of seven divisions, two British and five American, not to mention Robert Frederick's 1st Special Forces Brigade. Clark's force on the Garigliano consisted of only

Clark's Change of Direction toward Rome

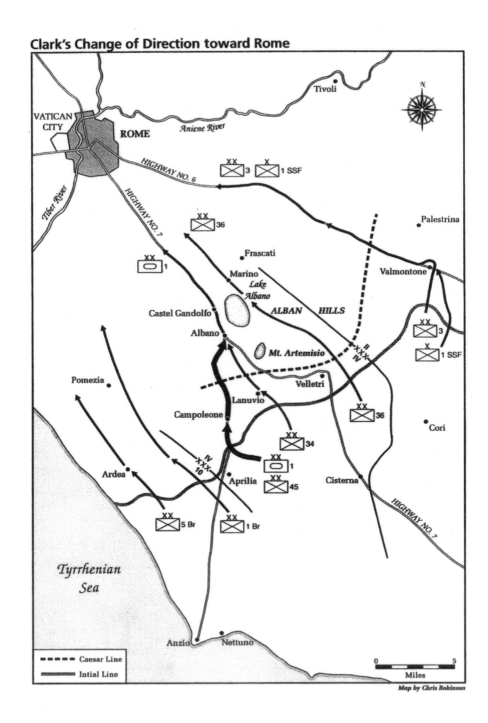

six divisions: two American in the II Corps and four French in the FEC. He had also been relieved of responsibility for the Liri Valley and Monte Cassino. His heart, naturally, was where the bulk of the American divisions was located.

Another issue between Clark and Alexander was the long-standing one, the direction of the main attack from the Anzio beachhead once VI Corps was ready to take the offensive. As always, Alexander continued to insist that there was only one possible direction, that is, northeastward through Cisterna, Cori, and Valmontone (Operation Buffalo). Clark was not convinced, but he was not disposed to argue on the matter. He seemed to comply with Alexander's views, but at the same time he instructed Truscott to continue planning for Operation Turtle—that is, an attack up the Albano road to the Alban Hills. He insisted that Turtle was being planned only as a supplement to Operation Buffalo to Valmontone.

As of the third week in May, the dispositions at Anzio were, from left to right, the 5th and 1st British Infantry Divisions, the American 45th Division on the Albano Road, the 34th Infantry Division, the newly arrived 36th Infantry Division (on the road to Cisterna), and the Devil's Brigade covering the right flank, on the Mussolini Canal. The 3d Infantry Division and the 1st Armored Division were being held back in reserve, ready to pass through the 36th to make the main effort to take Cisterna. O'Daniel's 3d Division was to assault the town of Cisterna itself; the 1st Armored Division was to attack to its left, and Frederick's Special Forces Brigade was to pass to its right. Once Cisterna was taken, the 36th was to continue the attack to Cori and beyond. The British divisions on the west were expected to make only limited attacks, mostly to confuse the enemy as to the direction of the main effort.

On the German side, the disarray had been heightened by the absence of the XIV Panzer Corps commander, Frido von Senger, when the Gustav Line had collapsed. When Senger arrived back at his headquarters at Frosinone on May 17, he was dismayed at what he saw.[1] His command post had been virtually destroyed by Allied air attacks, and what remained of it was overrun by staff members from Vietinghoff's Tenth Army, which had received the same treatment.

---

1. He deplored, for example, the fact that his pet 15th Panzer-Grenadier Division had been broken up, its components, parceled out to the defeated 71st and 94th Divisions, now fighting for their lives. He also learned that the 29th Panzer Division had been virtually destroyed because von Mackensen had delayed its departure from Fourteenth Army to fill a gap in the Hitler Line. Mackensen had been relieved of command.

Senger's mission was no longer to defend a position: it was to save what he could of his XIV Corps. As he surveyed the situation confronting him, he decided that his best move would be to concentrate his divisions, one by one, at Frosinone, where he could maintain contact with the LI Mountain Corps on his left and establish a position to stop the French, whose violent attack was beginning to slow down. He would move most of his troops across secondary roads because of the pressure of the Eighth Army in the Liri Valley and Allied airpower.

But Frosinone could be only a temporary position. In the eyes of von Senger, the key town was Valmontone, farther up the Saccho Valley.[2] Here he hoped—though he admitted it might be too late—to concentrate his forces in preparation for moving in an orderly manner into what the Germans informally called Kesselring's "C" position.[3] Senger's plans were disapproved, but it is noteworthy that Valmontone was prominently on the minds of three top generals, two of them Allied: Alexander, Clark, and von Senger.

Alexander finally gave the order to launch Operation Buffalo on the morning of May 23. Clark, who had moved into his command post at Nettuno, joined Truscott at an observation post in the 3d Division sector to watch the attack as it was launched. The accounts of the two men throw some light on the differences in their personalities.

Clark:

> Before dawn on the morning of May 23 I went with Truscott to a forward observation post on the Anzio front, where just before six o'clock some 500 pieces of artillery opened up on the enemy, whose positions were concealed by a morning haze. The smoke and haze hid our movements, but in the next hour or so we could hear our tanks moving forward to the attack and there was a dull rumble of aircraft overhead as bombers began to pour it on the German positions. A beleaguered Anzio garrison was about to break out with the town of Cisterna as the first objective.[4]

2. The corridor we refer to as the Liri Valley is actually the valley of the Saccho River. The Liri River flows in from the north at a point about twenty miles west of Cassino and thereafter the combined rivers are called the Liri. The valley that runs from Rome to Cassino is therefore the Saccho-Liri Valley.
3. Kesselring's name for that position was the "Caesar Line."
4. Clark, *Calculated Risk*, 354.

Truscott:

> 0545! There was a crash of thunder and bright lightning flashes against the sky behind us as more than a thousand guns, infantry cannon, mortars, tanks, and tank destroyers opened fire. That first crash settled into a continuous rumbling roar. Some distance ahead, a wall of fire appeared as our first salvos crashed into the enemy front lines, then tracers wove eerie patterns in streaks of light as hundreds of machine guns of every caliber poured a hail of steel into the enemy positions. Where we stood watching, the ground quivered and trembled. Day was now breaking, but a pall of smoke and dust shrouded the battle area. At the end of forty minutes, the guns fell silent. Then, from the southeast appeared three groups of fighters, and light bombers, their silvery wings glimmering in the morning light. Towering clouds of smoke and dust broke through the pall about Cisterna as their bombs crashed into the town and enemy positions. Five minutes later and the planes were gone. The artillery began anew. H hour had come and the battle was on.[5]

A few hundred yards from the observation post occupied by Clark and Truscott, Sergeant Audie Murphy, a squad leader in "B" Company, 15th Infantry, had a slightly more earthy view of the stupendous bombardment being laid on the German position at Cisterna. He and his men grinned as they exulted, "Hitler, count your children."

On a more practical side, Murphy exulted because the bombardment made the first phase of the attack easy: it reduced the German fire so that he and his men easily reached the enemy's main line of resistance, on the railroad track just south of Cisterna itself. Unfortunately for Murphy and his men, the railroad tracks ran through a deep cut that crossed the company sector, and the men were forced to slide down the bank and clamber up the other side while under heavy German fire. Murphy, as squad leader, sent his men across one by one: "Brandon! Jones! Valero! Flack!" All the men made it except for Corporal Flack, who for some unknown reason paused just a second. A second was enough. A German machine gun cut him down with one burst.

With all his men across, Murphy slid down the embankment, only to find himself grabbed from behind; the entrenching tool fastened to his back had wedged between a couple of rocks. One of his comrades, Kerrigan, sprang back across the cut to come to his aid. By then, however, Murphy had pulled himself loose and made it to safety.

---

5. Truscott, *Command Missions*, 371.

"You ignorant bastard," Kerrigan shouted. "Are you hurt?"

"No, just a slight heart attack and a nervous breakdown." Asked why the hell he hadn't looked where he was going, Murphy answered with the bravado that dogfaces wore as a front: "I was interested in the scenery."

With his squad assembled on the north side of the railroad cut, Murphy was aware that the platoons of "B" Company could well be cut off from each other. Maybe they had walked into a trap. In front of Murphy's eyes, however, Sergeant Lusky, platoon sergeant of the 1st Platoon, took matters into his own hands.

Yelling for his men to follow him, Lusky moved off toward the nearest German position, which was posing the greatest threat. Lusky's path took him across a flat field, totally lacking in cover, so he was quickly knocked down. Almost instantly he sprang back to his feet with a bleeding shoulder, only to be knocked down again. As Murphy and his comrades watched in fascination, Lusky went down a third time. When he got up again, it was obvious that his right arm was shattered. Nevertheless he cradled his gun in his left armpit and continued on until ten horrified Germans threw up their hands and surrendered.

That was all that Murphy saw, and it would be gratifying if the story ended that happily. Unfortunately it did not. Sergeant Lusky, it was learned later, had ignored the pleas of his men to send for the medics. Instead, he got up and started on toward another position. His men, "inspired by his valor and half-insane with rage," stormed the German emplacement and captured it. When they returned to their fallen leader, he was dead.[6]

In a day, 3d Division had broken the German defenses at Cisterna. The 7th Infantry occupied the town; the 30th Infantry crossed the railroad tracks on its left to the northwest, and the 15th Infantry continued southeast of the town. Still, from Audie Murphy's viewpoint, the enemy, though "reeling like a punch-drunk fighter," was still pounding the Americans with artillery and small arms. By this time the dogfaces were deathly tired but aware that they had to continue to keep the enemy off balance.

At one point Murphy's platoon reached a small forest, which the Germans had recently evacuated. In their hunger and thirst the Americans scrounged through garbage and around the area searching for something to eat or drink. All of a sudden, a heavy barrage of enemy artillery came

---

6. Murphy, *To Hell and Back,* 120–22.

in. Obviously there was nothing for a dogface to do—this was a job for American counterbattery artillery—Murphy dived into an abandoned foxhole, pulled his helmet on tight, and bent over so that the helmet would protect him from above. Hardly had he assumed that position than a body fell on top of him. When Murphy looked, he saw that the new-comer was Horse-Face Johnson, his comrade from the days when the 3d Division was in North Africa.

Johnson was not himself. He was ashen gray and his smile was feeble. But at first both men made light of his condition. Murphy asked if the Krauts had finally scared him. But all Johnson wanted was some water, which Murphy provided. When the canteen slipped through his friend's fingers, Murphy became alarmed and tore Johnson's shirt off. The wound in his chest was small. "I think I strained my back," Johnson said. "Nothing but a scratch, a goddamned silly scratch."

Murphy prepared to leave the foxhole to fetch a medical corpsman. At first Johnson protested. "The shells out there are thicker than whores at an Elks' convention." When blood began gurgling from Johnson's mouth, however, both he and Murphy became truly alarmed. "If I get any mail from South Carolina," Johnson urged, "burn it. Might be forwarded to the wife. Damned Army efficiency at the wrong time." This was the old Horse-Face. Habitually he had always been full of stories, most of them lies. But this time he seemed serious.

Despite the shells hitting around, Murphy left the foxhole to find a medic. When he found one, the man was frightened, too frightened to go with him until Murphy threatened to kill him with his bare hands. The distance back to Johnson's foxhole, Murphy later recalled, was short, but when they arrived, Private Abraham Homer Johnson, otherwise known as Horse-Face, was no longer living.

Murphy closed his eyes. A roar surged through his brain, muffling the noise of the incoming shells. "Knowed an old boy in the Army once. Named Horse-Face. He was a pal."[7]

Not far from Murphy, in the 3d Battalion,[8] another soldier still in his twentieth year was going through an entirely different experience. Whereas Murphy was a veteran, Sergeant John Shirley, assigned to a sled team, was facing his first serious combat, concerned about how he would act. In a house near a woods that temporarily camouflaged the tanks of his

---

7. Ibid., 123–25, *passim*.
8. By coincidence, also of the 15th Infantry.

tank-sled team, Shirley watched the sky darken as American artillery pounded the German lines. Since the sled team was designed to pass through and exploit a breakthrough made by the rest of the 3d Battalion, its employment was delayed an hour.

Finally the word came by radio. Shirley watched as the platoon leader and his squad leaders conferred over a map, though they left him, a mere assistant squad leader, in the dark as to what was up. On order, the men climbed into their sleds, faces down, having no inclination to raise their heads while the tanks and sleds moved out on the road.

Soon Shirley felt the sled being towed off the road to the left. After another turn, this one to the right, Shirley heard the shouted order to dismount. Rolling out of the sled, Shirley found himself in a field of tall wheat. Two wooden stakes were stuck in the ground right in front of him and another was next to his left heel. Shirley was a new replacement, but his training had been good enough that he recognized the stakes for what they were: German antipersonnel mines brought to the surface by recent rains. He could see nobody, so he decided to leave. He made his way around the mines to his front and was lucky enough to make it out of the field without encountering any more. It was twelve minutes since they had stopped, he remarked, and to his surprise he was still alive.

Shirley had sense enough not to stand up, but he knew the general direction to go. He then did an "infantry crawl" on his knees and elbows for some sixty yards and then, to his surprise, he found himself looking over the edge of a wide antitank ditch. Even more to his surprise, he saw what was left of the 3d Battalion, all three rifle companies, huddled in the bottom. He estimated that the battalion had lost half its men in the course of an hour! He slid down the embankment to join his comrades in "I" Company.

The sled mission was obviously a failure, because the teams had been committed behind frontline companies that had not achieved a breakthrough. But the lieutenant commanding the sled team did not consider his mission finished. He gathered up the six men he could find and headed them to the small house on the other side of the ditch that had been their assigned objective. Using fire and movement—the BAR[9] man covering the others as they rushed—the small group charged inside the house, only to find it empty. But only a few feet away from the house was a German trench, the position being protected by the antitank ditch. Apparently without waiting for the other men of the team, Shirley jumped into the trench.

9. Browning Automatic Rifle, a sort of semi-machine gun assigned one to each rifle company.

Sergeant John Shirley, Company I,
15th Infantry. Courtesy Dr. John
Shirley.

Shirley's luck had held up. The trench was dug in a zigzag pattern, and
the twelve-foot section he landed in was unoccupied. Shirley crept carefully to the first bend, a ninety-degree turn to the right, and as he turned
the corner he saw a German soldier firing over the parapet. Shirley let
loose with his tommy gun into the German's back. He had, Shirley
thought to himself, just killed his first German soldier.

On he went. The next segment of trench went to the left. Again as
Shirley turned, a lone German occupied it, this time firing a light machine
gun. Shirley emptied his tommy gun into the figure but found to his dismay that only three rounds had remained from his first burst. Without
waiting to see if the German was still alive, Shirley reacted: "I ran forward
the 10 or 12 feet and hit him on his helmet with the butt of my tommy-gun.
I broke the wooden stock at its narrowest place. I kicked off the helmet
and struck him again with the metal part of the gun. He had probably
been dead since my first bullets struck him."[10]

What followed was almost anticlimax. As Shirley looked over the parapet, he could see the rest of the 3d Battalion moving out in his direction,
making him fear that the Americans might not realize that he was one of
them. He headed back down the trench and stopped off to check the first
man he had killed. Like other American soldiers, Shirley was eager to take
souvenirs, and a Luger pistol was a prize. On looking at the man's holster,

10. Shirley, *I Remember*, 9–10.

however, Shirley found it red and sticky. So sticky that he passed up the chance to have a memento of his first moments in combat.

His participation was not quite over, however. Some fifty yards beyond Shirley's trench was another. There one of the sled team, a strange little man they called Flash, crept right up to the trench, apparently oblivious to his own safety. A flurry of "potato-masher" grenades flew out of the trench, and Flash was killed. However, in an instant about twenty-five Germans came up under a white flag in surrender. Some of them were wounded. Shirley, his weapon still broken but reloaded and usable, marched them back. On the way they passed the company commander of "I" Company. Shirley felt a tinge of satisfaction: "Our eyes met; no words were spoken, but there was an expression and admiration on his face. For whatever motive he had for sending Flash and me to the sled team, I knew he was pleased with what we had done."[11]

The 23d of May is not enshrined as one of our national holidays such as D-Day in Normandy, which occurred two weeks later. But the day was incredibly bloody; the preponderance of strength the Allies had amassed had failed to solve the problem of prepared positions, manned by the highly professional and hardened German infantry. The 3d Infantry Division alone, which had borne the brunt of the attack, lost 950 dead during the break-through, that is, one of every nine infantrymen in the division.

Heroism was hardly confined to O'Daniel's dogfaces. At least two Medals of Honor were awarded to men participating in "secondary" attacks, one from the 45th Division and one from the 34th. The 45th Division, on the left of the 3d, was charged with attacking in the area of the so-called Thumb, the scene of such bitter fighting on the part of the British the previous February. Technical Sergeant Van T. Barfoot, a tall, thin Choctaw Indian, was in the 157th Infantry.[12] Near the division objective of Carando near Campoleone, Barfoot's platoon ran into heavy German resistance on commanding ground. He took matters into his own hands and moved off alone toward the enemy left flank. Reaching a machine gun position, he wiped it out with one well-placed hand grenade.

11. Ibid., 11. Apparently the trench that Shirley attacked was an outpost line, considering it was so lightly held. Written in later years, his account is vague as to whether he entered the trench alone or with others. The implication is that he was alone.
12. Barfoot's Indian ethnicity was a matter of his own choice. It was not noticeable to the author when the two were classmates at the Army Command and General Staff College in 1954. The Cherokees required only one eighth Indian ancestry to be allowed to claim Cherokee citizenship. The same may apply to the Choctaws.

He then moved to the next machine gun emplacement and with his tommy gun killed two Germans and captured three. Another machine gun crew, witnessing the fate of the others, surrendered. Before the day was over, he had captured a total of seventeen enemy soldiers and consolidated his position on favorable ground. With the inevitable counterattack, he took a bazooka and stopped three advancing enemy tanks, killing at least some of the escaping crew with his automatic rifle. Then, despite his exhaustion, he helped two wounded men back to the rear.[13]

Barfoot survived to finish a successful career in the army, retiring as a brigadier general. Not so fortunate, however, was Captain William W. Galt, of the 34th Division. Galt, a battalion operations officer in the 168th Infantry, went forward from the battalion command post to see what had held it up. Volunteering to lead the next attack, Galt discovered that one tank destroyer[14] had not joined in the attack, whereupon Captain Galt hopped up on the rear deck. Galt was totally exposed as he stood on the rear deck of the vehicle, but he made full use of its .30-caliber machine gun and of hand grenades. When the TD trapped forty German soldiers in a large trench, Galt gave them the option to surrender. When they refused he killed all forty—or so the reports claimed. At that time an incoming German artillery shell took Galt's life.[15]

The losses of the VI Corps, including its British divisions were staggering on May 23 and May 24, but Mackensen's lines had been broken.

As the Allied offensive was going into its third week, the American II Corps, on the Tyrrhenian coast, had begun pushing ahead so rapidly that they caught up with their dashing French neighbors on their right. The talk at headquarters was now centered around a media event rather than an important one: the linkup between the forces coming from the Gustav Line and those from the Anzio Beachhead. The war correspondent Eric Sevareid, on the evening of May 24, was writing a broadcast script predicting the juncture, expected soon. On finishing his text, he fell asleep on the floor awaiting the time for his broadcast. Someone shook him by

---

13. *The Medal of Honor*, 335–36.

14. The tank destroyers were a separate branch of the Army during World War II. The M4 Sherman's 75 mm gun (later even the 76 mm) was no match for the armament of the German Mark V Panzer or its successor, the Mark VI Tiger. The TD, with its ninety-mm gun, was a match for either of them. It was a specialized weapon, designed for use against tanks. It had very little armor on the sides and no overhead cover. For work with infantry, the M4 Sherman was preferable. The infantry liked the TD's, partly because of the attitude of aggressiveness inculcated in their training.

15. *Medal of Honor*, 340.

"My God! Here they wuz an' there we wuz."

Drawing copyright 1945 by Bill Mauldin, courtesy of the
Mauldin Estate.

the shoulder; it was General Clark's censor. The colonel seemed embarrassed but he said his piece: "Eric old boy, I'm sorry to wake you up. I just wondered if you would do me a favor and change that script to read: 'There will be one *Fifth Army* front in Italy.'"[16]

Sevareid's luck, however, failed him in his efforts to witness the important story, the juncture between the Anzio force and the II Corps coming up to meet them. He slept in late, and when the other journalists were alerted and sent forward, they did not, for some reason, awaken him. Sevareid later learned that Lieutenant Francis Buckley of Philadelphia had encountered Captain Ben Souza of Honolulu at a small blown bridge. "Where the hell do you think you're going?" Souza demanded.

16. Sevareid, *Not So Wild a Dream,* 398.

"I've come to make contact with the Anzio forces," Buckley answered. "Well," said Souza, "You've made it."

So the Anzio beachhead was no longer a separate entity. It had all happened so quickly that General Clark, arriving late, was forced to stage a reenactment for the photographers.

By the evening of May 24, the end of the second day of the attack out of Anzio, General Lucian Truscott, in command, was relatively well satisfied. The 3d Division, though it had sustained fearsome losses in the first two days of battle, had surrounded Cisterna, and the 7th Infantry had nearly finished digging the last stubborn defenders out of the rubble of the town. The other two regiments of the division were continuing to drive ahead to its north and south. On the left of the 3d, a combat command of the 1st Armored Division was probing to the northwest toward Velletri, a key town in the Alban Hills. On the right of the 3d, Frederick's Devil's Brigade had driven ahead, perhaps too aggressively. Going so far as to lose touch with units on its flanks, the brigade had been forced back by German counterattacks but was still in a strong position. To the northwest, the 45th Infantry Division was engaged in heavy combat and was inflicting heavy loss on the enemy. Since the Cisterna attack had gone so well, Truscott abandoned his original plan to pass the 36th Division through the 3d to continue the attack on Cori. The 3d would push ahead, at least for now.

That afternoon, Truscott received a visit from General Clark. After having been brought up to date, Clark asked what Truscott would think of abandoning, or at least downgrading operation Buffalo, toward Valmontone, and putting the main effort northward along the road to Campoleone and the Alban Hills (Operation Turtle). This was the issue that Clark and Alexander had been playing cat and mouse over for some time.

Truscott paused. The switch, he said, should not be made unless two conditions should develop. One was that the enemy should have begun withdrawing to the northwest along the front of the 45th Division. The other condition would be one in which the enemy should decide to establish a strong defense of Valmontone.[17] With those two conditions met, it might be desirable. The terrain between Cori and Valmontone was rugged, ideal for defense, and an attack to the northwest might be easier, but only if those two conditions were to develop.[18]

17. Truscott, *Command Missions,* 372–73, estimates that the Anzio Beachhead was faced by five German divisions. Three potent German divisions were elsewhere and might be available to defend Valmontone. These were the Hermann Goering, the 3d Panzer Grenadier, and the 4th Parachute, all first-class units, 374.

18. Ibid., 372–74.

The attack went well, though the fighting remained hard. Two days later, on May 25, Truscott returned to his command post at Nettuno feeling satisfied. Waiting for him was Brigadier General Don Brann, Fifth Army G-3 (Operations), the man Clark used habitually to convey bad news.

Brann's message was a shocker. "The Boss wants you to leave the 3d Infantry Division and the Special Service Force to block Highway 6," he said, "and mount that assault you discussed with him to the northwest as soon as you can."

Truscott, as he later described himself, was dumbfounded. The conditions he had laid down had not materialized. The Germans were not defending the hills in front of Valmontone with any great strength, and there was no sign of any withdrawal in the Campoleone area. Without these conditions, there should be no change in plans. He refused to obey the order unless he could talk with Clark in person.

Brann, however, stood his ground. Clark, he said, was not in the beachhead and could not be reached even by radio. Clark wanted the order carried out.

Truscott had no choice. The glitter of Rome rather than the destruction of Germans was the grand prize. Such was the order, he later wrote, "that turned the main effort of the beachhead forces from the Valmontone Gap and prevented the destruction of the German X Army."[19]

Clark's decision to change direction without Alexander's approval was the most controversial he ever made. Though not so publicized as the failure at the Rapido, where his hands were largely tied, this decision represented a clear-cut case of insubordination.

The degree to which it damaged the Allied effort to destroy the German Tenth Army is not clear-cut. There were many secondary roads that von Vietinghoff could use. Most people side with Truscott in his condemnation of the action but few are so categorical. Clark's adversary, von Senger, later wrote that he thought Clark's action to move northward was the right one. He cited the principle of the parallel pursuit.

In any event, what actually happened was that von Vietinghoff's Tenth Army lived to fight another day.

19. Ibid., 375.

CHAPTER 23

VELLETRI

Fred Walker's Finest Hour

*Generally the army commander is credited with winning the
battle, but . . . the battle of Velletri was all Walker's; it was his
plan, he directed it, and he led it. He put his head in the noose
for instant hanging if it failed to work. For my part, I was only
the pick-and-shovel but trying to do what the boss wanted done.*
  Colonel Oran C. Stovall, Division Engineer, 36th Division

When Clark changed the direction of VI Corps from Valmontone to
the Alban Hills, he caused Truscott a great deal of anguish. Aside
from the resentment Truscott felt over what he considered Clark's
erroneous tactics and defiance of Alexander's orders, he and his VI Corps
staff were now burdened with headaches galore. The switch entailed an extensive shift in troop dispositions, the most drastic of which involved the 1st
Armored Division. "Old Ironsides" had to be withdrawn from its position
driving north toward Valmontone and sent south and east of Velletri, crossing the supply lines of the 34th and 45th Divisions in the process. It also required Truscott to displace practically all of the corps artillery, as well as all
affected command posts and communications. Since the area was small and
congested, with a limited road net, Truscott later complained that "a more
complicated plan would be difficult to conceive."

Despite Truscott's travails, however, the VI Corps was able to meet
these challenges. In his memoirs, Truscott tells of the feat with a touch of
swagger, attributing its success to the thorough preparations by his staff,
his well-trained and disciplined troops, and incidentally mentioning that
the enemy lacked the strength and mobility to prevent it.[1]

1. Truscott, *Command Missions,* 375–76.

Breakthrough at Velletri--36th infantry Division, 31 May-2 June 1944

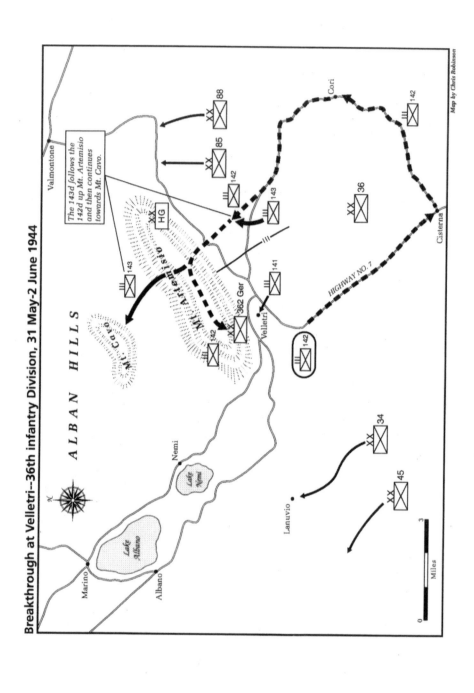

The 143d follows the 142d up Mt. Artemisio and then continues towards Mt. Cavo.

ALBAN HILLS

Mt. Cavo

Mt. Artemisio

Lake Albano

Lake Nemi

Marino

Albano

Nemi

Lanuvio

Velletri

Valmontone

Cori

Cisterna

HIGHWAY NO. 7

88

85

142

143

HG

143

141

362 Ger

142

142

36

142

34

45

Miles

0   3

Map by Chris Robinson

All of this might have been worth the effort had the change been a switch from an assault on an enemy position of strength in favor of a soft spot; in fact it was quite the contrary. Sometime earlier, German Field Marshal Albert Kesselring had decided to defend Rome not at Valmontone in the Saccho Valley but along the southern rim of the Alban Hills. He had begun work on the so-called Caesar, or "C," Line at about the time he had begun preparing the Hitler line at Cassino. The result was a strong defensive position about thirty miles long, stretching between the Tyrrhenian Sea and Valmontone. Of necessity it was thinly held, because only five German divisions were available to the Fourteenth Army. Of the five, however, four were high-quality units, nearly up to strength.[2] The position, therefore, represented a formidable obstacle.

Truscott's new direction of attack was approximately northward. The key towns facing him at the foot of the Alban Hills were, from west to east, (a) Carano, near Campoleone; (b) Lanuvio in the center; and (c) Velletri, astride Highway 7, on his right. Valmontone remained the objective of the 3d Division and the Special Forces Brigade—only now they were without the 1st Armored and the bulk of the corps artillery and engineer support.[3]

Under these circumstances, the attack toward the Alban Hills and Rome went slowly. For four days, from May 26 through the 29th, the 45th Infantry Division attacked toward Campoleone, the 34th toward Lanuvio and the 1st Armored (after a second relief by the 36th at Velletri) on the left. None of these efforts attained their objectives, and each day of bloody fighting produced only a couple of miles of gain.

The reason for the slowness was not enemy strength so much as the nature of the terrain. The winding roads through the mountains were simply not suited for rapid exploitation of success. The experience of John Shirley, of Company "I," 15th Infantry, 3d Division serves as an example.

After having been in combat for only four days, Shirley had risen from the position of assistant squad leader to that of acting platoon sergeant. His platoon, originally forty men, was down to nineteen. It had only one other NCO, a corporal.

2. From southwest to northeast, they were the 4th Panzer-Grenadier, the 65th Panzer-Grenadier, the 3d Panzer-Grenadier, the remnants of the 362d Infantry and the Hermann Goering Divisions. See map, 423, Walker, *Texas to Rome*. All but the 362d were in good condition.

3. The fact that the 3d Division and the Special Service Force were still making the attack justified Clark's giving Alexander assurances that he was obeying the AAI Commander's specific instructions. Alexander was not fooled; he knew where the weight of the attack was directed.

The 3d Division, though in a secondary role against a supposedly beaten enemy, was to drive rapidly to Valmontone by way of a small town named Artena, only two miles short of the objective. The lead elements were following a winding road, but Artena had been reported as unoccupied. Fifty feet out ahead of Shirley's truck was a jeep carrying a driver and two lieutenants from 3d Battalion Headquarters.

Under these conditions—or at least the conditions as understood by the men of "I" Company—safety in an exposed area lay in speed. Thus, even in those mountain roads, the drivers kept up a pace of fifty miles per hour. By so doing, they calculated, they could avoid the effects of observed enemy artillery fire.

When the truck convoy approached a bend in the road about two miles from Artena, a single shell, probably fired from a German 88, exploded on the shoulder of the road only a few feet from the truck in which Shirley was riding. "Shell fragments, rocks, dirt, and a rush of hot air" engulfed the truck as it swerved to an abrupt stop.[4] The two men in the front seats of the truck had been killed, and the two lieutenants in the jeep up ahead had been wounded. The men in the truck dived into the ditches beside the road, and Shirley feared that they made a perfect target for an enemy artillery barrage. None came, but the men were forced to continue on by foot. The lead element of the 3d Division was eventually held up for three hours by a single German artillery piece.

The officers and men of "I" Company still assumed Artena to be unoccupied, but the shell that had so delayed them served as something of a warning. By the time Artena was taken, "I" Company was now commanded by its only surviving officer, a second lieutenant. And Shirley, whose 3d Platoon was now down to sixteen men, was given the eight survivors of the 2d Platoon. Together the original total of eighty men was down to twenty-four, commanded by a buck sergeant who had been in action for only four days.[5]

At this point, General Truscott decided to commit his reserve, Fred Walker's 36th Infantry Division. It was a big move on Truscott's part, because a commander can do little to affect the course of a battle once all his troops are in action. But there was no reason to leave the 36th idle. It was the only unit in VI Corps that was not depleted and worn-out. The division had landed at Anzio only on May 22, as the attack to break out of

4. Shirley, *I Remember*, 16.
5. Ibid., 17.

the beachhead had begun, and it was nearly up to strength and relatively retrained and rested.

The 36th had its problems, however. Even though three whole months had passed since its disastrous repulse at the Rapido, it was still looked upon as a "hard-luck" outfit; bad luck had continued to dog it. Immediately after its withdrawal from the Rapido, for example, it had been assigned the mission of seizing the mountaintops west of Cassino. Even had the division been fresh, the mission would have been doubtful, but in its depleted condition, the task was impossible. Needless to say, the 36th had failed to attain its objective.

As a result the 36th Division had been kept in reserve ever since, rebuilding. It had been trained in mountain warfare, in preparation for an attack across the Garigliano into the Esperia, the territory in which Juin's FEC later so distinguished itself. Most recently it had been held in reserve near Naples as part of Alexander's deception plan. Clark's change in emphasis, however, had resulted in the division's being sent to Anzio rather than the Garigliano. Fortuitously the mountain training had fitted the 36th for the kind of warfare it was about to face.

But processing new replacements and training the division as a whole were not the only serious problems that Walker had been forced to contend with. The morale of his units, especially among the older members of the division, had been seriously injured by some callous moves on the part of General Clark himself. Soon after the Rapido failure, Clark, possibly attempting to shift blame onto the division itself, had replaced Walker's three regimental commanders, his assistant division commander, his chief of staff, and his operations officer. He left Walker himself in command of the division, but he did not consult him in the process of replacing all of his important subordinates. The wonder is that under these circumstances Walker did not demand relief himself, though he expected that he would be next to go.[6]

It was under this cloud that the 36th Division moved up into the line on the evening of May 26, 1944, relieving the 1st Armored Division facing Velletri. From the outset, Walker had a strange feeling that the sector was mysteriously quiet. Patrols on the front facing Velletri were finding enemy activity surprisingly light. Under orders from Truscott to cut the railroad

---

6. Walker was a reasonable man. When his new chief of staff and new operations officer reported in on February 6, Walker noted, "I have discussed with them the manner in which they are to perform their duties. I shall help them in every possible way for I do not blame them for the manner in which they happened to be assigned here" (Walker, *Texas to Rome*, 326).

line in front of Velletri without getting in a fight, Walker had instructed the commander of the 141st Infantry Regiment, Colonel John W. Harmony, to avoid becoming too seriously engaged. Harmony coped with those instructions by sending out aggressive patrols while holding his main body back. Those patrols, like the ones before, returned reporting no German activity. Harmony therefore set up his main line just a mile south of the railroad while keeping the railroad under surveillance by heavy patrolling.[7]

On May 27, Walker called his staff and commanders together to discuss the possible assignments the division might be given in the near future. The worst employment, in Walker's mind, would be to replace either the 34th Division facing Lanuvio or the 3d, now nearing Valmontone, both sadly depleted by heavy fighting. Much as he would dislike either mission, Walker was confident. "We are," he later recorded, "prepared for almost anything."[8]

But Walker could not get his mind off that possible gap in the enemy lines. Following his meeting of Saturday, May 27, he decided to make a personal reconnaissance of the front of the 143d Infantry. There he was told that patrols had met no strong resistance since moving into position. Based on that information, Walker consulted his division engineer, Lieutenant Colonel Oran C. Stovall, to discuss the possibility of constructing a road up the north end of Monte Artemisio, a long, three thousand-foot hill that ran southwest to northeast behind Velletri. If that critical hill could be taken and supported with tanks, he might be able to place the bulk of the division behind the Germans defending Velletri. The next morning Stovall reported favorably. The road could be built, he said; he and his staff had made personal surveys of the region and were confident that it could be done.[9]

Walker was determined to be certain beyond reasonable doubt. He therefore made another personal reconnaissance, this time from the observer's seat of a Piper Cub. He looked carefully at Monte Artemisio, and he detected almost nothing by way of field works, guns, or emplacements. On return, therefore, he directed his air photo section to search through the available aerial coverage of the area. Finally, based on all this evidence, Walker was convinced that he could send two regiments up the northern slopes of Monte Artemisio practically undetected. The problem now was to convince General Truscott.

7. Wagner, *Texas Army*, 162.
8. Walker, *Texas to Rome*, 372.
9. Stovall was not so confident as he appeared to Walker. The night before reporting to Walker, he later admitted, he could not sleep.

Truscott, to Walker's disappointment, was not at the moment receptive to new ideas. His testy mood was in evidence at the meeting he held on the evening of May 29 in his headquarters beneath Nettuno. It was a formal affair, considering the circumstances, with about sixty officers attending. The map on the wall was large and elaborate. Truscott, possibly out of frustration, was putting on a show for what had to be a somewhat discouraged group of officers. In that setting, Truscott rebuffed Walker's efforts to get his idea across.

Truscott's decision that evening was just the one that Walker had feared. The 36th Division was to pull out of the line the next morning and move south, replacing the weary 34th Division in its attack on Lanuvio. The T-Patchers, as Walker saw it, were being "shoved into another impossible situation."[10]

The next morning, May 30, Walker assembled his staff and unit commanders to make arrangements to move to Lanuvio, starting at noon. As he left the meeting, he was surprised to see Truscott pull up to his command post in a jeep. Apparently Walker's futile efforts to get his point over the previous evening had made some impression. In all likelihood, also, Truscott himself was dissatisfied with the unimaginative plan he had announced and was open to any new ideas.

This was the moment that Walker had been hoping for. With his plan for infiltrating around Velletri up Monte Artemisio matured in his mind, he explained it in detail and with conviction. Truscott studied his words and mulled them over seriously. "You may have something there," he said. "I'll call you back in an hour." On Truscott's departure, Walker quickly suspended the order he had given that morning for leaving their present position: no further movements until his commanders heard from him.

As promised, Truscott called at about 11:00 A.M. He had talked with General Clark, he said, and Walker should go ahead with his plan. Walker was elated, but, ever-touchy, he was hurt when Truscott added, "You had better get through."[11] At the same time, however, Truscott demonstrated his support by attaching several units, including the 36th Combat Engineer

---

10. Walker, *Texas to Rome,* 374.

11. Ibid., 375. Walker had a dire interpretation of these words, translating them to mean, "If you don't succeed, you'll be on your way back to the States. . . . I accept none of the responsibility." Truscott's account mentions no such threat. In all likelihood, Truscott, being only human, was a little irked that a subordinate had found a solution contrary to that which the corps commander had presented to a large audience the evening before. Truscott was also tired.

Regiment and some tank units, invaluable additions to Walker's fighting power.[12] The die was cast; the responsibility for the success of the Velletri operation by way of Monte Artemisio was squarely on Walker's shoulders.

Walker's plan was relatively simple. Harmony's 141st Infantry was to remain in place facing Velletri on the south. Colonel Paul D. Adams's 143d Infantry, on Harmony's right, was to be relieved by the 16th Engineer Regiment, fighting as infantry. The 142d, under Colonel George E. Lynch, in reserve at the moment, would lead the attack round to the right, up the gap on the northeast slope of Monte Artemisio.

The immediate objective of the 142d Infantry would be to seize the Machio d'Ariano and Hill 931, at the northeastern end of the mountain. The 143d Infantry would follow the 142d until the 142d reached the crest, at which point the two would continue in different directions. The 142d would turn left and proceed to the southwest, occupying the entire Artemisio hill mass, and ready to attack enemy forces at Velletri from the rear. The 143d would first take Monte Cavo and the Roca di Papa, the highest points on the mountain and behind Monte Artemisio. It was then to continue northwest toward Albano, well behind enemy lines on Route 7, the Road to Rome.

It was a tricky maneuver for Lynch's 142d Infantry. Currently located on the west end of the division line, it could not proceed to the right, where it would make its attack, because enemy observation and fire would make it impossible. As a result, Lynch was forced to put his men in trucks and send them southward from its reserve position west of Velletri to Cisterna, then east to Cori, and then northward to the east of Velletri. Those towns were places that had been in German hands only a few days before. To move the four miles across the front, the truck trip was about twenty-five. Lynch stayed behind to greet the regiment when it returned to the combat zone.

Walker himself was understandably nervous. When Eric Sevareid found him at about this time, he gave the correspondent a brief, curt nod, not typical of Walker. Sevareid called Walker a "solemn, self-contained man," and noted that he had never seen the general in such a state of perturbation.[13] Walker was aware of his nervousness, and realized that he was taking his feelings out on his subordinates. At one point he bypassed the chain of command and pounced on a platoon leader who was preparing to move forward. "Lieutenant," he barked, "get your men up and get going. Get going."

---

12. Other attachments included the 805th Tank Destroyer Battalion, the 605th Tank Destroyer Battalion and two companies of the 751st Tank Battalion, Wagner, *Texas Army*, 163.
13. Severeid, *Not So Wild a Dream*, 404.

Major General Fred Walker plans attack. U.S. Army, Eisenhower Library.

The lieutenant, a young man about to risk his life and unimpressed by the "brass," looked askance. Emphasizing each word, he said, "General, I'm going, but I'm not going until I get ready."

Walker knew that the lieutenant was right. "In other words," Walker wrote later, "he was saying, attend to your business and let me attend to mine."[14]

Colonel Lynch, also, was concerned that some frightened young soldier might compromise secrecy by firing his gun inadvertently or in a moment of panic. He therefore ordered all troops to move with loaded magazines but no ammunition in the chambers of either rifle or pistol. "Any killing," he announced forcefully, "was to be done by bayonet, knife, or any other quiet means." The directive worked. Lynch later recalled that he did not hear a single shot all night until the dawn.[15]

Shortly after midnight of May 30, the 142d Infantry, in a column of battalions, began making its way up the southeast slope of Monte Artemisio,

14. Walker, *Texas to Rome*, 377.
15. Adelman and Walton, *Rome Fell Today*, 24.

following the white tape laid on the ground by the engineers. The members, from colonel down to private, were tense, anticipating discovery at any time. At first they had good concealment in the form of parallel rows of vineyards. As they passed through this area, the men could hear a steady exchange of machine gun fire off to their left, which indicated that the fight of the 141st for Velletri was under way. The men listened for anything—a random shot, barking dogs, and even the braying of a jackass.

At around 3:00 A.M., the men of the 142d witnessed an enemy air action overhead. The German planes came uncomfortably near, and the Americans hugged the ground, hoping that the flares would not pick them up. Soon, however, it became apparent that the 142d was not the enemy's target. In fact the men were relieved when they realized that "it focused attention away from our sector to over in front of Velletri where it was taking place." The flares did, however, cause a delay of a half hour before the men could move on again.

As a result of delays, Colonel Lynch was concerned with the coming of daylight, the first of which began at 4:15. When it arrived, the head of the column was just beginning its ascent up Monte Artemisio. Fortunately, a heavy haze protected them from enemy view, and the 142d picked up the pace. As Lynch later reported, "There was no one to oppose us. The infantrymen clambered up the slopes."[16]

The Americans climbing Monte Artemisio, unbeknownst to them, were actually going through a gap in the German lines, the boundary between two German corps, the 4th Parachute Corps on the west and the 76th Panzer Corps on the east. The 362d Grenadier (Infantry) Division— or the remnants thereof—was on the left flank of the 4th Parachute Corps and the Hermann Goering Panzer Division was on the right flank of the 76th Panzer Corps. The gap between those units was a full two miles.

The exposed flanks had not escaped the notice of the German commanders, though they were unaware of the magnitude of the threat. The commander of the Hermann Goering Division, General Wilhelm Schmalz, had become aware of it as early as the night of May 27–28. He sent patrols out to find the 362d, which he knew was somewhere on his right, and those patrols confirmed the extent of the gap. Though they had not encountered many Americans, Schmalz reported the gap to Mackensen's Fourteenth Army Headquarters.

16. Regimental Commander's Comments—Operations in Italy, May, 1944. Headquarters, 142d Infantry, U.S. Army, July 1, 1944, 5. Quoted in Adelman and Walton, *Rome Fell Today,* 23–24.

He also took action himself. In desperation, Schmalz stationed an engineer platoon on Castel d'Ariano. Hardly a combat unit but at least a listening post. Throughout the 28th and 29th of May he pleaded with Fourteenth Army to order the 4th Parachute Corps to do at least the same. His appeals, however, went unheeded.[17] Fortunately for the Americans, Schmalz's engineer listening post did not detect the arrival of the 142d Infantry; instead it reported only that it had been "engaged with some American infantry" when it reported back to Schmalz.[18]

The lead elements of Lynch's 142d Infantry arrived at Machio d'Ariano at 6:35 A.M., but it was early afternoon, May 31, before General Schmalz realized that he had a significant penetration on his hands. Ironically he learned it from Fourteenth Army, not his own security units. His resources to eradicate the penetration were meager, however; he was able to throw in only an understrength battalion of panzer grenadiers, no tanks. The attack of one weak battalion against two American infantry regiments was foredoomed to failure.

In the meantime, Stovall's engineer units were feverishly building the tank trail. For the moment, aggressive action had to await their efforts. Walker would not commit his infantry to serious combat without tank and tank-destroyer support.

The next step, according to Walker's plan, was for Lynch's men to occupy the entire Artemisio Ridge. As early as 6:40 A.M., right after arriving at the crest of the hill, the 142d Infantry commander sent an order for his 1st Battalion to begin the southwest move. With virtually no resistance, the 1st and 2d Battalions had reached Hill 821, on the west end, by the end of the day.

By 7:30 P.M., May 31, Schmalz, and his counterpart Heinz Greiner, of the 362d Grenadier, realized the full extent of their peril. Their position was hopeless; six thousand American troops were in their rear, overlooking the main road from Velletri to Nemi and Albano beyond.[19] In contrast to so many heartbreaking actions of the Italian campaign, the American casualties in this flanking movement had been light: The 142d had lost sixty-one men, only eight of them killed. The 143d had incurred even lighter losses: fourteen casualties, of whom only three had been killed.[20]

17. Fisher, "Monte Artemisio," 426, of Walker, *Texas to Rome.*
18. Ibid., 429. The 142d also caught a small group of artillery observers, one of them taking his morning bath.
19. Wagner, *Texas Army,* 166.
20. Fisher, in Walker, *Texas to Rome,* 430

On the next morning, June 1, 1944, the 141st Infantry resumed its attack on Velletri. One battalion came from the south, the Velletri-Valmontone Road, while the other two, from the Velletri-Nemi Road, came in from the northwest. By 4:30 that afternoon, the regiment had penetrated to the center of town. There was plenty of evidence that the Germans had intended to hold on to it:

> The place was in ruins. Enemy dead and materiel littered the streets, and in the remaining buildings numerous dead and wounded were discovered. Hundreds of prisoners were routed from the extensive fortifications, tunnels, and reinforced gun positions—mute evidence of the important role Velletri was to play in the German defense plans. Despite the stubborn resistance of survivors of the enemy garrison, the 141st incurred few casualties—one man killed and 38 wounded.[21]

It was the next day, June 2, that the 143d Infantry was able to move out toward its more ambitious objective of Monte Cavo. The fact that it went northward instead of toward Velletri to the south stands as evidence that the enemy was beaten. The advance was deliberate, not because of enemy action but due to the need to allow the competent but overworked engineers to complete a road capable of carrying tanks and tank destroyers. Once under way, the 143d seized the high point at Roca di Papa and Monte Cavo. The road to Rome was open to the 143d.

The evaluation by the military historian Ernest F. Fisher summarizes the action:

> General Walker's stratagem had worked. An entire American infantry division now moved into the Alban Hills. Field Marshal Kesselring's last defense line south of Rome had been shattered, and General Truscott's 6th Corps, led by the 36th Infantry Division, now pursued the Germans across the fabled Roman Campagna toward the historic city.[22]

The noted correspondent Eric Sevareid expressed his triumph, along with a slight disdain for Walker's superiors: "Rome must now fall. General Alexander and Clark would soon receive the key to the city, but surely it was General Walker who turned the key. From him they were really receiving it."[23]

21. Ibid., 431.
22. Ibid.
23. Sevareid, *Not So Wild a Dream*, 408.

But Walker's greatest tribute was more impressive because it came from his enemy, Heinz Greiner, former commander of the 362d Grenadier Division:

> . . . in my book I have called special attention to your admirable deed, and may I—23 years after the war's end—personally express to you my high regard for this deed. . . . You can really be proud of your courage and presumably of your correct estimate of the situation. . . May I, as your former opponent, express to you my high regard.[24]

24. Heinz Geiner to General Fred Walker, Oct. 17, 1968, cited in Walker, *Texas to Rome,* 433.

CHAPTER 24

ROME

The roads leading into Rome had become the Italian Grand Prix, with every unit and every war correspondent racing to be the first to enter the Eternal City. Keyes's II Corps, barreling up the flat, straight Highway 6 into Valmontone, was hell-bent on beating Truscott's VI Corps, coming a shorter distance but via a more twisting and easily defended road from the Alban Hills. Every parallel side road, and even flanking fields, were filled with olive-drab American jeeps, command cars, trucks of all sizes, tanks, and tank-destroyers—all heading flat out for Rome.

Flint Whitlock

With the rupture of the Caesar Line at Velletri, Kesselring's organized defensive position collapsed. Though many German units still had plenty of fight in them, Kesselring's objective was now confined to extricating his Tenth and Fourteenth Armies. He declared Rome an open city and made no attempt to establish a defense line behind the Tiber. He planned to make his next stand on the Arno, another strong barrier to the north.

Kesselring was not feeling defeated. On the contrary, he was heartened by the fact that von Vietinghoff's Tenth Army, by going through the mountains at Subiaco and Tivoli, had escaped entrapment and would soon join up with the Fourteenth to fight another day.[1]

---

1. Kesselring, *Memoirs*, 203.

As the German divisions made their way back, their rear guards fought with their usual fortitude. Sometimes their tactics were underhanded. False pretensions of intentions to surrender were common, but Audie Murphy, of the 15th Infantry, reported a new angle. A German unit sent a tank toward the American lines with two American prisoners perched on the front. As the tank approached, the American lieutenant commanding the intended target made a quick though painful decision: he opened fire with all guns available. One round stopped the tank but unfortunately killed one of the American prisoners. The other man was more fortunate; he hopped off and ran for safety.[2] By the loss of a single life, the defending lieutenant had undoubtedly saved several other Americans.

As of June 4, the Americans were using only two of the three major roads leading into Rome from the south and southwest. Truscott's VI Corps, bolstered with the 1st Armored Division, was using Route 7 through Velletri, and on its right Keyes's II Corps, consisting of the 3d, 85th, 88th Infantry Divisions and the Devil's Brigade, was following Route 6 from Valmontone. The third main road, Route 5, came into Rome from Pescara, on the Adriatic, and though the British Eighth Army was astride it, that road was rejected as an approach to Rome. Since it crossed directly in front of the Fifth Army advance, its use would cause confusion and possibly the tragedy of friendly casualties.

A spirit of competition therefore began to develop between American units, which developed into a race to see who could get into the Eternal City first. The issue as to who won was never decided. Nobody really knows which unit was actually the first to cross the Roman city limits. Still the race provided an intriguing excuse for making bets and creating headlines for the newspaper reporters: Which corps would get there first? The VI on Route 7 or the II, on Route 6?

Almost everyone placed their bets on II Corps on Route 6. One who did so was Eric Sevareid, who sat frustrated in front of a microphone beside the road, where he hoped to get a report from anyone heading toward the rear. It was the afternoon of June 4, and nobody in the vicinity had appeared with much of anything to say. Sevareid's spirits suddenly perked up, however, when he spotted a couple of generals conferring a short distance away. One of the conferees was Frederick, and the other officer was Geoffrey Keyes, of the II Corps. Sevareid moved up within earshot to eavesdrop.

---

2. Murphy, *To Hell and Back,* 129. Murphy did not specify the weapons used. They were probably recoilless rifles and bazookas.

Keyes, according to Sevareid, seemed impatient. "General Frederick," he asked, "what's holding you up here?"

"The Germans, sir," Frederick answered curtly.

"How long will it take you to get across the city limits?"

"The rest of the day. There are a couple of SP[3] guns up there."

Keyes seemed perturbed. "That won't do!" he exclaimed. General Clark, he said, was scheduled to be across the city limits by four o'clock in order to have a photograph taken for the next day's newspapers.

Frederick said nothing for a long time, staring Keyes straight in the face. Finally he answered, "Tell the general to give me an hour." Though apparently somewhat disgusted, Frederick was as good as his word. The guns were silenced within the hour, possibly at the extra cost of a couple of lives.[4]

Clark arrived by jeep at the appointed hour, having visited Artena, Valmontone, and Velletri along the way. Keyes and Frederick, who had remained on hand, gave him a report. Clark was pleased, especially when Frederick informed him that elements of his brigade were now on the edge of Rome. Other flying columns were entering the city, but all were being opposed by German rear guards.

As Sevareid watched, the three generals began to climb a small hill nearby, in Clark's words, "to take a look." When they reached the top, they found facing them a large sign with the magic name on it: ROMA. Clark instantly decided that he wanted to have that sign as a souvenir. For the moment, nobody was able to retrieve it because firing in the area continued. They waited patiently, however, until all seemed to be quiet. Then Clark and Frederick started up to secure Clark's treasure. At the top they paused to accommodate the urgent requests of shouting photographers, who very much wanted to record the moment. Flashbulbs popped, immortalizing the event for history. Suddenly everyone heard another pop, much louder and obviously no flashbulb: it was a shot from a German sniper. As Clark later recorded the moment, "I doubt that anybody ever saw so many generals duck so rapidly." Clark and Frederick beat a hasty retreat. But Clark was to have his prize. Frederick later went back and retrieved the sign and sent it to him.[5]

Farther south, in the outskirts of Rome, a somewhat similar incident occurred. Truscott and Harmon had met on Route 7 to plan the final stages of the 1st Armored's entry into the city. Absorbed in the problem at

3. Shorthand for "self-propelled."
4. Sevareid, *Not So Wild a Dream*, 410–11.
5. Clark, *Calculated Risk*, 363–64.

Generals Mark W. Clark and Geoffrey Keyes on the outskirts of Rome, June 4, 1944. National Archives.

hand, the two men were busily struggling with unwieldy tactical maps and paying no attention to their surroundings. All of a sudden a German machine gun broke loose from the walls of a stone outhouse. Only then did the two generals show energy; they both plunged into a nearby ditch.

As Truscott and Harmon hugged the ground, a whimsical thought passed through Harmon's mind. "This," he thought, "was the ultimate anti-climax. The two of us, who had gone through so much together, were to be killed by fire from an Italian privy."[6] Eventually an American Sherman tank came clanking up the highway. Harmon shouted and pointed. The tank commander understood. He did not bother to use his

6. Given Ernie Harmon's reputation for salty language, it is possible that this account toned down the words he used at the time.

75 mm gun; he simply turned his tank and drove across the field, ramming straight into the building. When the Sherman had finished its handiwork, Harmon recorded, "there was neither machine gun, outhouse, or German." The tank commander saluted the generals from his turret and drove off. Harmon and Truscott picked themselves up, "resumed the tatters of [their] dignity, and went back to being generals again."[7]

Back in the Velletri area, Fred Walker was giving his weary troops no respite after the breakthrough on Monte Artemisio. Leaving his assistant division commander to coordinate the movements of the other two regiments, he left to find for himself where the lead elements of the 141st Infantry were. He found them at Marino. Colonel John Harmony had mounted many of his foot troops on tanks and tank destroyers to make progress as rapid as possible. Walker noted, however, that very few Germans were being taken prisoner. He quickly concluded that Harmony's column was not moving rapidly enough.

Eventually, the lead troops of the 141st reached the all-important Route 7, only to find that they had met up with Combat Command "A" (CCA) of the 1st Armored Division. Its commander, Colonel Louis V. Hightower, claimed that the 1st Armored had been given priority on that road and that the 141st Infantry should follow behind him. Walker, however, was not going to stop. He exercised his rank and directed a compromise: Hightower's troops, he declared, would march on the left side of the road and Walker's on the right. Hightower was not pleased, but he had to obey.[8] The two columns started out together, neither one of them going as rapidly, of course, as it would had it been accorded the exclusive use of the road. The double column eventually reached the outskirts of Rome, where they encountered the corps commander, General Truscott.

Truscott, who was anxious for Hightower to get into Rome and secure the bridges over the Tiber River, told Walker sharply that he was out of his zone, and ordered him to move the 141st Infantry to another road a mile off to the right. Walker complied cheerfully. Once into the city, he knew, he would have plenty of streets to follow. On the auxiliary route, Walker and his men continued on their way. They met resistance and the going was slow, but they were into Rome!

Truscott was impatient. Once Walker had departed for the auxiliary road, he turned to Hightower and asked what his orders were. "To take the bridges over the Tiber," Hightower responded.

7. Harmon, *Combat Commander*, 192.
8. Walker, *Texas to Rome*, 382.

"Well, what are you waiting for?"

Hightower saluted and left.

Truscott then turned to one of his favorite war correspondents, Michael Chinigo, who had faithfully stuck with VI Corps even though advised otherwise by Clark's headquarters. "Mike," Truscott said, "if you want to be the first correspondent in Rome, you had better follow that tank." Chinigo, grateful, climbed into his jeep and left. Chinigo later reported great success.

That evening elements of the 1st Armored Division seized the bridges over the Tiber intact. The 45th Infantry Division also reached the river, and the engineers began constructing and repairing other bridges.

Truscott, unlike Clark, had no ambition either to tour the city of Rome or to be seen in public. He was preoccupied with his efforts to bring the pieces of his VI Corps together. His activities were interrupted, however, by orders to report to Clark at Capitoline Hill. With a driver and his Italian-speaking aide, he returned to the spot where he had met with Walker and Hightower the previous day. The pace of his jeep was slow, hindered by crowds of people offering "glasses and bottles of wine, fruit, bread, and embraces."

Like Clark, Truscott and his aides soon became lost. They solved their problems much as Clark did, by commandeering the services of an Italian boy, who sat on the front of the vehicle and gave directions. First they went to Capitoline Hill, only to find it devoid of any official party. They then headed for the Excelsior Hotel. About halfway to the hotel they met Clark's official entourage and joined it. Following the army commander, Truscott, Keyes, and Juin dutifully played their roles, though Truscott was anxious to get back to planning the pursuit of the enemy across the Tiber.

Then, to an enthusiastic crowd, Truscott heard General Clark make a talk that began, "This is a great day for the Fifth Army."[9]

The reason for undertaking the landing at Anzio—the capture of Rome—had been attained.

The next morning, June 6, 1944, the British and Americans stormed the beaches of Normandy.

9. Truscott, *Command Missions*, 380.

EPILOGUE

Rome had fallen! Nine months of struggle, death, and misery had finally culminated in attaining the goal so profoundly desired by the Anglo-Americans in general and Winston Churchill in particular. The event did not, of course, mean the end of the Italian campaign. Eleven more months of fighting lay ahead before the end of the war in Europe. Nevertheless, the psychological benefit was obvious. Rome was the first of the three capitals of the Axis to be taken. Berlin and Tokyo would come later, but Rome was a significant beginning.

Taking Rome had another effect. It provided encouragement to those people who particularly desired to keep the Italian campaign active. The Mediterranean Theater was of great importance to the British, because it gave them a combat area in which they were dominant, as were the Americans in northwest Europe. And besides that matter of national prestige, Allied control of the Mediterranean was vital to the maintenance of the lifeline to India through the Suez Canal.

The timing was perfect. The Allies in Italy had succeeded in taking Rome before the Normandy invasion could take place, so they could savor their moment of victory before being upstaged in the headlines by Overlord. Up to June 5, 1944, the campaign in Italy had been the only arena in which American and British troops were engaging the forces of Hitler. All the eyes of the world were focused on them. From that day on, however, Italy would be regarded as a "secondary" theater. And the deemphasis on Italy was to become even more drastic because of the transfer of Allied troops from Italy to France.

The Mediterranean Theater, it will be recalled, had already lost seven experienced divisions as the result of transfer to the United Kingdom. Now it was fated to lose seven more as the result of decisions made by the Big Three at Tehran in November 1943. There the United States, Britain, and Soviet Russia had confirmed that the Western Allies should attack northwest Europe in the spring of 1944, and that a sizeable force (Operation Anvil, later Dragoon) should be landed simultaneously at Marseilles. The Dragoon force, led by the VI Corps, would drive northward up the Rhone River until it met Eisenhower's force coming from Normandy. At that time, it would come under Eisenhower's command as the U.S. Seventh Army. Churchill, who quipped that he had been "dragooned" into the agreement, never considered the Tehran agreements to be set in concrete. Roosevelt, however, had viewed the agreement as his own personal commitment to Stalin. As a result, three American and four French divisions began withdrawing from the Italian front immediately upon the capture of Rome.

All the Dragoon divisions were to come from Italy, in fact from Clark's Fifth Army. The VI Corps and the French Expeditionary Corps were earmarked for the operation. The plan was for the three American divisions of VI Corps to make the assault, later to be followed up by the four divisions of the French Expeditionary Corps. Clark was not allowed to choose which divisions to send, because that choice had been made at a higher level of command.[1] And if that fact were not painful enough, Clark would also lose Lucian Truscott. For some strange reason, Juin was not slated to command the French Expeditionary Corps in France.

From a military point of view, it is difficult to argue with the decision of the Combined Chiefs of Staff, ratified by their respective governments, to concentrate all possible force in Overlord, the main Allied force fighting Germany. The arguments against the transfer, therefore, centered around political considerations. Viewpoints, pro and con, generally ran along national lines, with nearly all the British opinion opposing it and American favoring it. Clark was the exception among the Americans. He professed to harbor no objection to the basic concept of a landing in southern France, and he could understand the strong desire of the French troops to fight on their own soil. He maintained, however, that the French could have executed Dragoon by themselves, leaving the VI Corps, with its three American divisions, in Italy:

> For various reasons . . . our team was broken up and the Fifth Army
> was sapped of a great part of its strength. A campaign that might have
> changed the whole history of relations between the Western World
> and Soviet Russia was permitted to fade away, not into nothing, but

1. The 3d, 36th, and 45th Infantry Divisions.

into much less than it could have been. . . . Not alone in my opinion, but in the opinion of a number of experts who were close to the problem, the weakening of the campaign in Italy in order to invade southern France instead of pushing on into the Balkans was one of the outstanding political mistakes of the war.[2]

Nevertheless, though Churchill fought against Dragoon to the bitter end, it was delayed but never canceled. The landings occurred on August 15, 1944.[3]

Though he had lost Rome, German Field Marshal Albert Kesselring found cause for satisfaction in the situation that faced him in early June 1944. Over the objections of such an influential figure as Erwin Rommel, he had convinced Hitler to take the gamble of defending Italy south of Rome. He had delayed the Allies for nine months, longer than anyone had previously predicted, and had extricated both his Tenth and Fourteenth Armies from the Allied pincers and had successfully brought them across the Tiber, damaged but far from destroyed.

Kesselring had long been planning his next step. He had prepared a major defensive position, the Gothic Line, to protect the all-important Po Valley. The Gothic Line ran roughly between Pisa on the Tyrrhenian Sea on the south and Rimini on the Adriatic to the north, a position nearly as strong as that of Monte Cassino on the Rapido. To give his engineers and the attached Todt organization units time to prepare the Gothic Line, Kesselring occupied a strongly held delaying position along the Arno River, much the same concept as that he had employed at the Winter Line of late 1943.

Alexander did not pause to regroup his forces after taking Rome. Unlike Clark, Alex professed to regard that city's capture not as an end in itself but as only an incident in his all-out attempt to destroy Kesselring's retreating forces. He therefore continued his offensive without letup, and for a while the flat terrain beyond the Tiber favored him. The port of Civitavecchia fell on June 7 (where the Allies found Anzio Annie) and the French seized the island of Elba on June 18. So well were things going that Alexander believed that he could break the Gothic Line and reach the Po Valley as early as August.[4]

2. Clark, *Calculated Risk*, 368.
3. When the landings were made, Churchill witnessed them from a British warship.
4. *West Point Atlas*, Map 105.

The situation then changed. An alarmed Hitler sent Kesselring an additional eight divisions of varying size and quality, and with this augmentation Kesselring was able to slow Alexander's progress nearly to a halt. It was early August, therefore, before the Allies even reached the line of the Arno, a distance of only about 180 miles, against a delaying action executed by what had recently been considered a shattered enemy. Alexander eventually reached the Gothic Line, but it took him until January 1945. It was spring before the last great Allied offensive was launched.

December of 1944 saw significant changes in the Allied high command. The death of Field Marshal Sir John Dill, the British representative on the Combined Chiefs of Staff in Washington,[5] called for a replacement with diplomatic skills. The nod for that vital position went to General Sir Henry Maitland Wilson, the Supreme Commander, Mediterranean. Wilson's departure from Algiers provided Churchill the opportunity to elevate Alexander to the position of Supreme Commander, Mediterranean Theater of War, a recognition that many thought was overdue. Clark, with Churchill's staunch support, was then elevated to the command of Allied Forces in Italy. The Prime Minister had held a special affinity for Clark from the early days of the war. Command of the Fifth Army was then passed to Lucian Truscott.[6] There the command structure stood until the end of the war.

The German high command also underwent significant changes. During the fall of 1944, Kesselring was injured in a vehicular accident and was kept out of action for weeks. Von Vietinghoff filled his shoes until his return. Then, during the last weeks of the war, a desperate Hitler removed his old warhorse, Field Marshal Gerd von Rundsted, from command of the Western Front in France and Germany. He called on Kesselring, the man once so maligned in the German officer corps, to replace him. It thus fell to von Vietinghoff, in late April 1945, to make the final surrender to Clark. This disagreeable chore he delegated to Frido von Senger, who was forced to make a perilous journey through partisan-infested country to Clark's headquarters in Florence to go through the formalities. Senger deserved better.

5. General George C. Marshall was so fond of Dill that he arranged for Dill to be represented by an equestrian statue in Arlington National Cemetery, an honor unthought of in the twentieth century.

6. Truscott was reluctant to return to Italy, even to command an army. He believed that he had a chance for promotion with Eisenhower, and he would have preferred to stay with Ike rather than return to Italy. But the transfer was not negotiable.

A collection of colorful personalities played roles in the twenty-month Italian campaign. Some of the participants had significant careers ahead of them, and these are summarized in the appendix. The two main characters in these pages, however, are too important to be engulfed in a list with others. They are, of course, General Sir Harold Alexander, commander of the 15th Army Group, and Lieutenant General Mark Wayne Clark, commander of the American Fifth Army.

The two men shared some superficial characteristics. Both were handsome soldiers, smooth in manner, showing the world a serenity they did not feel. In different ways, both were controversial. And both, though they managed to conceal their attitudes, considered the armed forces of their allies as inferior to their own. Alexander, in Tunisia, was reported to have thought of the Americans as "our Italians," whereas Clark's distaste for such British generals as McCreery and Penney was obvious to all.

In other, more important ways, Alex and Clark made a study in contrasts. Alexander was generally viewed as the most experienced high-level commander in both the British and American Armies. Clark, on the other hand, though a wounded veteran of the First World War, was a novice in high command. Alex was quiet to the point of being self-effacing; Clark was outgoing and unabashed in his zeal to call attention to himself.

Of the two, Alexander is to this author the more interesting because of the inconsistency of opinion about him. Those who admire him do so extravagantly. Truscott called him "outstanding among the allied leaders,"[7] and it was no secret that General Eisenhower—all the Americans, for that matter—harbored forlorn hopes that it would be Alexander, not Montgomery, who would command the British Commonwealth forces for the invasion of northwest Europe, Overlord.

Yet there are those who consider Alexander overrated, even among the subordinates who owed him loyalty. Sometimes, in fact, his subordinates were the worst. Just after the landing at Salerno, Montgomery was probably speaking seriously when he advised Clark to simply ignore Alexander's orders at will. Clark, though pretending to do otherwise, followed that advice to an extraordinary degree. His most flagrant defiance of Alexander's orders occurred when he redirected the main thrust of the VI Corps attack from the direction of Valmontone to Velletri on May 26, 1944. Clark was an ambitious man, and if he seriously feared Alexander's wrath, he would

---

7. Truscott, *Command Missions,* 547. Eisenhower, in *Crusade,* 211, wrote: "I regarded Alexander as Britain's foremost soldier in the field of strategy. He was, moreover, a friendly and agreeable type; Americans liked him."

never have taken such action. In a way, Alexander's shortcoming has been compared to the gentlemanly reticence of General Robert E. Lee, in the American Civil War.

Some of Alexander's apparent lack of force is inherent in the position of an Allied commander. Conscious that he was a tactical, not an administrative commander, he treated the Americans with kid gloves. Thus, while he felt strongly that Dawley, Lucas, and probably Clark were incompetent, he rightly felt that he had no direct authority to relieve the officers of another nationality. In that he was correct. Eisenhower, for example, had no authority to relieve Montgomery when their relationship temporarily broke down in the winter of 1944.[8] Alexander's relationship to the Americans in Italy was exactly the same.

The opinions of some American historians also deserve respect. Carlo d'Este, for example, has portrayed Alexander as somewhat lazy, at least detached, especially when compared to his onetime subordinate, the more colorful Montgomery. The late Martin Blumenson apparently felt the same way. These two historians have done extensive work on the Mediterranean campaigns.

Clark's is a different case, because he managed to earn the dislike of so many of his subordinates. His occasional high-handedness could be astounding. Fred Walker, for example, was well justified in resenting Clark's action in relieving all the regimental commanders and important members of the 36th Division staff without consulting Walker himself. Veterans of the 45th Division have never forgiven Clark for easing out the much-loved Troy Middleton on a flimsy excuse. Another cause for resentment against Clark was his obvious thirst for personal publicity. His efforts to bring attention to the Fifth Army too often appeared to be efforts to bring attention to himself. Such posturing sits poorly with men bleeding in the mud. The resentments, however, had little to do with the conduct of the campaign.

Yet, when Clark's contributions to the Allied cause are considered, there is much to be admired. Both Churchill and Eisenhower were among his most staunch supporters because, if either wanted a difficult job done, they knew that Clark would carry the hod for them. He was certainly courageous; his perilous submarine trip to the Algerian coast to confer with possible French allies in October of 1942 was not the deed of a coward. The guilt for the Rapido disaster on January 20, 1944, was by no means all his. He was a superb American representative on the Allied

8. During and just after the crisis of the Ardennes Campaign in December of 1944, Eisenhower considered Montgomery's insubordination to be such that he nearly presented the Combined Chiefs with an ultimatum to choose between them. He could not, however, relieve Montgomery as overall British commander on his own authority.

Control Council for the occupation of Austria after the end of the war. And he was probably better qualified than anyone else in the American Army to fill the shoes of Douglas MacArthur as commander of United Nations forces in the Far East nearly a decade later. Unfortunately for Clark's reputation, his greatest accomplishments were attained before and after the days covered in this book—and these are the days for which he is best remembered.

In summary, both Alexander and Clark were outstanding men, both with flaws and both easy to misunderstand. Given the impossible problems they both were called on to confront, they performed their roles well.

Since this story of the Anzio Beachhead is only a part of a long and arduous campaign, it is inevitable that the question should arise, Was the campaign worth it? Are those rows of crosses and Stars of David in the Anzio cemetery symbols of needless death? The question is not idle, especially since the Americans, especially General George C. Marshall, were always looking for ways to deemphasize it. Should the Italian campaign have ever happened at all?

From a humanitarian viewpoint, one must wish that the Italian campaign could have been avoided. It was, after all, an operation of attrition, something much to be deplored. Trading a life for a life without having a decisive end in sight—the "soft underbelly of Europe" was a farcical argument—is a repellent thought. And yet the Allied invasion of Italy and its subsequent pursuit were inevitable in the management of the war.

When the Sicilian campaign came to an end in late July 1943, many Allied divisions were spread out in the Mediterranean from Morocco to Sicily, all of which would remain idle for the next eleven months if not employed in Italy or Sardinia. Even those troops scheduled for deployment to the United Kingdom would have no place to fight until the Allies crossed the English Channel in the spring of 1944. Could the Allies have left all those divisions idle? The answer has to be No. A suspension of Allied activity in the Mediterranean would have allowed the Germans to make use of some sixteen additional divisions in Russia or France. What would have been the effect of that situation on the Soviet Russians, who were fighting so valiantly on the Eastern Front, if the Americans and British were fighting absolutely nowhere in Europe?[9]

9. The decision, it can be argued, had been inevitable for over a year, ever since Roosevelt and Churchill, during the summer of 1942 had opted to occupy North Africa rather than attempt to cross the English Channel in 1942. When the Germans resisted in Tunisia, it required so much force to reduce them that *Overlord* was rendered impossible in 1943.

And finally, did the Anzio beachhead further the Allied purpose to seize Rome? Alexander thought so. In his 1962 *Memoirs* he wrote, "Anzio played a vital role in the capture of Rome by giving me the means to employ a double-handed punch—from the beachhead and from Cassino. . . . Without this double-handed punch, I do not believe we should ever have been able to break through the German defenses at Cassino."[10]

Others disagree, and we seem to find a dichotomy of opinion between the favorable views of the individuals who had personally participated and those of later historians. Martin Blumenson, for example, subtitled his book on the Anzio campaign *The Gamble That Failed*.

None of these questions carry a great amount of relevance today. In the final analysis, one is left with only one lasting impression: the heroism of the men and women who suffered through Anzio and the rest of Italy. Paying a fearsome price, they brought the day of Allied victory that much closer.

10. Alexander, *Memoirs*, 124.

APPENDIX

AFTERYEARS

The Italian campaign, because of the nature of the terrain and the fact that neither the Germans nor the Allies enjoyed a great preponderance of strength, afforded no opportunities for any spectacular maneuver that makes for exciting reading. An account of the campaign would therefore be a dreary subject indeed were it not for the collection of colorful personalities that played roles in those twenty months of fighting. Some of them, listed alphabetically, had significant careers ahead at the end of the war.

Darby, Brigadier General William O. After the destruction of his three Ranger battalions, Bill Darby was temporarily out of a job. But not for long; he was soon given command of the 179th Infantry Regiment, 45th Division. He served in that capacity only a short while before Clark decided that he had taken too many risks and arranged for him to be transferred back to the War Department. Soon, however, Darby became restive behind a desk and asked to be sent once more overseas. He was returned to Italy and given a plum, the position of assistant division commander, 10th Mountain Division. His luck, however, had run out; he was killed by a shell fragment only a few days before the end of the war. He was thirty-four years old at his untimely death.

Dagit, Lieutenant Avis, later Avis Schorer. This plucky nurse, on demobilization from the army, remained in nursing, specializing in anaesthesia. She returned to her home in Minnesota, where as of this writing she continues to be active in civic affairs.

Dawley, Major General Ernest J. Unlike the more-favored John P. Lucas (see below), Ernest Dawley was treated harshly after his generally agreed failure at Salerno. Sent home as a colonel, he seemed to have no option other than retirement. General Marshall, however, recognized Dawley's worth and placed him in command of various training and replacement establishments. He retired as a brigadier general in 1947, at which time he was awarded a second star, thus restoring his full wartime rank. He died in September 1973, age eighty-seven, having survived most of his wartime associates.

Frederick, Major General Robert T. Upon the wounding of Major General William Eagles in December of 1944, Robert Frederick took command of the 45th Infantry Division, guiding it competently to the end of the war. He retired from the army after having earned two Distinguished Service Crosses, two Distinguished Service medals, and many other lesser decorations, including eight Purple Hearts. He died in November 1970.

Harmon, Major General Ernest N. Ernie Harmon, though more than once an acting corps commander, never attained permanent command at that echelon and with it the third star of lieutenant general. Nevertheless, as one of the handful of truly outstanding division commanders, he is far better remembered than many who attained the hollow prize of another star. On December 24, 1944, for example, Harmon's 2d Armored Division, near the Meuse River in Belgium, destroyed its German counterpart, the 2d Panzer, thus stopping the westward German drive in the Bulge. Harmon's roar of triumph was typical: "The bastards are in the bag!!" On retirement, Harmon became superintendent of Norwich Military Academy, where he had been a cadet years before. He assumed a quieter demeanor and that of a devout family man until his retirement in 1965, at age seventy. He died in December 1980.

Hyde, Captain James F. C., Jr. In early May 1944, Jim Hyde underwent the shattering misfortune of losing his eyesight due to a grenade exploding in the pocket of a companion. Nevertheless, despite his blindness, he hired readers and attended law school after his discharge. He went on to a successful career that included twenty-five years in the Office of Management and Budget (formerly the Bureau of the Budget), an arm of the White House. He attended the National War College and achieved a master's degree, teaching there as an adjunct professor of political science. He died in 2006, after having contributed generously to this story.

Kesselring, Field Marshal Albert C. Following his capture at the end of the war, Kesselring was tried by an Allied court as a war criminal for signing a document ordering the execution of Italian partisans when the Germans took control of Italy after the Italian surrender. General Westphal was a fellow defendant. Both were sentenced to death. It is significant and somewhat amusing that photos of the two just after their death sentences show a remarkably happy-looking Kesselring. Their sentences were commuted to life imprisonment, however, and Kesselring ironically became nearly despondent. He could not bear to think of the riffraff he would have to live with for the rest of his life. Released for poor health in 1950, he died in 1960.

Leese, General Sir Oliver. Shortly after the fall of Rome, this capable, congenial, and informal general left the Eighth Army to take command of the ground forces in the India Theater, where he had Americans as well as British under him. He remained active in veterans and other civic affairs for some years after the war. He died in 1978.

Lucas, Major General John P. Though General Mark Clark did what he could to avoid hurting Johnny Lucas's pride, there was no gainsaying that he had been relieved from command of VI Corps because of dissatisfaction with his performance, especially on the parts of Alexander and Churchill. Nevertheless, the treatment he received was far more considerate than that meted out to the luckless Dawley, relieved of command after Salerno. Lucas retained his rank as a major general and was given command of the Fourth Army, at San Antonio, Texas. Later he headed the advisory group in Nanking from 1946 to 1948. He died in 1949. Sentimentalists may feel that Lucas died of a broken heart, but the causes of his somewhat early demise were completely natural.

McCreery, General Sir Richard. Upon the departure of Oliver Leese, Richard McCreery assumed command of the British Eighth Army, thus making him the counterpart of Mark W. Clark until the latter's elevation to army group command. When the Allies moved northward into Vienna after the end of the war, McCreery and Clark again became counterparts as fellow members of the Allied Control Council, each representing his own country.[1]

Senger und Etterlin, General der Panzertruppen Frido von. To Senger, as noted, fell the distasteful task of actually making the German surrender to Clark in late April 1945. Imprisoned for a year after the war for some unknown reason, he was released from captivity in 1946, and returned home, where he led a useful life as a civilian until his death in 1963. His memoir, called *Neither Fear nor Hope* in the United States, is one of the war's masterpieces.

Shirley, John. Sergeant John Shirley was extremely fortunate to survive the war with the 3d Division. At its end, he had been promoted to the

---

1. The author, as a lieutenant in HQ, Allied Forces in Austria, observed the two working together indifferently. Unaware of the past animosity that had existed between them, in a diary I wrote in Spring of 1946, I described McCreery: "The British member of the Allied Council, General McCreery, is a thin, toothy, sharp-looking Irishman who commanded the British Eighth Army up through Italy. Reputedly adored by his soldiers, he is not an impressive figure in the council chamber. Nobody's fool, he holds his own against the occasional attacks made on him by Konev, and puts his foot down solidly when interests of the British Empire are at stake. He leaves soon, and Britain will have a hard time replacing him."

grade of first lieutenant and commanded "L" Company, 15th Infantry. Following his discharge he became a veterinarian and is still active in the affairs of the 3d Division Association.

Truscott, General Lucian K., Jr. By the end of the Italian campaign, as noted, Lucian Truscott was in command of Clark's old Fifth Army. In October of 1945, after General George S. Patton was relieved by General Eisenhower for unacceptable political remarks while governing Bavaria, Truscott was called upon to assume command of the Third Army. Patton, bearing no rancor, made exceedingly complimentary remarks at the changeover ceremony. Retired somewhat early for medical reasons, Truscott was awarded the retirement rank of full general, to the applause of the army officer corps. He died in 1965.

Walker, Major General Fred L. One of the ironies of the Italian campaign is the fact that Fred Walker, whose brilliant maneuver at Velletri saved the day for Truscott and Clark, was relieved of command of the 36th Division on July 7, only a short time after the fall of Rome. Although he had anticipated this move,[2] he was surprisingly bitter because of the affection he had developed for his 36th Division Texans. Clark denied any role in the decision to remove Walker, and as evidence he pointed to a letter he had received from General Marshall himself saying that he would like to have Walker's services as commandant of the Infantry School, Fort Benning, Georgia.[3] Marshall must have been sincere, because he was not one to indulge in chicanery. In any event, Walker stayed close to the veterans of the 36th, but did not take an active role in the much-publicized resolution of the 36th Division Association in 1946 calling for a congressional investigation of Clark's part in the Rapido River debacle after the war. He died in 1969 at age eighty-two.

Wells, Lloyd. Once discharged from the army, Lloyd Wells began a long career as an author and a professor of political science at the University of Missouri–Columbia. At the same time, Wells maintained an unusual interest in the study of the Italian campaign, and the fact that his account of his own adventures was written with considerable study of official sources made it unusually valuable as a source. He died in 2000, at age eighty. His colleagues wrote that they were content that "his was a life truly worth living."

---

2. Walker's logic was justified. After Clark had relieved his regimental commanders and key members of his staff shortly after the Rapido operation—without consulting Walker as to the replacements—he rightly surmised that Clark, while having confidence in him as a division commander, wanted to "get rid" of him personally. See Walker, *Texas to Rome*, 393.

3. Clark, *Calculated Risk*, 383.

BIBLIOGRAPHY

Books

Adelman, Robert H., and George Walton. *The Devil's Brigade.* New York: Bantam Books, 1966.

———. *Rome Fell Today.* Boston: Little Brown, 1968.

Alexander, Field Marshal Earl of Tunis. *Memoirs, 1940–1945.* London: Cassell and Co., 1962.

Altieri, James. *The Spearheaders.* New York: Popular Library, 1961.

Anders, Wladyslaw. *An Army in Exile.* Nashville: Battery Press, 2004.

Barnett, Correlli, ed. *Hitler's Generals.* New York: Grove Westenfeld, 1989.

Blaxland, Gregory. *Alexander's Generals.* London: William Kimber, 1979.

Blumenson, Martin. *Anzio: The Gamble That Failed.* Philadelphia: J. P. Lippincott Co., 1963.

———. *Bloody River: The Real Tragedy of the Rapido.* Boston: Houghton Mifflin Company, 1970.

———. *Salerno to Cassino, Mediterranean Theater of Operations.* Washington: Center of Military History, US Army in World War II, 1969.

Boatner, Mark. *The Biographical Dictionary of World War II.* Novato, Calif.: Presidio Press, 1996.

Breuer, William B. *Agony at Anzio.* New York: Jove Books, 1990.

Bryant, Arthur. *Triumph in the West, 1943–1946: Based on the Diaries and Autobiographical Notes of Field Marshal the Viscount Alanbrooke.* London: Collins, 1959.

Burhans, Robert D. *The First Special Service Force: A History of the North Americans, 1942–1944.* Nashville: Battery Press, 1996 (reprint).

Butcher, Harry C. *My Three Years with Eisenhower.* New York: Simon and Schuster, 1946.

Churchill, Winston S. *Closing the Ring.* Cambridge: Riverside Press, 1951.

Clark, Mark W. *Calculated Risk.* New York: Harper and Brothers, 1950.

Darby, William O., and William H. Baumer. *Darby's Rangers: We Led the Way.* San Rafael, Calif.: Presidio Press, 1980.

D'Este, Carlo. *World War II in the Mediterreanean, 1942–1945.* Chapel Hill: Algonquin Books, 1990.

———. *Fatal Decision: Anzio and the Battle for Rome.* New York: Harper Collins, 1991.

Doyle, Charles H. *Stand in the Door.* Williamstown, N. J.: The 509th Parachute Infantry Battalion Association, 1988.

Eisenhower, Dwight D. *Crusade in Europe.* Garden City, N.J.: Doubleday, 1948.

———. *The Papers of Dwight David Eisenhower, The War Years.* 5 Vols. Edited by Alfred D. Chandler, Jr., and Stephen E. Ambrose. Baltimore: Johns Hopkins Press, 1970.

Ellis, John. *Cassino: The Hollow Victory.* New York: McGraw-Hill, 1984.

Graham, Dominick, and Shelford Bidwell. *Tug of War: The Battle for Italy, 1943–1945.* New York: St. Martin's Press, 1986.

Hapgood, David, and David Richardson. *Monte Cassino.* New York: Congdon and Weed, 1984.

Harmon, Ernest N., with Milton MacKaye and William Ross MacKaye. *Combat Commander: Autobiography of a Soldier.* Englewood Cliffs, N.J.: Prentice Hall, Inc., 1970.

Hickey, Des, and Gus Smith. *Operation Avalanche: The Salerno Landings, 1943.* New York: McGraw-Hill, 1983.

Höhne, Heinz. *Canaris, Hitler's Master Spy.* New York: Cooper Square Press, 1999.

Howe, George F. *The Battle History of the First Armored Division.* Washington: Combat Forces Press, 1954.

Irving, David. *Hitler's War.* Vol 2. New York: Viking Press, 1977.

Kesselring, Albert. *The Memoirs of Field-Marshal Kesselring.* 1953. Reprint, Novato, Calif.: Presidio Press, 1989.

Lewin, Ronald. *Ultra Goes to War.* New York: McGraw-Hill, 1978.

Macmillan, Harold. *The Blast of War, 1939–1945.* New York: Harper and Row, 1967.

Majdalany, Fred. *Cassino: Portrait of a Battle.* London: Wellington House, 1957; New York: Cassell Military Paperbacks, 1999.

Macksey, Kenneth. *Kesselring: German Master Strategist of the Second World War.* Greenhill, 2000.

Marshall, Charles F. *A Ramble through My War: Anzio and Other Joys.* Baton Rouge: Louisiana State University Press, 1998.

Matloff, Maurice. *Strategic Planning for Coalition Warfare, 1943–1944.* Washington, D.C.: Office of Chief of Military History, Department of the Army, 1959.

Moran, Lord. *Churchill, Taken from the Diaries of Lord Moran.* Cambridge: Houghton Mifflin Company, 1966.

Morison, Samuel Eliot. *History of United States Naval Operations in World War II.* Vol. 9, *Sicily–Salerno–Anzio.* Boston: Little Brown, 1984.

Morris, Eric. *Circles of Hell: The War in Italy, 1943–1945.* New York: Crown, 1993.

———. *Salerno: A Military Fiasco.* New York: Stein and Day, 1983.

Murphy, Audie. *To Hell and Back.* New York: Holt, Rinehart, and Winston, 1949. Reprint, New York: Bantam Books, 1968.

Murphy, Robert B. *Diplomat among Warriors.* New York: Doubleday, 1964.

Nicolson, Nigel. *Alex: The Life of Field Marshal Earl Alexander of Tunis.* London: Weidenfeld and Nicolson, 1973.

Parker, Matthew. *Monte Cassino: The Hardest-Fought Battle of World War II.* New York: Doubleday, 2004.

Pogue, Forrest C. *George C. Marshall: Organizer of Victory, 1943–1945.* New York: Viking Press, 1973.

Pond, Hugh. *Salerno.* Boston: Little Brown, 1961.

Price, Frank J. *Troy H. Middleton: A Biography.* Baton Rouge: Louisiana State University Press, 1974.

Pyle, Ernie. *Brave Men.* New York: Grosset and Dunlap, 1944.

Schorer, Avis D. *A Half Acre of Hell: A Combat Nurse in WW II.* Lakeville, Minn.: Galde Press, Inc., 2000.

Senger und Etterlin, General Frido von. *Neither Fear nor Hope.* New York: E. P. Dutton, 1964.

Sevareid, Eric. *Not So Wild a Dream.* New York: Alfred A. Knopf, 1946.

Shapiro, Lionel S. B. *They Left the Back Door Open: A Chronicle of the Allied Campaign in Sicily and Italy.* London: Jarrolds, 1944.

Shirley, John. *I Remember: Stories of a Combat Infantryman in World War II.* Copyright John B. Shirley, 1993, 2003.

Starr, Charles G., ed. *From Salerno to the Alps: A History of the Fifth Army, 1943–1945.* Washington, D.C.: Infantry Journal Press, 1948.

Summersby, Kay. *Eisenhower Was My Boss.* New York: Prentice Hall, 1948.

Sun-Tzu. *The Art of War.* Armed Services edition, translated from the Chinese by Lionel Giles. New York: Dover Publications, 2002.

Tomblin, Barbara Brooks. *With Utmost Spirit: Allied Naval Operations in the Mediterranean, 1942–1945.* Lexington: University Press of Kentucky, 2004.

Trevelyan, Raleigh. *The Fortress: A Diary of Anzio and After.* London: Buchan and Enright, 1956.

Truscott, Lucian K., Jr. *Command Missions.* New York: E. P. Dutton, 1954.

United States Government. Historical Division, Department of the Army. *Anzio Beachhead (22 January 1944–25 May 1944)*. 1947.

Vaughan-Thomas, Wynford. *Anzio*. London: Longmans, 1961.

Wagner, Robert L. *The Texas Army: A History of the 36th Division in the Italian Campaign*. Austin, Tx.: Robert L. Wagner, 1972.

Walker, Fred L. *From Texas to Rome: A General's Journal*. Dallas, Tx.: Taylor Publishing Company, 1969.

Warlimont, Walter. *Inside Hitler's Headquarters, 1939–1945*. Translated from the German by R. H. Barry. Novato, Calif.: Presidio Press, 1962.

Wells, Lloyd M. *From Anzio to the Alps: An American Soldier's Story*. Columbia: University of Missouri Press, 2004.

Westphal, General Siegfried. *The German Army in the West*. London: Cassell and Company, 1951.

Whitlock, Flint. *The Rock of Anzio: From Sicily to Dachau, the History of the 45th Infantry Division*. New York: Westview Press, 1998.

Articles

Dolan, James. "From the Rangers to POW Camp." *Remembering World War II*. Durham Caldwell, ed. Ludlow (Massachusetts), Ludlow Historical Commission, 2000.

Fisher, Edward F. "A Classic Stratagem on Monte Artemisio." *Military Review,* date unknown, also Appendix D, in Walker, *From Texas to Rome*.

McManus, John. "Bloody Cisterna." *World War II* (Jan. 2004): 58–64.

Ramsey, Winston S., ed. "The Battle for San Pietro." *After the Battle,* London: Battle of Britain Prints, Inc., Plaistow Press, 1977.

Walker, Major General Fred L. "The 36th Was a Great Fighting Division." *Southeastern Historical Quarterly* 72 (July 1968).

Unpublished Manuscripts

AFHQ. MSG to War Department, dated Oct. 4, 1943.

AFHQ. Supreme Commander's Dispatch, Italian Campaign, Sept. 3, 1943, Jan. 8, 1944.

Balch, Laura Ruth. Undated. "Experiences as an Army Nurse at Salerno and Anzio." Courtesy Robert Uth.

GMDS. The German Operation at Anzio: A Study of the German Operations at Anzio Beachhead from Jan. 22, 1944, to May 31, 1944.

Produced at GMDS by a combined British, Canadian and U.S. Staff, April 9, 1946. National Archives.

HQ. Fifth US Army, General Instruction No. 5, dated Oct. 2, 1943.

HQ. Fifth US Army, Report of G-3 Operations, Sept. 9–30, 1943, dated Nov. 4, 1943.

HQ. Fifth US Army, Report of G-3 Operations, Oct. 1943, dated Nov. 10, 1943.

Hyde, James F. C., Jr., Esq. Letters to author, Feb. 6 and Mar. 30, 2006.

Kauffman, Kenneth F. "German Artillery Guns Firing on the Anzio Beachhead." York, Pennsylvania, 1985.

Vietinghoff, Heinrich von. "The Campaign in Italy: 71 Inf Div in Italy (German), May 1944." NARA. Foreign Military Studies Collection, US Army Europe Historical Division, RG 549, #CO25.

Walker, Fred L., Jr. "Mission Impossible at Cassino: The First Assault across the Rapido River near Cassino in World War II, January 1944."

Interviews

Davison, General Michael. July 24, 2003. Interview by author, Arlington, Virginia.

Duer, A. Adgate. July 30, 2004. Interview by author, Oxford, Maryland.

Kerwin, General Walter. April 2, 2002. Interview by author, Alexandria, Virginia.

———. Letter to author, Oct. 1, 2004.

Kesselring, Field Marshal Albert. *U.S. News and World Report,* Sept. 2, 1955.

Schorer, Avis Dagit. Telephone interview by author, Aug. 6, 2004.

Seiler, Siegmund, 2d Lieutenant, 2d Company, 6th Technical Unit, German Army. Interview by Captain W. Jellinek at Fifth Army Stockade, Jan. 25, 1944.

Official Orders

Headquarters, Allied Armies in Italy, Order Number 1. May 5, 1944. Courtesy National Archives.

Fifth Army OUTLINE PLAN—AVALANCHE, 26 Aug 1943. Courtesy National Archives.

Fifth Army, Caserta, Italy, Operations Instruction Number 10, 160900A Nov. 1943. Courtesy National Archives.

INDEX

Page numbers in italics refer to illustrations.